A SHORT GUIDE TO TRADITIONAL CONSERVATISM

How the Philosophy that Built the West Can Restore It

A SHORT GUIDE TO TRADITIONAL CONSERVATISM

How the Philosophy that Built the West Can Restore It

Adapted from Part Four of **CHRIST OR COLLAPSE:**
The Case Against Godless Government

DAVID MILLARD HASKELL

The audiobook for this work, other shorter, excerpted editions, and the full version of *Christ or Collapse* are available at **CollegePress.com**

College Press Publishing
1307 W 20th Street
Joplin, MO 64804
www.collegepress.com

Library of Congress Cataloging-in-Publication Data

Names: Haskell, David Millard, 1968– author.
Title: A short guide to traditional conservatism : how the philosophy that built the West can restore it / David Millard Haskell.
Other titles: Christ or Collapse. Part four. Adapted.
Description: First edition. | Joplin, Missouri : College Press Publishing, 2026. | Adapted from Part Four of Christ or Collapse: The Case Against Godless Government. | Includes bibliographical references.
Identifiers: ISBN 978-0-89900-470-9 (print) | ISBN 978-0-89900-477-8 (e-book) | ISBN 978-0-89900-482-2 (audiobook)

Subjects: LCSH: Conservatism—United States. | Conservatism—Canada. | Religion and politics—United States. | Religion and politics—Canada. | Church and state—United States. | Church and state—Canada. | Political participation—United States. | Political participation—Canada.

Classification: LCC JC573.2.U6 2026 (print) | LCC JC573.2.U6 (e-book) | LCC JC573.2.U6 (audiobook) | DDC 320.52

Contents

Introduction

This book, *A Short Guide to Traditional Conservatism: How the Philosophy that Built the West Can Restore It,* is an excerpt from the larger work, *Christ or Collapse: The Case Against Godless Government.*

In total, four shorter volumes, each containing two to four chapters from the larger work, have been created. Because this book is an excerpt, readers will occasionally encounter references to ideas or remarks found in chapters not included here. Though this may at times give pause, such references can be safely overlooked, as no essential concepts required to understand this volume are missing, and the discussion remains complete and intelligible on its own.

This compact volume you're about to read brings together Chapters 9, 10, 11, and 12—which comprise Part Four of *Christ or Collapse.* Like all the shorter books in the series, it begins by defining the political philosophy of Traditional Conservatism and outlining its core principles, clarifying that its aim is for Christian norms and values to inform governance. It then explores the deeper theological foundations that undergird Traditional Conservatism and explains how traditional conservative laws from the past can serve as a blueprint for the present.

The discussion also addresses why the Christian moral framework of Traditional Conservatism is incompatible with certain actions and policies currently sanctioned by the state. The volume concludes by outlining practical strategies for advancing Traditional Conservatism today.

If you find the ideas in this volume compelling, I encourage you to continue with the other excerpts in the series or the full text itself. All are available as books or audiobooks.

The first volume in this collection of shorter works, titled *Our Foundation for Flourishing: Christianity's Positive Influence on Government and Society* presents Part One of *Christ or Collapse* and is comprised of Chapters 1, 2, and 3. After defining the core tenets of Traditional Conservatism, it demonstrates that the philosophy's mission to have Christian norms and values shape the nation's laws is nothing new. In fact, it's been the default position of both America and Canada since their respective beginnings. The book concludes by presenting a vast array of studies demonstrating the unique social benefits associated with the practice of Christian norms and values. By providing empirical evidence of the good produced by these norms and values, it supports Traditional Conservatism's call for those principles to again guide public life and policy.

The second excerpt in the series is titled *Our Unanchored Society: How Progressivism, Classical Liberalism, and Libertarianism Have Set Us Adrift*. It presents Part Two of *Christ or Collapse* and combines Chapters 4, 5, and 6. It traces the historical development of progressivism and other liberal ideologies, then, drawing on empirical evidence, it examines the damage that occurs when the "social justice" of progressivism replaces genuine justice. It concludes by showing how the "unrestrained freedom" championed by Classical Liberals and Libertarians is a pathway to enslavement.

The third volume is titled *Sameness Is Our Strength: The Need for Nationalism and a Common Culture*. It features Part Three of *Christ or Collapse* and brings together Chapters 7 and 8. It begins with a clear explanation of healthy nationalism, then presents extensive research showing that mass immigration can significantly undermine a nation's safety, civility, and economic stability. It concludes with strategies for building a common culture that can restore unity in the United States and Canada.

At the end of every shorter volume—and also at the end of the full work, *Christ or Collapse*—I've included a two-page Postscript that invites those persuaded by the ideas of Traditional Conservatism to join with others who share their conviction. Perhaps I'll be hearing from you.

In the meantime, I hope you enjoy *A Short Guide to Traditional Conservatism: How the Philosophy that Built the West Can Restore It.*

1

Principles of Traditional Conservatism

The Advantages and Disadvantages of Excerpts

As the cover of this book—and the Introduction you just read—makes clear, this volume is an excerpt from the larger work *Christ or Collapse: The Case Against Godless Government*. The full book develops its argument across more than 550 pages and draws on over 1,000 corroborating references, bringing together historical analysis, philosophical reasoning, and empirical evidence. An excerpt like this allows readers to engage deeply with one important portion of that broader argument—perhaps an area that particularly interests them. In that sense, it serves both as a lens and a gateway: it offers a focused look at one major theme while also inviting readers to explore the full work for a more comprehensive understanding.

At the same time, reading an excerpt from a larger work has its limitations. In the full book, many of the central ideas and assumptions are introduced and developed earlier. When a shorter volume is drawn from later chapters of a much larger work—as this one is—some of that earlier conceptual groundwork is necessarily absent. As a result, readers may encounter later arguments whose deeper foundations were laid out earlier in the first few pages.

To address this and fill in the most likely definitional gaps, this chapter—Principles of Traditional Conservatism—introduces several of the key ideas from the introductory pages of *Christ or Collapse.* These provide the philosophical tenets that inform the arguments developed throughout the book. By outlining them at the start, readers are given the essential framework needed to understand the analysis that follows.

Introducing Traditional Conservatism

This book champions Traditional Conservatism as a distinct political philosophy, separate from Christianity as a religious system. Though related, they are not identical. One need not believe the supernatural claims of Christianity to embrace Traditional Conservatism. However, one must believe the evidence that societies thrive—achieving peak individual freedom, social cohesion, and economic prosperity—when they adhere to a Christian ethos.

In straightforward terms, Traditional Conservatism holds that Christian norms and values should shape a nation's practices and policies. It recognizes that laws cannot be ethically neutral—all laws mandate some kind of moral stand—and therefore it forthrightly requires that laws, explicitly and implicitly, reflect Christian morality (because it produces the best results).

At the same time, the philosophy holds that government leaders must acknowledge society's pluralism and respect the electorate's preferences regarding how Christian norms and values are translated into law. For example, the electorate signals whether laws and policies informed by Christian biblical standards should directly cite Scripture or theology. Also, respectful of today's ideologically diverse society, Traditional Conservatism holds that laws should incorporate natural law principles or be supported by appeals to logical reasoning and empirical evidence—rather than resting solely on "because Scripture says so." What is not negotiable for a democratically elected traditional conservative government is the legalization or endorsement of what historical Christianity has consistently prohibited.

While advocating for laws rooted in Christian principles, this philosophy also maintains that the nation's statutes must respect the freedom of conscience of non-Christians and must not compel adherence to any particular religious belief. However, freedom of conscience and religion does not extend to groups or movements that promote violence or seek to overthrow Christianity or the traditional norms, values, and culture of the West. Freedom of conscience and religion protects only those who practice their faith—or no faith at all—without attacking the civilizational foundations of the nation. Apart from that caveat, under Traditional Conservatism, laws that steer society's actions toward the common good are acceptable; those that compel individual belief are not. In this, the philosophy safeguards the distinction between public and private spheres, ensuring the state's role is primarily confined to the former.

By insisting that the state's role be strictly limited to a few essential areas of public concern—and should not extend to controlling thought or imposing religious beliefs—Traditional Conservatism draws extensively from some of the key principles of Reformed Protestant theology. And while certain theological notions underpin much of Traditional Conservatism, its broader definition lets anyone—Christian or not—adopt it as a rational choice based on a preponderance of facts, not compelled faith. Through historical and empirical examples, traditional conservatives demonstrate to those who will listen that their political philosophy surpasses others in promoting societal well-being; it's on this evidentiary foundation that they present their argument for public consideration.

Furthermore, as it is explained in these pages, Traditional Conservatism as a political philosophy need not be linked to any specific political party. Throughout Western history, there have been various parties that did not carry the "conservative" label yet still upheld the principles of Traditional Conservatism. Many politicians touted as "liberal" years ago would qualify as traditional conservatives today, even if only in part. On the flip side, many established political parties that include "conservative" in their name today don't uphold the core tenets of the philosophy. Therefore, for the greatest clarity, remember that the true measure of Traditional Conservatism is the degree to which a party, politician, or individual aligns with the core principles of the philosophy outlined in this chapter.

Since Christianity and Traditional Conservatism are so closely interwoven, readers should expect frequent detours in these pages where I emphasize unpacking the faith more than the philosophy itself. As the two are inseparable companions, it's worth noting that when I show how Christianity—through its orthodox values and practices—surpasses other religious and ideological systems in promoting societal well-being, this conclusion applies equally to Traditional Conservatism. Put simply, Christianity is the soul animating the body of Traditional Conservatism, so exploring the societal benefits that the faith yields also reflects the benefits that Traditional Conservatism provides. To champion Christianity is to champion Traditional Conservatism—they rise together. As Christianity grows, so does Traditional Conservatism. I've pointed out that you don't need to be a believer to adopt this political philosophy; yet, when both heart and mind align, embracing it becomes more likely, and one's dedication to the cause grows far more passionate.

Why "Traditional Conservatism"?

I deliberately use the term "Traditional Conservatism" to distinguish it from contemporary political ideologies that label themselves "conservatism" yet diverge from, or even contradict, the foundational traits of the original political philosophy. For example, in some cases, Neo-Conservatism has been little more than warmongering to aid globalist imperialism. The Traditional Conservatism I endorse is grounded in British common law and Christianity, in particular, Reformed Protestantism. However, I believe that a devout Catholic who appreciates Thomistic thought would find this perspective largely in harmony with their own. Traditional Conservatism *conserves* those *traditions* of British law and Christian belief; other "conservatisms" do little or nothing to maintain the enduring moral order and divine intent that ground a stable society.

I explain Christianity's influence on this political philosophy in detail starting below and then throughout this book. Conversely, I will describe how British common law inspires Traditional Conservatism only briefly.[1] In short, common law provides a framework for turning the customs of a nation's people—worked out incrementally over time—into the official law of the land. From the Middle Ages, judges traveled throughout Britain, resolving disputes based on local conventions. Their rulings set precedents, ensuring consistency across similar cases. This incremental process transformed informal customs into a coherent legal system known as common law.

British common law, by valuing established customs, opposes the swift imposition of rigid decrees by a small elite driven by new theoretical ideas (something that's the norm today). That is to say, in its practice and process, judges do not seek to change popular custom to conform to their own world-view and sensibilities; instead, they work to protect popular custom by establishing legal precedents based on those time-honored traditions. This bottom-up approach—this judicial acquiescence to the people's prerogative—led British common law to gradually adapt in order to protect individual rights like property, liberty, and fair hearings.

It's important to note that many of our most valued legal protections grew out of the Christian-influenced customs of the British people. In other words, in England, customs based on a biblical understanding of individual and community life developed first. Historians tell us that the biblical worldview was widely accepted by the Norman Conquest in 1066,[2] and even earlier—about two centuries before—under Alfred the Great and his immediate successors.[3] Because the Bible emphasizes property rights, personal liberty, and fair hearings, British customs came to reflect these values. When judges later codified these customs into common law, they effectively enshrined biblical principles.

Though Traditional Conservatism originated in Britain, this philosophy has been embraced and refined across the Anglosphere in nations historically linked to the UK and predominantly English-speaking, such as the United States, Canada, Australia, and New Zealand. As these countries attest—at least historically—the success of Traditional Conservatism lies in its ability to adapt and evolve for the common good while preserving core truths, a balance made possible by blending British common law and Christianity.

Below, I'll list and explain nine of the core tenets of Traditional Conservatism. My list of Traditional Conservatism's traits is by no means exhaustive. Many before me have compiled their own definitions of conservatism, often including a broader range of points. Notably, the influential American political theorist Russell Kirk articulated ten principles of conservatism,[4] and these were, in large part, a distillation of the tenets that Englishman Edmund Burke put forward in the late 1700s.[5] That said, I'm confident that my version would not be found lacking by Kirk, Burke, or other foundational thinkers. Though my language and emphasis may differ, the underlying philosophy remains unmistakably aligned.

Core Tenets of Traditional Conservatism

1. Traditional Conservatism Relies on Christian Moral Absolutes

As I've suggested, the paramount feature of Traditional Conservatism is its unwavering dependence on the moral absolutes of Christianity for civic direction. Christian norms and values serve as the unchanging, non-negotiable touchstones by which all other elements of public life must ultimately orient themselves. Importantly, they are the ground from which all other elements of the political philosophy grow. Supported by historical and current evidence, the philosophy contends that a society lacking laws rooted in Christianity's moral absolutes inevitably falls into moral relativism and disorder or becomes tyrannical.

As I enumerate each of the other tenets of Traditional Conservatism, I'll touch on how they originate in scripture. I'll also mention that by explicitly linking Traditional Conservatism to Christian doctrines, my presentation of this political philosophy stands apart from most contemporary voices. In fact, my account may strike some readers as more overtly religious than even the works of Edmund Burke or Russell Kirk—Christians both, and the foremost architects of this philosophy. I attribute that difference to historical context.

Writing in the late 18th and mid-20th centuries, respectively, Burke and Kirk could assume their readers were already steeped in Christian belief and ethics—they took for granted the moral absolutes of the faith. Thus, when Burke affirmed that conservatism is rooted in "one law for all, namely that law which governs all law, the law of our Creator,"[6] and Kirk declared that "the conservative believes that there exists an enduring moral order. That order is made for man, and man is made for it: human nature is a constant, and moral truths are permanent,"[7] neither found it necessary to elaborate on who the Creator was or what His moral law entailed. Additionally, Kirk's reluctance to explicitly acknowledge conservatism's debt to Christian doctrine may reflect the cultural climate of his time. In the aftermath of World War II, even among conservatives, there was a growing tendency to downplay overt references to Christianity in public discourse—viewed as a way to promote broader social cohesion in an increasingly pluralistic society. As society careens toward the abyss, we now recognize the folly of that notion. Today's Traditional Conservatism begins by acknowledging its reliance on Christian doctrine.

2. Reluctance to Abandon Established Customs and Traditions

As a political philosophy, Traditional Conservatism posits that society's customs and traditions have developed for good reason: their longevity implies usefulness. Therefore, it advises skepticism when faced with the radical removal of norms and values that have stood the test of time. Following this same line of thought, the philosophy holds that traditions and customs provide a nation with stability, continuity, and a sense of identity and belonging. This isn't to say that the philosophy prohibits or avoids change. Change is welcome when it meets the following criteria: it follows prudent deliberation; it's a response to proven necessity, such as the elimination of explicit harm; it works to restore tradition; and, importantly, it doesn't erode established moral absolutes.

This political tenet—continuity of custom—finds its inspiration in Christian doctrine. To trace the line back further, Christian doctrine itself is grounded in God's Word as revealed in the established texts of the Old and New Testaments. Among God's people, therefore, the order has consistently been this: God's Word gives rise to doctrine, and doctrine gives rise to enduring custom.

For example, in Matthew 22:37–40, summarizing the core commandments, Jesus says: "'Love the Lord your God with all your heart and with all your soul and with all your mind.' This is the first and greatest commandment. And the second is like it: 'Love your neighbor as yourself.' All the Law and the Prophets hang on these two commandments." This divine command became, in very large measure, custom across the West.

Some have misinterpreted scripture to argue that Jesus' mission was to tear down established tradition. This is not so. Jesus himself addressed this issue, saying, "Do not think that I have come to abolish the Law or the Prophets; I have not come to abolish them but to fulfill them. For truly I tell you, until heaven and earth disappear, not the smallest letter, not the least stroke of a pen, will by any means disappear from the Law until everything is accomplished" (Matthew 5:17-18). When one examines the examples that supposedly suggest that Jesus was intent on tearing down tradition, it's clear that his efforts were not to override but to restore, correcting people's flawed understanding of ancient wisdom and custom so they might follow them better (for example, Matthew 5:21, 43).

Apart from the words of Jesus found in the Gospels, other books of the New Testament call for the veneration of inherited insight and practice. In 2 Timothy 3:16-17, the early church leader, the Apostle Paul, celebrates the tradition of the faith as a timeless guide for human life, writing, "All Scripture is God-breathed and is useful for teaching, rebuking, correcting and training in righteousness, so that the servant of God may be thoroughly equipped for every good work." Elsewhere, in Romans 1:21-22, Paul warns that turning away from God's established law results in both moral and intellectual decline. Similarly, James 1:25 praises those who persevere in following divine norms and values, highlighting the benefits that arise from adherence: "But whoever looks intently into the perfect law that gives freedom, and continues in it—not forgetting what they have heard, but doing it—they will be blessed in what they do." By extension, scripture proposes that people find unity in their common adherence to core beliefs and time-honored standards (for example, Galatians 3:28).

Old Testament scriptures equally underscore the enduring authority of ancient instruction, portraying it as a sacred inheritance to be honored and upheld. For example, veneration of ancient wisdom is vividly expressed in Psalm 119, a lengthy hymn of devotion to God's law. Verse 97 declares, "Oh, how I love your law! I meditate on it all day long," while verse 105 states, "Your word is a lamp for my feet, a light on my path."

Similarly, Deuteronomy 4:5-6 reinforces this reverence when the prophet Moses instructs the Israelites: "See, I have taught you decrees and laws as the Lord my God commanded me, so that you may follow them in the land you are entering to take possession of it. Observe them carefully, for this will show your wisdom and understanding to the nations, who will hear about all these decrees and say, 'Surely this great nation is a wise and understanding people.'" In this context, following God's ancient statutes transcends mere legal duty, serving as the foundation for a nation's identity and a shining example to others.

Later, in Deuteronomy 6:6-7, Moses instructs the Israelites, "These commandments that I give you today are to be on your hearts. Impress them on your children. Talk about them when you sit at home and when you walk along the road, when you lie down and when you get up." This passage underscores the duty to safeguard the spiritual heritage—the commandments and promises given to their forefathers—by passing them intact to the next generation. Psalm 78:4-6 expands this vision, declaring, "We will not hide them from their descendants; we will tell the next generation the praiseworthy deeds of the LORD, his power, and the wonders he has done ... that the next generation might know them, the children yet unborn, and arise and tell them to their children."

3. Obligation to Ancestors and Descendants—Stewardship of Inheritance

As touched on previously, much of Traditional Conservatism is influenced by Englishman Edmund Burke (1729-1797), who emphasized the importance of "the contract of eternal society."[8] His notion indicates that society is a partnership between those who are living, those who are dead, and those who are yet to be born. The traditional conservative principle of cherishing ancient traditions, norms, and values—explained just above—is one aspect of Burke's concept. However, in addition to passing down intangible cultural treasures to provide an ethereal sense of belonging across generations, Burke also envisioned the protection of tangible assets as part of his contract. That is, beyond specific custom, concrete holdings such as land, resources, or institutions that tangibly scaffold the foundations of society must be protected and preserved.

This protection and preservation are not optional but an obligation to one's forebears arising from gratitude for the material benefits they have bequeathed. The current generation, knowing they are enjoying the fruit of trees they neither planted nor brought to full bloom, feels duty-bound to ensure those tangible treasures are not neglected or given to strangers with neither history nor love for them. Instead, they must devotedly tend and even multiply them for the countrymen who follow. From the perspective of the forebearers, they can feel contented knowing that what they sacrificed to achieve will not be lost; their sentiment is: "I'm pleased to leave you this treasure; all I ask is that you take care of it."

While Traditional Conservatism insists that the current generation of countrymen is obligated to protect and preserve the land, resources, and institutions created and enhanced by past generations, it recognizes that this mission is significantly compromised when a population is overwhelmed by newcomers with no connection to the builders of the civilization. Newcomers may feel an obligation to the ancestors of their own birthplace, but they have little emotional connection to the deceased citizens whose work and sacrifices created the new environment they now enjoy. With no historical connection, there is no contemporary obligation.

To address this problem—to ensure that the duty to past generations is fulfilled and the tangible resources created by previous countrymen are not squandered or lost—leaders within the Traditional Conservatism movement are beginning to contemplate an expansive notion of rightful inheritance. While the details are slowly emerging, a society should recognize, as a starting point, that past public contributions must have a bearing on present and future public benefits. A family or group that has, for generations, given their time, talents, and treasure to establishing an outpost of civilization—through clear ing land, constructing roads and buildings, creating community organizations, and contributing to public projects through decades of taxation—should have their historical and current involvement honored. Their voice in public matters—especially those related to preserving what they and their ancestors produced over generations—should be given more recognition and sway. Exactly how this should be done is a point of debate. This sentiment reasserts itself in the philosophy's core principle of nationalism, and thus it will be explored more fully there.

What is beyond dispute is that those with deep emotional connections to land, resources, or institutions are more likely to preserve and protect them. One of the most powerful examples of deep emotional connection to the land leading to preservation and protection is found among hunters and anglers—most of whom lean heavily conservative and tend to have a longstanding connection to their native land. In the U.S., hunters and anglers have contributed more financial and physical support to wildlife habitats and management than any other group: "Sixty percent of budget funding for state fish and wildlife agencies, which are tasked with responsible wildlife management, is generated by hunters and anglers... Altogether, hunters pay more than $1.6 billion a year for conservation programs."[9] Similarly, in Canada, hunters and anglers are the largest financial contributors to wildlife habitat conservation.[10]

In its emphasis on protecting the land and institutions passed down generationally, Traditional Conservatism parallels the Christian view of wise stewardship over what one is gifted. Scripture consistently frames this duty to preserve our ancestors' legacy and improve it for future generations as both a moral imperative and a covenantal trust. The sentiment is rooted in gratitude for what has been received and hope for what is yet to come.

The story of Adam and Eve in the Garden of Eden, as recounted in Genesis 1:26-28 and 2:15, serves as an early biblical example of human stewardship over the land, emphasizing both authority and responsibility. In Genesis 1:26-28, God creates humanity in His image and grants them dominion over the earth's creatures and resources, instructing them to "subdue it" and "fill the earth," which implies a role of active management and care rather than mere exploitation. This stewardship is further clarified in Genesis 2:15, where God places Adam in the garden "to work it and keep it," a phrase that combines cultivation (enhancing the land's fruitfulness) with protection (preserving its integrity). The narrative positions Adam and Eve as caretakers of creation, tasked with maintaining and improving the garden under God's guidance—until their disobedience disrupts this harmonious role.

Later in the Old Testament, this theme of inheritance as both a divine right and an obligation appears. In Numbers 27:1-11, Zelophehad, an Israelite man, dies without sons, leaving his five daughters. As women, there was dispute over whether they could inherit their father's land. God, through Moses, affirms their claim, ensuring that the material good accrued by prior generations is preserved for the descendants, rather than lost to those who contributed nothing.

Elsewhere, the Old Testament describes improvement for the future as a duty. Proverbs 13:22 states, "A good man leaves an inheritance to his children's children," suggesting that righteousness involves not only maintaining what was received but multiplying it for posterity.

The New Testament deepens this principle. The parable of the talents (Matthew 25:14-30) is commonly understood among Christians as a teaching that urges individuals to actively contribute to and enhance the world beyond what they inherit. The servants in the story are entrusted with their master's goods, expected not just to preserve them faithfully but also to multiply them wisely. The one servant who merely buries the coins he was given—preserving without improving—is condemned, while those who invested and increased their initial sum are praised. Beyond a strictly religious context, the moral lesson is that people have a duty to multiply the resources entrusted to them, improving the world and leaving it better than they found it.

4. Acceptance of Social Hierarchies

Traditional Conservatism is at ease with a hierarchical social order where roles and responsibilities are clearly defined and distributed according to natural competencies and records of greater obligation or sacrifice.

Regarding competencies, it admits that some are more suited than others to certain roles, and when character, capacity, and career align, stability, peace, and prosperity follow. To say that some are more suited than others to certain roles is to rebuke the notion that "all men are created equal"—at least as today's progressives would understand it.

Weaving a narrative fit for a fantasy or science fiction novel, progressives today promote the idea that innate differences between people are virtually nonexistent (with the exception that Whites are innately more racist). For them, it's not a lack of skills, talent, or competence that prevents certain people from occupying particular positions; it's systemic bigotry. Because they believe people are fundamentally equal, like identical twins, they conclude that if someone falls behind, the cause must be nefarious and social, not natural or individual.

This near-literal belief that people are innately equal inspires progressives to take dramatic corrective action, specifically calling for the removal of criteria based on merit and competency and the imposition of criteria based on gender, sexual orientation, or skin color. This often involves government interventions—such as affirmative action, diversity quotas, or wealth redistribution—to ensure equality not just in opportunity but also in actual outcomes across gender, racial, and social lines.

Traditional conservatives hold that the principle "all men are created equal" is fundamentally a legal concept—referring to equality before the law and in natural rights—rather than a claim about biological sameness or sociological uniformity. Therefore, enforcing equality of outcome is to do violence to the very principle of equality, undermining liberty and property rights. They hold that differences in talent, effort, and circumstance naturally produce varied outcomes, and that government should safeguard fairness, not force uniformity. It's not the business of the state to make people equal in fact, but to ensure that the laws are equal.

When hierarchies emerge justly based on merit, traditional conservatives maintain that, at the societal level, subordinates in fields such as business, religion, the military, or other institutions should willingly and harmoniously follow those in higher positions—except in cases where a superior commands actions that clearly violate established moral principles. Likewise, within the family, traditional conservatives—particularly those rooted in the Christian faith—affirm the husband as the head of the household and uphold the expectation that children honor and respect their parents.

This call to defer to those in leadership above you does not equate to support for oppression, but rather to honor given for greater obligation, respect for different societal roles, and a desire for optimal functionality. Related to the latter, from a leadership theory perspective, organizations and teams—even families—function best when there's a clearly recognized point of ultimate responsibility, ensuring decisive action and coherent direction. In terms of checks and balances, those who receive the elevated status that comes from greater authority only maintain that status and authority insofar as they willingly accept and fulfill their greater responsibilities. Key among their responsibilities is securing—through their own sacrifice if necessary—the best circumstances for those under their authority.

In all circumstances, Traditional Conservatism consistently honors sacrifice made in service to others, granting greater status and influence—essentially a higher place in the social hierarchy—as a key form of recognition. This approach reflects the Christian ideal that true greatness comes through selfless service, as Jesus taught: "Not so with you. Instead, whoever wants to become great among you must be your servant" (Mark 10:43).

At the societal level, the philosophy's acceptance of a ranked, social pyramid of positions reflects the Christian notion of believers forming the "Body of Christ," a hierarchical yet caring communal structure where everyone has a role that aligns with their natural abilities, fostering maximum benefit and mutual respect (for example, 1 Corinthians 11:3 and 12:12-27).

At the level of families, the notions of male headship and honoring of parents also have a Christian pedigree. Christian scriptures, such as Ephesians 5:22-24 and Colossians 3:18-19, emphasize that wives are to submit to their husbands as the highest authority in the family, portraying this dynamic as a reflection of Christ's headship over the church. Ephesians instructs wives to submit "as to the Lord," with the husband as "head of the wife," while Colossians reinforces this submission "as is fitting in the Lord," framing it as a divine order. However, this authority isn't absolute or oppressive; it's paired with the husband's obligation to love his wife sacrificially, mirroring Christ's self-giving love for the church, thus balancing headship with mutual care and responsibility. Related to honoring parents, Christians find this commanded in Exodus 20:12 and Ephesians 6:1-3, where obedience and respect are linked to God's design for family and societal stability more generally (a topic I'll return to in the next subsection).

Among the foundational principles of Traditional Conservatism, few provoke greater indignation from non-conservatives—and even from conservatives outside the traditional sphere—than the concept of hierarchy as it applies to a man being head of the household. Indeed, this concept of "male headship" clashes so sharply with modern attitudes that non-conservatives struggle to imagine even a single plausible justification for its legitimacy.

While it's beyond the scope of this book to examine in detail the reasons why traditional gender roles promote societal flourishing, the books of George Gilder, in particular *Sexual Suicide*[11] and *Men and Marriage*,[12] provide fact-based arguments in support of that claim. More recently, Louise Perry's work *The Case Against the Sexual Revolution: A New Guide to Sex in the 21st Century* presents its own unique arguments for rejecting contemporary norms and values surrounding sex and relationships.[13]

5. Promotion of Nationalism

Nationalism, a core tenet of Traditional Conservatism, prioritizes the needs and interests of one's countrymen above those beyond the homeland's borders, reflecting a commitment to communal loyalty and sovereignty. Though not a perfect match, some substitute the term *fraternity* for nationalism when discussing this tenet of the philosophy—perhaps because it makes for better alliteration when grouping it alongside other principles of the philosophy like faith, family, and freedom. Fraternity refers to a sense of brotherhood, solidarity, and mutual support among members of a group or community with shared values. To feel a sense of fraternity, group members need not be direct kin, but because of their character and worldview, they share a bond as "your people." Whether using fraternity or nationalism as the descriptive term, central to this notion are the questions: "Who qualifies as one's 'countryman'?" and "What makes someone 'your people'?"

For Traditional Conservatism, a countryman starts with those holding official citizenship, but the right disposition is as important as proper documentation. The correct disposition involves embracing and defending the home nation's heritage—its language, culture, and historical traditions. In addition to documentation and disposition, the philosophy considers one's historical dwelling when assessing a countryman. It unashamedly proclaims that a multi-generational record of residence—with familial evidence of constructing and contributing to the infrastructure, community, and culture of a place—elevates one's status as a true countryman. As discussed previously, greater sacrifice (in this case, generational outlay to one's nation) also equates to greater honor within Traditional Conservatism.

A family or kin group that has proven its loyalty and commitment to the nation's well-being through decades or even centuries of sustained contributions deserves a stronger voice in shaping its future. Traditional Conservatism argues that the principle of "obligation to ancestors and descendants" demands such recognition, while the principle of "acceptance of social hierarchies"—in which greater contributions merit greater honor—justifies it.

However, building on the earlier discussion in the *Obligations to Ancestors and Descendants* section, this perspective does not endorse creating preferential laws or allocating additional public benefits to individuals based on their history of deep-rooted contributions to the country. Honoring them means giving their opinions, not their votes, greater weight. How this is to be done is currently a point of discussion among traditional conservatives and has not yet been resolved. What's becoming clear, however, is that the toil and treasure of decades—or centuries—are dishonored when they are casually handed over to those who neither appreciate nor merit them. That is to say, many traditional conservatives today maintain that something must be done to significantly slow current citizenship processes across the West.

A growing consensus holds that the current paths to citizenship in both the U.S. and Canada demand too little of newcomers. Granting insider status with such undue haste and with so little contribution from applicants is a humiliation to those who have given so much for so long. A more rigorous model that honors those who built the foundations we stand on demands an extended process toward citizenship—a decade or two is not unreasonable—during which applicants, and their families if applicable, must demonstrate successful assimilation and true allegiance. This dedication to their new nation is to be demonstrated not only in language and cultural customs but also through steady contributions to the tax base, the strengthening of social cohesion, and the betterment of their communities.

By contrast, those who refuse to adopt the national language or customs, or who prove to be financial burdens, social disruptors, or shirkers of civic duty, would be returned to their country of origin at the first clear evidence of a failure to integrate or provide a consistent net benefit to the nation.

In addition, even those who achieve citizenship after arriving from abroad must be restricted from holding government, military, or bureaucratic positions, and dual citizenship should be prohibited. While their second-generation descendants may participate, the original immigrants themselves cannot. These measures are not intended to judge ability but to ensure that key responsibilities remain in the hands of individuals deeply rooted in the nation's culture, history, and civic traditions. By tying governing or civic authority to long-term investment in the country, traditional conservatives aim to preserve stability and continuity while still allowing fully committed newcomers to earn their place as true countrymen once they meet all integration requirements.

Such requirements are hardly novel or unduly harsh, as they echo the standards imposed upon earlier generations of European immigrants who built the United States and Canada from their founding eras into the mid-twentieth century. With no government subsidies, welfare programs, or institutional safety nets to fall back on, their welcome was tacitly conditional: they were expected to labor, adapt, and contribute in ways that tangibly strengthened the societies they entered. In other words, belonging was never an entitlement but a covenant, sealed by the immigrant's ability to improve the nation that received them.

The greater honor given to a countryman because of his predecessors' longstanding loyalty does not diminish the legitimacy or fundamental rights of those who become citizens through the rigorous new extended process. Provided they meet the measures outlined above, newcomers become true countrymen. While they are not required to abandon the language or benign customs of their ancestral homelands, these must be secondary to the language, customs, and culture of their new nation. This full acceptance of the home nation's identity—combined with the rejection of political loyalties to former countries—transforms them from mere residents within the nation's borders to countrymen who embody the nation's established character. In expecting new citizens born elsewhere to assimilate fully, traditional conservatives express their desire for continuity through unity. What traditional conservatives are not expressing, however, is racism.

Whereas racism seeks to exclude based on immutable traits like skin color, nationalism, as promoted by today's traditional conservatives, ignores race as a divide and seeks to include anyone of goodwill through cultural assimilation. For the traditional conservative today, nationalism's impulse is based in collective allegiance, not biological determinism. A supporter of Traditional Conservatism of European background can easily share authentic fraternity with other countrymen who support the philosophy and hail from different ethnic backgrounds. If they share devotion to traditional Christian faith, the bond is even deeper, as they move from alignment of the head to alignment of the heart.

Currently, an overwhelming number of newcomers have taken up residence in countries of the West, and Traditional Conservatism's definition of nationalism provides a lens for assessing the success of that immigration project. Is there evidence that the masses of newly invited refugees and "citizens" embrace the nation's linguistic, cultural, and historical traditions as their own? Have they rejected political and cultural allegiances to any prior heritage? Are they making steady contributions to the tax base, the strengthening of social cohesion, and the betterment of their communities?

Perhaps more importantly, has anyone in authority asserted that they must meet those requirements? A traditional conservative leader would!

Naturally, the most reliable way for a country to ensure that newly arrived citizens fully adopt its linguistic, cultural, and historical traditions—while relinquishing political and cultural ties to previous heritages—is to primarily accept Christian immigrants. Traditional conservatives view this approach as not only reasonable but, given the current societal contexts of America and Canada—where many newcomers explicitly voice hatred for all things Western—essential.

Unlike some forms of nationalism, the nationalism promoted by Traditional Conservatism rejects racism because the philosophy aligns with Christianity. The faith clearly opposes racism, as demonstrated by key scriptural teachings affirming the unity and equal value of all people in Christ. Colossians 3:11 declares that in the new self, "Here there is no Gentile or Jew, circumcised or uncircumcised, barbarian, Scythian, slave or free, but Christ is all, and is in all," showing that racial distinctions are irrelevant in the process of sanctification and unity in Christ. Similarly, Galatians 3:28 states, "There is neither Jew nor Gentile, neither slave nor free, nor is there male and female, for you are all one in Christ Jesus," emphasizing equality across ethnic lines. Revelation 5:9-10 illustrates that Christ's redemption extends to "every tribe and language and people and nation," uniting diverse groups in worship and purpose. Ephesians 2:15-16 highlights the cross's role in abolishing enmity between groups, creating "one new humanity" through reconciliation. Finally, Deuteronomy 1:17 and Matthew 5:44 call for impartial judgment and love for all, condemning racial malice or pride as sin.

Other aspects of the philosophy's understanding of nationalism are also drawn from the Bible and Christian tradition. The Old Testament first justifies nationalism by portraying nations as divine inventions; for example, Deuteronomy 32:8 reads, "When the Most High gave the nations their inheritance, when he divided all mankind, he set up boundaries for the peoples..." From the start, nations were presented as part of God's design to order mankind and allow diverse people groups to co-exist while retaining their unique languages or customs (for example, Genesis 10:31–32; Genesis 11:1-9; Psalm 86:9; Acts 17:26).

Related to the duty to prioritize one's countrymen over citizens of other nations, that notion begins in the Ten Commandments when God states: "Honor your father and your mother" (Exodus 20:12; Ephesians 6:2). Although this edict is primarily tailored to familial bonds, it lays the foundation for a greater sense of loyalty and responsibility toward one's people, encouraging individuals to prioritize the well-being and stability of their own community before extending their concerns outward. Honor for forebears is linked to the sustainability of a nation, with God stating, "so that you may live long in the land the Lord your God is giving you." Sociological and anthropological research confirms that close-knit relationships based on ancestral connections provide the most solid foundation for social cohesion, reducing conflict and encouraging mutual support.[14]

Moving outward, the obligation to fellow citizens is explicitly commanded in Deuteronomy 15:7-8: "If anyone is poor among your fellow Israelites [your countrymen] in any of the towns of the land the Lord your God is giving you, do not be hardhearted or tightfisted toward them. Rather, be openhanded and freely lend them whatever they need."

While the New Testament demands benevolence toward strangers (even one's enemies), the overriding obligation to first care for one's own people is reinforced. In Mark 7:9-13, Jesus condemns those who would allocate resources to other matters at the expense of their family. Paul reiterates this principle, emphasizing that assistance to extended family and the larger Christian community takes precedence: the faithful are told to provide first "for their own relatives" (1 Timothy 5:8) and to prioritize good works "to those who are of the household of faith" (Galatians 6:10). From a Christian perspective, working to benefit one's country's citizens—especially the poorest and most vulnerable—is the clearest application of the golden rule: love your neighbor as yourself.

The traditional conservative's ideas surrounding who qualifies as a countryman and the obligations newcomers must meet to be considered legitimate citizens also have a biblical foundation. Scripture teaches that newcomers to an established nation must adopt the country's existing laws and customs to fully belong as citizens. This principle stems from a respect for God-given order, preservation of shared identity, and the need to guard against cultural erosion caused by those who reject or oppose the nation's social norms and values. The story of Ruth illustrates this principle when the eponymous Moabite immigrant vows to fully adopt Israel's traditions and faith, declaring: "Your people shall be my people, and your God my God" (Ruth 1:6).

The legal code of Judaism reinforces this principle. Leviticus 18:26 mandates that immigrants conform to the nation's laws: "But you must keep my decrees and my laws... the native-born and the foreigners residing among you." Similarly, Leviticus 19:33-34 instructs Israel to love sojourners (foreigners) and treat them fairly but also expects them to live as the native population.

In the New Testament, 1 Peter 2:13-14 commands: "Submit yourselves for the Lord's sake to every human authority: whether to the emperor, as the supreme authority, or to governors," framing obedience to a host nation's authority as an obligation. Additionally, scriptures such as 2 Corinthians 6:14-15, "Do not be yoked together with unbelievers. For what do righteousness and wickedness have in common?" and Ephesians 5:11, "Have nothing to do with the fruitless deeds of darkness," caution against associating with those who reject God's established principles. This suggests an obligation on longstanding citizens to develop strategies that will ensure newcomers embrace their nation's customs and traditions, which will safeguard the nation's traditional norms and values against erosion.

Like male headship, Traditional Conservatism's push for nationalism—especially a version insisting on one unifying culture—is resisted in a society steeped in the ideals of equity and inclusion. As one of the philosophy's most divisive tenets, nationalism earns a robust defense in two chapters of its own.

6. Support for Family

Although family may appear later in the list of characteristics, it holds paramount importance in Traditional Conservatism as a central pillar of support and emphasis. While the philosophy regards a Christian ethos as the intangible foundation of a thriving society, it views stable families as the tangible bedrock of social order. Families are the most basic social institution and serve as the primary training ground for positive civic engagement. For instance, children taught to honor their parents within the home learn to respect legitimate authority figures outside of it. Through family chores, they acquire a sense of duty that later translates into diligence in their external work. Daily interactions with parents and siblings foster teamwork, collaboration, and conflict resolution—skills that prepare them to navigate society more effectively. Above all, stable and loving families are essential for passing down customs and values, ensuring the continuity of cultural and moral heritage.

As is clear from the explanation above, Traditional Conservatism's elevation of family intertwines with its commitment to cultural continuity, hierarchical social order, and loyalty to one's countrymen. Given the profound good that flows from thriving families and their broader social impact, Traditional Conservatism actively supports their formation and preservation through political means, such as tax structures that benefit married couples, policies that elevate traditional marriage over other models and parental authority over state control, and governmental systems designed to strengthen rather than replace family life.

Traditional Conservatism's support for family is also grounded in scripture. In earlier discussions, we have already seen several biblical references affirming that family must be a priority (for example, Exodus 20:12; 1 Timothy 5:8). To these we may add the foundational teaching that marriage and children are central to God's purposes for humanity: "That is why a man leaves his father and mother and is united to his wife, and they become one flesh" (Genesis 2:24), and together they are commanded to "Be fruitful and increase in number; fill the earth and subdue it" (Genesis 1:28).

The primacy of parents in raising children is reinforced throughout scripture. Proverbs 22:6 captures the biblical vision of parents as divinely appointed educators, charged with "training their children in the way they should go." Deuteronomy 6:4–7 expands this responsibility, presenting the family as the primary vehicle for transmitting cultural, moral, and religious norms. God instructs parents: "These commandments that I give you today are to be on your hearts. Impress them on your children. Talk about them when you sit at home and when you walk along the road, when you lie down and when you get up."

The Apostle Paul echoes these principles in the New Testament, admonishing fathers: "Fathers, do not exasperate your children; instead, bring them up in the training and instruction of the Lord" (Ephesians 6:1–4). Here, Paul confirms the authority of parents while also emphasizing a balanced approach that fosters both spiritual growth and emotional well-being.

7. Limited Government

As seen above, Traditional Conservatism is dedicated to maximizing the social standing of the family; conversely, it seeks to minimize the size and role of government. Its call for limited government rests on two convictions: greater power breeds greater corruption, and a more active state produces a less active citizenry. In the former conviction, it mirrors the Christian teaching on humanity's propensity for sin (Romans 3:23); in the latter, the Christian teaching on industriousness and self-reliance (e.g., 2 Thessalonians 3:10–12; Proverbs 6:6–11;

Ephesians 4:28).

That said, traditional conservatives hold that certain functions must remain within the sphere of government: the defense of the nation, the protection of individual rights (including the enforcement of contracts and security of property), and the maintenance of the rule of law through courts and law enforcement. Beyond these, responsibilities such as health care, welfare assistance, education, marriage licensing, and other social services are best shifted to families and churches (or other community organizations)—groups that, when freed from heavy taxation and burdensome regulation, can provide these services with equal or greater effectiveness.

In this respect, traditional conservatives share some ground with libertarians or classical liberals. Yet they depart sharply from the libertarian impulse to treat all rules as oppression. Conservatives are willing to assign government a more activist role in curbing depravity and encouraging decency for the common good, measuring both against the time-tested norms and values of Christianity.

The Apostle Paul's letter to the Romans (13:1–7) outlines the proper role of the state, and Traditional Conservatism aligns closely with his vision of legitimate and illegitimate power. Paul instructs believers—as a general rule—to submit to governing authorities, recognizing them as instituted by God to maintain order, punish wrongdoing, and promote the good of society. He also commends individuals to fulfill civic duties such as paying taxes and respecting rulers. Yet even here, the state's role is confined to upholding justice, maintaining order, and protecting citizens—functions that resonate with the limited-government convictions of traditional conservatives. Paul does not extend government's reach to economic redistribution, social engineering, or even education (which in modern contexts has often become the chief vehicle for social engineering).

Moreover, Paul's call to submit to rulers is not absolute. His command assumes that authorities act as "God's servant for your good" (Romans 13:4), fulfilling a divine mandate to promote justice and order. When a government departs from this mandate—commanding actions that violate Christian moral law or forbidding those required by faith, such as worship—the duty to obey shifts to a duty to resist. This principle is expressed in Acts 5:29, where Peter declares, "We must obey God rather than human beings!" affirming divine authority over human authority in cases of conflict (see also Exodus 7:14–18; Esther 5:1–2; Daniel 3:16–18; Daniel 6:10).

Thus, both Paul's instruction and Traditional Conservatism's view of the state rest on the same foundation: government is to be respected and obeyed insofar as it upholds justice and order under God, but it is never to be treated as an absolute power.

8. Support for Personal Freedom

I've just stated that Traditional Conservatism will employ the power of the state to curb or incentivize behavior in order to achieve the common good, with the "common good" understood as aligning with the historical Western-Christian worldview. Therefore, it may seem paradoxical to claim that this political philosophy also supports "maximum personal liberty." After all, to say that it's willing to use the state to discourage or encourage some behavior is to say that it's willing to quash the freedoms of those who want to do the opposite. Incidentally, this is the major complaint of libertarians and classical liberals against conservatives, and it leads them to point a finger and scream, "See! They want to take away your freedom! They're authoritarians just like the Progressives!" However, this supposed contradiction can be reconciled by understanding two key aspects of traditional conservative thought.

First, Traditional Conservatism does not equate liberty with unfettered freedom but sees unfettered freedom as leading to slavery. At the individual level, uncontrolled freedoms lead to addiction, financial instability, criminal acts, relationship damage, social isolation, health issues, and failure to reach one's goals. At the level of society, to the extent that unfettered freedom creates masses of degenerate individuals with anti-social behavior, it creates dependent, dysfunctional, crime-ridden hellholes (think of cities with a long history of radical progressive leadership). Multiply the dysfunction caused by unfettered freedom to the level of a nation, and you create the preconditions for tyrants to rise. A population, desperate for order to be restored, is willing to exchange its rights for an assurance of safety and civility.

Rather than unfettered freedom, Traditional Conservatism advocates for "ordered liberty," where individual freedoms are balanced against the promotion of individual excellence and the need for societal stability. The philosophy defines maximum liberty as the most freedom each citizen can enjoy without undermining the social order, concluding that maximum liberty for the maximum number of people is only sustainable within a framework of laws, customs, and values informed by Christianity. However, as a safeguard against overcontrol and tyranny, the philosophy insists that this regulatory framework cannot be arbitrary or untested but must have a long record of balancing freedom against the maintenance of civil society. It will come as no surprise that traditional conservatives appeal to history to show that the laws, customs, and values formed in the Anglosphere under the influence of Christianity meet these criteria.

Beyond asserting that regulations informed by Christianity are best suited to maintain the balance between liberty and social order, Traditional Conservatism makes a related, yet more dramatic, claim. It posits that a citizenry immersed in the norms and values of Christianity is prone to self-regulation, honesty, cooperation, and responsibility. This leads to a society where individuals act in ways that naturally support social harmony, reducing the need for state oversight in personal conduct. In short, when sharing a "common moral language" supplied by Christianity, personal freedoms can be maximized because people do good and forgo evil of their own accord, requiring no external intervention.

From the Old Testament account of the Hebrews being led out of bondage in Egypt to liberty in the Promised Land, the Bible provides examples of how a people can and must be free. As with its other tenets, Traditional Conservatism's advocacy for and understanding of maximum liberty are dependent on stories and concepts from scripture.

The philosophy's position that unfettered freedom, or freedom out of balance, harms the individual and society is frequently attested in the Old and New Testaments, and it finds succinct expression in the Apostle Paul's first letter to the church in Corinth. After asserting that he has found true freedom in Christ, he details how that freedom must be used to become the best version of oneself, writing, "I have the right to do anything—but I will not be mastered by anything.... I have the right to do anything—but not everything is constructive" (1 Corinthians 6:12; 10:23).

Similarly, in 1 Corinthians 8:9, Paul discusses how one's freedom might impact others, warning, "Be careful, however, that the exercise of your rights does not become a stumbling block to the weak." He goes on to emphasize that those who are naturally self-disciplined or morally stronger should, for the common good, create a public environment that helps avoid the downfall of the temperamentally vulnerable (1 Corinthians 8:10-13; see also Romans 14:13–21).

One of the most iconic biblical passages on freedom is found in Jesus' words. In John 8:31-32, he declares, "If you hold to my teaching, you are really my disciples. Then you will know the truth, and the truth will set you free." On a spiritual level, this freedom delivers individuals from the bondage of sin, fostering a life-changing connection with God. However, on the level of personal character, this teaching echoes the traditional conservative vision of "true" freedom coming from the knowledge of the good, which allows individuals to realize their fullest potential, becoming their "best selves."

While the New Testament clearly defines freedom as liberation from sin or spiritual freedom rather than personal autonomy or self-governance, there are key passages where freedom is plainly extolled as the ability to act, speak, or think without restriction from external forces. In addition to his comments in 1 Corinthians mentioned above, in Galatians 5, Paul declares that Christians are to live freely according to their conscience guided by faith. In Romans 14 he discusses believers' freedom to choose their own course in matters not explicitly forbidden by scripture. His idea reflects Old Testament verses such as Deuteronomy 4:2, "Do not add to what I command you and do not subtract from it," which warn against human additions to divine law. The idea—that "Man should not legislate where God has been silent" or "Human laws should not bind where God has left men free"—became a key focus of early Protestant doctrine and continues to heavily influence Traditional Conservatism's approach to state restrictions on liberty.

The philosophy's emphasis on individual liberty and autonomy also finds inspiration and greater clarity in some of the other early doctrines of Protestantism—specifically *sola scriptura* and the *priesthood of all believers* —which emerged during the Reformation in the 1500s.

Sola scriptura teaches that the Bible alone is the ultimate authority in faith and practice, encouraging everyone to read and understand it independently. This opposed the Catholic view, which discouraged personal access to Scripture, maintaining that ordinary people should rely on clergy for interpretation. The doctrine of the *priesthood of all believers* states that every Christian, not just professional clergy, has direct access to God and is equally capable of serving him in their own sphere of influence. Together, these Protestant ideas helped shape Western values of individual liberty by democratizing religious knowledge, promoting literacy, and reinforcing personal agency.

In particular, by challenging the Catholic Church's exclusive authority, Protestantism encouraged individuals to scrutinize all forms of unchecked power and to expand their personal autonomy. This shift laid the groundwork for Enlightenment ideas about liberty, influencing Western societies to maximize individual freedoms. As Protestant reform spread, the resulting religious diversity and tolerance helped develop principles of pluralism and civil liberties, eventually shaping the legal and political frameworks that protect freedom of thought, speech, and religion.

9. Free Markets

Like personal freedom, Traditional Conservatism adopts a balanced view of free markets. It generally favors less government intervention, believing that greater personal autonomy leads to economic success. Its default stance, similar to libertarianism, is to let businesses and individuals operate with minimal regulation. However, it recognizes the need for controls to prevent obvious harm or injustice. When such controls are in place, it argues that a laissez-faire economy—a free market—encourages innovation, efficiency, and prosperity. In this system, the qualities, prices, supply, and demand of goods naturally self-regulate through competition.

But the philosophy holds that eroding social cohesion, compromised moral values, or significant threats to the welfare of the community justify additional regulation. Because of their dedication to the common good, their obligations to ancestors, and their patriotic duty to their countrymen, traditional conservatives often support solutions that are less profitable. They may enforce protections that, while costly, improve health or save historic sites. They may place the needs and desires of workers over those of business owners in certain employment disputes. Direct evidence of this is found in traditional conservatives' resentment toward monopolies, job loss through offshoring, wage suppression due to labor oversupply, and job insecurity from restructuring or automation. In their inclination to put fraternity before fortune, they are at odds with libertarians and even other types of conservatives.

At this stage of our exploration, we are starting to see some overlap. Astute readers will recognize that the Christian doctrines we have discussed in relation to other aspects of Traditional Conservatism also inform its stance on free markets. For instance, the stewardship principle (Genesis 1:28), where individuals are seen as caretakers of God's gifts, resonates with the economic activities in free markets by suggesting a duty to use resources in a way that makes them "fruitful and multiply." Rather than repeating these connections, I'll leave it to readers to revisit and link these ideas. Nonetheless, there are a few more

Christian principles, not yet discussed, that support the free market perspective within Traditional Conservatism.

While Christians have occasionally chosen to hold property in common and are always called to voluntarily use some of what they own to benefit others, they have also championed the right to private property. They recognize the importance of owning land and goods, as well as the freedom to produce, buy, and sell for personal gain. This position is a necessary precondition for free markets. For free markets to exist, a country needs a system where goods and services are traded. For a single market—or a broader market economy made up of many markets—to function, citizens must have secure property rights. One of the clearest endorsements of property rights in Christianity comes from the Ten Commandments, where "You shall not steal" (Exodus 20:15) inherently recognizes the right to property ownership. This commandment would be meaningless if there were no concept of personal ownership.

In Matthew 20:1–16, Jesus tells the parable of workers in a vineyard, each receiving wages according to their agreement with the owner. This parable acknowledges that individuals have the right to negotiate terms for their labor and that the vineyard owner has the right to manage his property as he sees fit. Elsewhere in the New Testament, Ephesians 4:28 states, "Anyone who has been stealing must steal no longer, but must work, doing something useful with their own ha nds..." Here, stopping theft is linked to the idea of working to gain personal property, which people are then free to use and share as they choose.

Moving outward to free markets, the Bible provides a moral framework within which market activities should operate. The core Christian principle for all economic endeavors is to work diligently for profits and to be grateful for them; this gratitude should then manifest as social responsibility and voluntary service to the community. For Christians, several biblical passages highlight ethical resource management. Proverbs 14:23 links profit to hard work, stating, "All hard work brings a profit, but mere talk leads only to poverty," endorsing industriousness in market economies. Jesus' Parable of the Talents (Matthew 25:14–30), mentioned earlier, underscores the rightness of investment and productivity being rewarded and advocates for entrepreneurship. Paul's teaching in 2 Thessalonians 3:10, "The one who is unwilling to work shall not eat," supports personal responsibility and a productivity-based livelihood.

Of course, the Christian teachings I've referenced do not detail the intricacies and operations of a modern economic system; however, they do align with free market principles of stewardship, the work–reward connection, and personal accountability.

Reasserting and Adding to the Purpose of this Book

The aim of this book is to persuade readers that the cultural revitalization and very survival of Western nations—especially the United States and Canada—depend on a majority of citizens pursuing Traditional Conservatism.

Traditional Conservatism is the application of Christian norms and values to the governance of a nation.

In the preceding pages, I've highlighted both the core tenets of this political philosophy and the ways in which the Christian faith supports and inspires them. As mentioned, in the pages that follow, not all of those tenets will be examined individually for their specific contributions to societal well-being. Rather, their significance will be conveyed through the cumulative weight of varied examples.

For most devout Christians, the information I've relayed in this chapter, including my major claim, will be met with affirming nods but little action beyond that. They will agree that the Christian faith holds the prescription for what ails society, but most will say they're too busy or too worried about public backlash to act on it.

By contrast, non-Christians are likely to reject my prescription for our ailing nations outright. No matter how concerned they are about society's decline, they would rather take a pass than support a project where Jesus is the de facto leader. After all, they think, what has He ever done for them?

The question is provocative—and unavoidable. It demands an answer.

Endnotes for Chapter 1

1. For a more complete description of the relationship of conservatism and British common law, see Yoram Hazony, *Conservatism: A Re-discovery* (Washington, DC: Regnery Gateway, 2022).

2. John Blair, *The Church in Anglo-Saxon Society* (Oxford: Oxford University Press, 2005).

3. S. Keynes and M. Lapidge, eds., *Alfred the Great: Asser's Life of King Alfred and Other Contemporary Sources* (London: Penguin Classics, 1983).

4. Russell Kirk, "Ten Conservative Principles," lecture, The Heritage Foundation, Washington, DC, March 20, 1986, ; also see Russell Kirk, *The Politics of Prudence* (Wilmington, DE: ISI Books, 1993); and Russell Kirk, *The Conservative Mind: From Burke to Santayana* (Chicago: Henry Regnery Company, 1953).

5. Edmund Burke, *Reflections on the Revolution in France*, ed. Conor Cruise O'Brien (London: Penguin Classics, 1986).

6. Edmund Burke, *The Works of the Right Honourable Edmund Burke*, vol. 7 (London: Henry G. Bohn, 1857), 90.

7. Russell Kirk, "Ten Conservative Principles," 3.

8. Edmund Burke, *Reflections on the Revolution in France*, ed. J. C. D. Clark (Stanford: Stanford University Press, 2001; originally published 1790), 261.

9. Rocky Mountain Elk Foundation, "Hunting Is Conservation," December 27, 2019, .

10. Canadian Wildlife Federation, *The Role of Hunters and Anglers in Conservation* (2018), .

11. George Gilder, *Sexual Suicide* (New York: Quadrangle/New York Times Book Co., 1973).

12. George Gilder, *Men and Marriage* (Gretna, LA: Pelican Publishing Company, 1986).

13. Louise Perry, *The Case Against the Sexual Revolution: A New Guide to Sex in the 21st Century* (Cambridge: Polity Press, 2022).

14. For example: Donna L. Leonetti and Benjamin Chabot-Hanowell, "The Foundation of Kinship: Households," *Human Nature* 22, nos. 1–2 (2011): 16–40, ; Benjamin Enke, "Kinship, Cooperation, and the Evolution of Moral Systems," *Quarterly Journal of Economics* 134, no. 2 (2019): 953–1019; Nicolette V. Roman et al., "Strengthening Family Bonds: A Systematic Review of Factors and Interventions That Enhance Family Cohesion," *Social Sciences* 14, no. 6 (2025): 371, .

2

Advanced Theology Behind
Traditional Conservatism

The Pull Toward Chaos

There is a pull in the universe toward confusion. It's everywhere and in everything. You can accelerate the deterioration (think progressivism). You can do nothing and it still gets worse, just at a slower pace (think Classical Liberalism). Or you can apply a positive force—something that pushes back in the right direction—and counter it with an antidote to ruin (think Traditional Conservatism).

In physics, this phenomenon is described in the Second Law of Thermodynamics. It states that in any system, entropy—a measure of chaos—tends to increase over time. Systems naturally move from states of order to disorder unless external energy is applied to maintain or increase order.

This iron law of physics is also mimicked in areas of human endeavor. Unless purposeful action to maintain truth is applied to religious, political, and other institutions of cultural formation, they devolve into corruption.

In examining the evolution of Christian churches and denominations over time, philosophers of religion such as Ernst Troeltsch[1] and H. Richard Niebuhr[2] identified what they described as a type of entropy within religious groups: the church-to-sect cycle. In their model, a breakaway unit of a larger religious tradition—or a newly formed tradition—begins as a "sect," a small, fervent group adhering more closely to strict tenets of faith and rejecting mainstream norms. Over time, as the sect grows and gains respectability, its members abandon more costly (especially stigmatizing) aspects of their beliefs and practices to accommodate societal expectations. No longer in high tension with the norms of the non-believers around them, they become a "church"—a larger, more bureaucratic, and moderate institution. This shift dilutes the original zeal of the founding group, prompting new sects to break away and restart the cycle.

In a sect, the newly formed religious community sees its passion and purpose revived through a bold recommitment to, and more rigorous adherence to, the faith's original teachings and principles. As was discussed at length in Chapter 3, congregations today that strictly follow Christianity's original doctrines demonstrate passion and purpose through the highest levels of charitable giving, volunteering, and life satisfaction. These biblically faithful congregations, full of the confidence that accompanies unwavering beliefs, are better at keeping existing members and excel at recruiting new followers.[3] While churches around them die, they grow—until the day they, too, surrender the very doctrines that once sustained their vitality.

It's very difficult to swim against the stream. Most churches today—including those that market themselves as "conservative," "evangelical," or "Bible-believing"—have watered down their messages to make them more palatable to secular culture. On occasion, in private, pastors or lay leaders may give lip service to their faith's more controversial doctrines; they might mention, half under their breath, that homosexuality is a sin, abortion is a sin, God created only men and women rather than multiple genders, male headship is required, or some other modern taboo. But in public, they are silent, having completely succumbed to the pull of the Left and, accordingly, pulling all their punches. Feeling they must remove any content that would offend progressive sensibilities, sermons become nothing more than self-help monologues with a side of "Jesus loves you no matter what."

If you are a churchgoer, take a moment to think about the sermons your own pastor delivers. Does he regularly speak out clearly and boldly on the hot-button cultural issues that directly overlap with the imperatives of scripture? If not, why are you still at his church? If you have children, you are almost certainly sabotaging their faith, as among all cultural influences outside the family, the most damaging to Christianity are pastors and other church leaders who are embarrassed of their own doctrine and unwilling to defend it publicly.

Because they do not repeatedly and convincingly provide biblically sound answers to questions surrounding sexual ethics, the sanctity of life, and other basic moral issues, their congregations—especially the youngest members who are still forming their beliefs—are left to fend for themselves. The person in the pew is forced to conclude one of two things, and both lead to ruin:

1. Christianity has no opinion on these topics, so progressive claims must be authoritative.

2. Christianity does have an opinion, but my pastor—the expert—is ashamed of it, so I should be too and therefore accept progressive claims as authoritative.

You might ignore my challenge and, in the short term, choose to stay at a church where the pastor is a coward, but in the long term you will have to move on. Study after study,[4] including my own research,[5] shows churches that do not actively promote and instruct *on all* of

Christianity's doctrines and requirements slowly grow in progressive beliefs and quickly decline in membership, until they ultimately close their doors forever. And keep in mind this ripple effect: as Christianity slips away, so too does Western civilization. Ironically, those conservative clergy who complain about the deteriorating culture share much of the blame for its decline.

Similar to the cycle of churches and sects, American historian and political theorist Robert Conquest observed that political and cultural systems within a nation also tend to drift leftward. His observations were not published as a formal "theory" in the academic sense, complete with empirical models or hypotheses, but rather as witty aphorisms on political and organizational behavior. They gained prominence in conservative and libertarian circles after being popularized by writer John Derbyshire in a 2003 National Review article, where he recalled them from conversations with Conquest.[6] Conquest's "theory of political drift leftward" is captured in the maxim: "Any organization not explicitly right-wing sooner or later becomes left-wing."[7]

Conquest posits a relentless tendency for institutions—governments, non-profits, churches, corporations, or bureaucracies—to shift toward progressive or collectivist ideologies unless actively structured to resist it. His point is straight-forward: the only way to withstand constant left-leaning cultural and intellectual pressure is to intentionally build conservative principles into an organization's foundation. Its charters, leadership choices, laws, policies, and everyday practices must be instrumentally conservative. Government institutions, he argues, need these safeguards most of all.

Traditional Conservatism—with its explicit codification of Christianity's norms and values into law and custom—is the exact antidote that Conquest would prescribe to correct North America's leftward political drift toward civilizational collapse. Abhorrence of government overreach, a commitment to equal treatment before the law, and a balance between individual liberty and concern for the common good place Traditional Conservatism—and it alone—in the Goldilocks zone of political philosophies. It's not too hot, nor too cold, but just right.

Why institutions, including the state, tend to drift left toward destruction comes down to humans' love of convenience and hatred of being told what to do. The first lesson of Christian theology—taken from the Book of Genesis and its account of the Garden of Eden—is that God has all power and authority, while humans persist in the illusion that they can seize it. This continues to play out today.

Given the choice, most of us prefer ease over effort, autonomy over duty, and pleasure over sacrifice. The irony is that, when we choose ease, autonomy, and pleasure as our immediate goals, we lose them in the long run and in greater measure. Be that as it may, when a leader—especially a politician—offers peace without conflict, actions without consequences, and personal choice over collective responsibility, the appeal is irresistible. These are the promises of the Left, and this is its greatest advantage.

Institutions, being run by humans, often drift Left because it feels easier in the short term. Less structure means less effort, so ambitious leaders frequently push policies that favor comfort and self-expression over rigor and restraint. Few will ever admit, "I want lower standards so I can indulge myself—or so I can win your approval." Instead, the decline is wrapped in lofty slogans: "We're breaking barriers for freedom" or "We're broadening access for inclusivity" (meaning lowering standards). It's self-interest and flattery dressed up as altruism. By contrast, the Right demands effort. It calls for upholding standards, enforcing discipline, and shouldering burdens. That vision can inspire, but it runs against the grain of human instinct. Left unchecked, societies—like the universe—drift toward entropy.

Traditional Conservatism—The Only Solution

I will reiterate that if we hope to resist societal entropy, there is only one solution. In the preceding chapters, we explored the core tenets of Traditional Conservatism, determining that it was the political philosophy most consistently employed since the founding of America and Canada. Its retreat from guiding and undergirding the actions of the state—beginning after WWII and accelerating through the 1960s—stands as a historical aberration. Through an examination of objective evidence, we concluded that the norms and values of Christianity, from which this philosophy draws its principles, are uniquely beneficial to both a people and their nation.

By contrast, the ideas behind progressivism come from anti-Christian, anti-Western Marxism and have proven uniquely harmful to social cohesion and national success. Likewise, Classical Liberalism and Libertarianism, with their lack of moral vision and tolerance for socially harmful behavior in the name of unfettered freedom, were revealed to be profoundly damaging to a nation's well-being. For good measure, we discussed why nationalism is needed. I trust that the weight of evidence presented so far has brought even non-Christian readers to see Traditional Conservatism as the only viable path forward. I recognize, as I've often acknowledged, that it's no small task for the unchurched to embrace a political philosophy rooted in a specific religious tradition. Yet when it comes to accepting this philosophy, my biggest concern is not with non-Christians. I worry more that it will be rejected by Christians themselves. Numerous communities of Christians in the West have been misled to think that their faith and the governance of their nation must always remain separate.

"Political Quietism"—Justifying Light Under a Bushel

I've already shown that banishing the Christian faith from a country's customs and laws was a concept foreign to our great-grandfathers and all earlier ancestors. It was only through a concerted effort of propaganda, supported by politicians, judges, and cultural leaders, that the ideological project known as the Post-War Consensus became the dominant, accepted view. As a result of this project, natural and passionate convictions for faith, family, and fraternity were stigmatized. Many Christians were indoctrinated; many still are. The view that Christians should refrain from political involvement, activism, or attempts to influence laws and governments is called *political quietism*. At its core, quietism treats politics as spiritually irrelevant, holding that true faith should focus on private piety, evangelism, and personal morality rather than public action. It also views politics as dangerous and corrupting, arguing that engagement with political power compromises faith and distracts from the gospel.

The Christians arguing that neither they nor their brethren should try to impose any aspect of their faith on governance justify their position, first, by emphasizing the importance of religious liberty in a pluralistic society. They are so thoroughly brainwashed by the propaganda of the Post-War Consensus that they now believe tolerating words and actions that violate God's commands is somehow more virtuous—more "Christian"—than openly urging people to obey those commands.

One wonders how such people would have responded had they stood beside John the Baptist when he rebuked King Herod for shacking up with his brother's wife (Mark 6:17–18), or watched Jesus drive corrupt merchants from the temple (Matthew 21:12–13), or heard Paul denounce homosexual practice as incompatible with faith and flourishing (Romans 1:26–27; 1 Corinthians 6:9–10; 1 Timothy 1:9–10). Doubtless, their zeal for pluralism, tolerance, and inclusion would have prompted them to pull these men aside and scold them for being "too judgmental." Instead of condemnation, they would have told them to welcome these people just as they are.

For Christians promoting quietism, their unqualified exaltation of pluralism and tolerance is accompanied and aided by an interpretation of Christ's Kingdom—Jesus' reign on earth today—as purely spiritual, detached from any tangible authority in the public sphere. They contend that Jesus himself rejected the conflation of his kingdom with political power. Their primary scriptural support for this view is John 18:36, where Jesus, appearing before the Roman governor Pilate just before his crucifixion, states, "My kingdom is not of this world. If my kingdom were of this world, my servants would have been fighting, that I might not be delivered over to the Jews. But my kingdom is not from the world."

Proponents argue that Jesus' refusal to engage in earthly power struggles, as evidenced by his submission to Pilate's authority, indicates that Christians should not seek to impose their faith through governance, but instead influence society through personal witness and ethical living.

Beyond their proof-text from John, their position also draws on Romans 13:1 and 4, where Paul instructs:

> Let everyone be subject to the governing authorities, for there is no authority except that which God has established. The authorities that exist have been established by God... For the one in authority is God's servant for your good. But if you do wrong, be afraid, for rulers do not bear the sword for no reason. They are God's servants, agents of wrath to bring punishment on the wrongdoer.

For them, this passage suggests that Christians should respect secular authorities, even non-Christian ones, as divinely ordained. The example of Paul's submission to Roman governance implies that believers can live faithfully without transforming governments into explicitly Christian institutions. They say it shows a prioritization of peaceful coexistence over political power. Finally, Matthew 22:21 is cited, where Jesus says, "Render to Caesar the things that are Caesar's, and to God the things that are God's." Jesus' distinction between civic and divine obligations is seen as a directive to maintain a complete separation between religious and political activity.

A Rebuke of Political Quietism

Insofar as they justify quietism and undermine Christian political activism, the scriptural interpretations above are mistaken. In the passage from John's Gospel, Jesus' point was to contrast his lasting kingdom, rooted in God's authority, with Pilate's limited and temporary power. He was not trying to confine his rule to a purely spiritual realm. To be sure, his refusal to have his followers fight applied specifically to his redemptive mission—to die and rise again—not as a universal ban on

Christian involvement in politics or governance. As will be elaborated shortly, many of Jesus' teachings directly address how the world should be ordered and make clear that Christians are expected to work to put these principles into practice.

In the other two examples, there is no basis for claiming a dualistic view that completely separates the sacred from the secular, since that idea is foreign to the Bible. Both the Old and New Testaments make the same point: everything—including the state—belongs to God and is under his authority. When Paul writes to the Romans, he is not endorsing some secular order insulated from Christian influence. By calling rulers "instituted by God," he presupposes their duty to govern in line with God's standards revealed in scripture. What he doesn't do is suggest that Christians must passively accept rulers or laws that defy God's will—an idea flatly contradicted by his own actions. In Philippi, after being beaten and jailed, Paul refused the magistrates' quiet order to slip away and instead demanded a public reckoning for their injustice (Acts 16:35–40). In Corinth, he kept preaching Christ even when dragged before the proconsul Gallio, who eventually threw out the case (Acts 18:12–17). Later, though fully aware that bold testimony would bring imprisonment, Paul proclaimed the gospel before the Sanhedrin, governors Felix and Festus, and even King Agrippa, refusing to soften his message to please the governing authorities or save his own skin (Acts 21–26). And when Festus sought to hand him back to Jerusalem, Paul openly defied that order of the governor and appealed to Caesar himself (Acts 25:10–11).

These episodes make clear that Paul never regarded earthly rulers as absolute; whenever man's command collided with God's, Paul chose God. In doing so, he stood in perfect continuity with the rest of the apostles, who declared to the authorities, "We must obey God rather than human beings" (Acts 5:29).

Put simply, for Paul, the call to obey authorities is not absolute and does not remove believers' responsibility to work toward and support laws that reflect biblical ethics. In fact, his description of a governing official as "God's servant for your good," who "bears the sword" to punish evil, suggests that governance should align with God's definitions of good and evil. Logic suggests that this is likely to occur only if Christians are engaged in politics.

Similarly, when Jesus says to render unto Caesar, the context shows that he was addressing the immediate issue of paying taxes, not prescribing a universal divide between faith and politics. At most, his statement supports the legitimacy of civil authority, but it does not exempt it from God's ultimate authority.

Interpreting these scriptures or others like them as prohibitions against Christian political engagement is at odds with Christian practice and tradition. When, during the Protestant Reformation, the newly formed Anabaptist churches outlawed political activities for their members (explored more fully in a later section of this chapter), they were doing something that the Christians around them viewed as unbiblical. Likewise, when Christians today abdicate their duty to engage politically, they are departing from the historic witness of the Church and embracing a distortion of Christian responsibility.

Understanding Why the First Christians Were Less Active Politically

It's true that in the first 300 years of the faith, Christians avoided public office and withdrew from direct political engagement. However, their abstinence was rooted more in practical necessity than theological prohibition. Simply put, in the first three centuries of Christianity—a time when the faith was illegal and paganism was enforced by an uncompromising, totalitarian state—a believer couldn't serve in any political role without being forced to explicitly renounce core doctrines. Roman authorities, who at the time ruled all the nations where the early Christians resided, required that any official of the state and all governmental actions acknowledge the deity of Caesar and give homage to the pagan gods—neither of which a practicing Christian could do. This early avoidance of political activity by Christians was pragmatic, driven by the impossibility of holding office without idolatrous compromise in a polytheistic system. How can we be sure? Because throughout scripture there are numerous examples of God's people actively participating in political pursuits. The Bible—the Christian's guide for life—celebrates faithful believers advancing justice and God's purposes through direct political intervention. There is Joseph, son of Jacob, as governor in Egypt (Genesis 41-47), Daniel as a lead advisor to the Babylonian king (Daniel 1-6), and Esther as queen influencing Persian policy (Esther 4-8). The distinct lesson from scripture is that participating in the affairs of state—if done to the glory of God and without compromising one's faith—is not only permissible but commendable. There are writings from certain Christian leaders of the first, second, and third centuries that ignored or misinterpreted this clear biblical precedent from the Old Testament in order to convince their contemporaries that God Himself forbids political engagement.[8] Like some Christians today, they twisted Jesus' command to render unto Caesar into a blanket prohibition on public involvement. But these arguments of early apologists—which are not authoritative to the faith—were ultimately rationalizations for inaction in what appeared to be insurmountable circumstances.

The dramatic reversal of Christians' behavior at the start of the fourth century further demonstrates that it was largely pragmatism, not theological prohibition, that kept early believers from engaging politically. In 313 AD, with the passage of the Edict of Milan, the Roman Emperor Constantine legalized Christianity and the political landscape changed. With civic participation no longer requiring idolatry, Christians began serving in government positions. By 380 AD, Constantine's successor, Theodosius I, had made Christianity the state religion, and the highest governing roles were filled by devout Christians. Under the influx of Christian policymakers, the laws of the empire began to reflect biblical norms and values.

Even before the legalization of Christianity in the fourth century, some bold believers of the second and third centuries participated in overt political activism. We have examples of early Christian intellectuals producing political writings that sought both legal protections and the promotion of Christian ethical principles, marking one of the earliest forms of advocacy for religious freedom. Quadratus of Athens, in his *Apology* to Emperor Hadrian (c. 125–129 AD), appealed for an end to arbitrary persecutions of believers.[9] A generation later, Justin Martyr addressed his *First Apology* (c. 150–155 AD) to Emperor Antoninus Pius and his sons, urging them to investigate false charges against Christians, while also commending the moral contributions Christians made to society through honesty, charity, and civic virtue.[10] Finally, Athenagoras, in his *Plea for the Christians* (c. 176–177 AD) to Emperor Marcus Aurelius and Commodus, refuted malicious slanders and pressed for Christians to receive the same legal protections as other subjects.[11] Together, these writings show that from its earliest centuries, Christianity was not politically silent.

What Did Jesus Say?

Of course, Jesus's words in the New Testament are the loudest call to the political engagement of Christians. His *Great Commission* is the first and clearest mandate. In Matthew 28:18–20, Jesus commands his followers: "Go and make disciples of all nations, baptizing them ... and teaching them to obey everything I have commanded you." "Nations" ("ethne" in Greek) doesn't refer merely to individual converts, but to entire peoples, cultures, and social orders. The task isn't only to bring isolated persons into the faith but to disciple whole national communities so that their collective life reflects alignment with the teachings of Christ.

Historically, the most enduring way societies have been "taught to obey" moral commands has been through law. As explored fully in Chapter 6, laws do not merely restrain behavior; they shape it, reinforce shared norms, and instruct the conscience of a people. To disciple nations, then, requires more than private evangelism or personal morality. It demands that believers—through legal, peaceful means—work to see Christ's commands embedded in the very structures that govern public life.

Political participation is not a distraction from the Great Commission but a vital outworking of it. Entering into the legislative and judicial arenas is one way Christians "go into all the world," bringing Christ's authority into the halls of power and ensuring that public policies reflect divine justice, protect families and the vulnerable, and encourage virtue. Political arenas thus become mission fields, essential to the comprehensive discipling of nations. The same truth resounds in the prayer Jesus taught his disciples: "your kingdom come, your will be done, on earth as it is in heaven" (Matthew 6:10). To pray these words with sincerity is to long for God's rule to be manifested in the concrete realities of earthly life. But this petition cannot be fulfilled if the structures that govern society remain hostile to or detached from God's will. For God's will to be "done on earth," it must take visible form in the institutions that shape human life—laws, courts, governments, schools, and economies. To pray the Lord's Prayer while rejecting political engagement is a contradiction; one cannot earnestly ask for God's reign to be manifest on earth while simultaneously refusing to labor for his standards to inform public law and policy. The prayer itself calls Christians into active participation in building a social order that mirrors heaven's righteousness.

Nowhere is this public dimension of the Christian faith clearer than in the Sermon on the Mount. Jesus' ethical teaching in Matthew 5–7 was never intended as a set of lofty ideals for private life alone. His pronouncements on anger, marriage, sexuality, truth-telling, justice, and even the treatment of enemies are principles meant to shape the whole of human society. Indeed, many of his teachings bear directly on governance. He instructs on how justice should be pursued, how disputes should be resolved, how oaths and contracts should be honored, and how violence should be restrained.

To take Jesus seriously means applying his words not only to private piety but also to public order. The most effective way for his principles to shape all of life is to see them codified into law, where they serve as guardrails for society and become teachers of conscience. Far from suggesting a privatized or apolitical faith, Jesus' words are the loudest call to Christian political engagement. To ignore that call is to truncate the great mission he gave his Church and to betray the very prayer he taught Christians to pray.

Do Quietists Renounce Christian Advancements?

Those who claim the name of Christian while advocating political quietism face a few embarrassing questions. First, if believers—who possess *the mind of Christ* (1 Corinthians 2:16)—are not equipped to shape laws and governments, then who exactly do they think is better qualified? Second, if the moral vision of Christianity is unfit to guide legislation, then what set of values do they imagine is more worthy to direct the life of a nation? To answer both questions with secular alternatives is not merely shortsighted—it calls into question whether such a person truly understands, or even belongs to, the faith they profess.

Those who claim the Bible as God's Word must choose whether their primary loyalty is to Christianity or to libertarian ideology. I've seen many Christians, when asked to support a law pleasing to God but unpopular in culture, take the libertarian escape route. In those moments, their strongest allegiance is to "freedom of speech" or "freedom of consensual behavior," placing the moral rule of "live and let live" above God's commands as if it were the highest law.

While freedom is highly valued in Christian thought—and Christians have been its greatest defenders—true believers recognize that it cannot override divine command. Yes, there are ways that the moral law of the Christian faith can be adapted to modern times. In fact, the next two chapters focus specifically on that. However, what I am condemning at this moment is compromise and inaction, not the careful, thoughtful application of scriptural principles to contemporary settings.

By citing libertarian ideas like "I'm for 'live and let live'" to justify silence or inaction, these so-called Christians reveal that they are more concerned with defending Enlightenment ideals than upholding biblical truth. Masking indifference in the language of liberty is not wisdom or restraint—it is compromise and a denial of the very King they claim to serve.

A final question exposes the utter folly and moral bankruptcy of political quietism: When Christians of the recent past—within the last 200 years—labored through political action to produce faith-informed laws that ended slavery, reformed prisons, rescued women from prostitution, and protected children from sexual and labor exploitation—alongside countless other advances for human dignity—were they defying the will of God, or fulfilling it? Was the Christian politician William Wilberforce wrong to use his political power to tear the shackles from enslaved Black men and women and crush the transatlantic slave trade?

Was the Christian politician Anthony Ashley-Cooper, the 7th Earl of Shaftesbury, wrong to stand in Parliament and put an end to children being sent into coal mines, factories, and chimneys where they were maimed, starved, and worked to exhaustion?

Was the Christian political activist Elizabeth Fry wrong to confront lawmakers until women and children were no longer crammed into filthy, disease-ridden prisons and treated like animals?

Was the Christian political activist William Booth, founder of the Salvation Army, wrong to expose the brothels of London where children were bought and sold, and to force Parliament to raise the age of consent and criminalize trafficking?

If the answer to each of these questions is "No—they were not wrong" (and what person of good conscience could say otherwise?), then how dare today's political quietists claim that Christianity requires withdrawal from politics? Their defense of quietism is to side with oppression, applaud indifference, and rewrite history as if heroism were sin and inaction were virtue.

Are these Christians Rejecting Politics or Just Right-Leaning Politics?

In many churches today, pastors and Christian leaders who claim that "faith and politics don't mix" reveal not neutrality, but hypocrisy. What they really mean is that conservative or right-leaning ideas should never be raised from the pulpit. Yet week after week, they demonstrate that it's perfectly acceptable for them to promote left-wing social agendas—preaching against the evils of "whiteness," championing diversity, equity, and inclusion, and urging congregations to adopt increasingly tolerant views on homosexuality and transgender identity.

What their congregations never hear are sermons on discrimination against Whites in hiring, the irreparable harm done to the genitals of transgender children,[12] the erosion of traditional marriage, or progressive policies that release violent criminals back onto the streets. They may call for open borders and attack officials who enforce immigration law, but they remain silent on parishioners struggling with housing affordability or limited access to healthcare caused by mass migration. Guilt over failing to combat climate change or systemic racism is acceptable, but criticism of sexual immorality is not. To them, progressive causes are part of the gospel, while conservative causes are "divisive" and "political."

This inconsistency is just as widespread in evangelical or conservative Christian institutions as it is in theologically liberal churches.

When politically conservative believers are told not to "inject politics into church life"—a warning that applies only to one side—it's often justified by an appeal to following a "third way."

"Third Way Christianity" is a recent approach within modern conservative Protestantism that tries to find a middle path between two perceived extremes: historic Christian belief (orthodoxy) on one side and compassionate social action (orthopraxy) on the other. It emphasizes a "both/and" approach instead of "either/or."

Third Way pastors often describe their churches as places that value truth tempered by love, rejecting hard stands that can cause polarizing debates. They criticize conservatives for being too rigid about doctrine or morality, especially on issues such as sexuality, gender, and science. They also criticize liberals for being too quick to accommodate culture or downplay the authority of the Bible. Instead, they say they want to create a space where questions can be asked safely, differences can be discussed, and everyone feels included.

In practical terms, creating a space open to questioning, where all feel included, requires avoiding strict literalism. For example, LGBT individuals are welcomed in a spirit of love and relationship but are never called to fully align with the moral rules and doctrinal boundaries of historic Christianity. In reality, Third Way Christianity is, at best, a gateway to theological liberalism, and, at worst, theological liberalism itself.

Its intention to avoid division may be noble, but it inevitably leads to compromise, with leaders rejecting or softening clear biblical teachings on sin, sexuality, and moral order. In their effort to be inoffensive—what they call "winsome"—they lose the moral clarity that scripture provides. By refusing to let the Bible set their boundaries, they instead allow the surrounding culture to define them. Ironically, these Third Way Christians populating evangelical churches have discovered the only "middle path" that always veers left.

Other Critics of the Mix of Christianity and Politics

It's not just certain Christians who prefer godless government. In their effort to keep Christianity from shaping politics, political quietists find themselves aligned with agnostics and atheists openly hostile to their faith. These secularists and moral relativists are desperate to ensure their worldview—a system of values at odds with biblical teachings—faces no challenges, so they portray Christian participation in the public sphere as illegitimate.

The fallacious arguments these secularists use to justify barring Christians from political life begin with a cry of "separation of church and state." They falsely suggest this notion (largely taken for granted in Western nations) equates to an absolute barrier preventing Christians from advancing their moral convictions at the ballot box or in public office. We saw in Chapter 2 that, as originally conceived, it actually means that the state cannot establish an official religion or interfere with religious freedom of peacefully practicing citizens. Nevertheless, these secularists assert that any policy inspired or underpinned by biblical principles is off-limits. Hypocritically, they maintain that policies generated out of *any other* ideological system should enjoy full consideration and reception within a country's legislatures. It's not faith they dislike, but Christian faith. Marxism, Environmentalism, or Queerness are faith systems complete with their own moral codes and enmeshed, esoteric beliefs. They demand blind acceptance and unquestioning assent, as witnessed in their calls to "trust the science" or declarations that "the debate is settled." Yet these faith systems are allowed to pass unchallenged, enforcing a double standard in which only Christian principles are excluded from shaping legislation.

Secularists know they must obscure the fact that every law springs from some moral code if they want to persuade others that Christian norms alone should not shape legislation. They must pretend that statutes shaped by their own secular humanist principles or other ideologies are somehow "value free" and neutral when in fact they advance a very specific agenda. Importantly, to get their way they must overturn foundational ideas of democracy and the principle of equal participation. That is, they must advance the illegal and unethical idea that only secular or leftist worldviews are eligible to inform legislation but not the worldview that emphasizes equality for all, love for one's neighbor, and moral accountability.

Another spurious reason used by secularists to keep biblical principles out of governance is the charge that Christians seek to "impose" their beliefs, framing faith-based advocacy as inherently authoritarian. Secularists often paint vivid pictures of theocratic dystopias, claiming that if Christians held political power, they would launch campaigns of forced conversion—something their doctrine forbids and that all practicing Christians today find abhorrent. I will more fully debunk this slander in the next section; here I will note that in modern Western societies the only group truly guilty of promoting forced conversion is progressives. In just the last decade progressives in government, business, and academia have used jail, fines, firings, and expulsions to force conversion to their doctrines.

To those who wish to deny Christians the right to political engagement, the inescapable fact is that Christians—like all communities in a pluralistic democracy—have a legitimate right to advocate for their convictions in shaping the law. History shows that Christians—especially Protestants—who have exercised political influence have, more often than other groups, tended to do so with an articulated concern for protecting broad civil rights and freedoms, not solely those of their own community. Equally praiseworthy, their moral code requires that they pursue influence through lawful and ethical means.

Aside from rare instances of resisting tyrannical overreach in defense of basic, God-given liberties, Christians have consistently rejected violence or revolution as a means of seizing power. In this, their political engagement stands in stark contrast to ideological systems such as Marxism and certain currents of contemporary progressivism, which openly embrace disruption, coercion, and even violence as legitimate tools of political change.

About Theocracy

In the first chapter of *Christ or Collapse* I wrote:

> The purpose of this book is to convince readers that cultural renewal—indeed, societal survival—depends on making the affairs of state and legal frameworks reflective of the norms and values of Christianity. For those squirming uncomfortably and murmuring that I'm advocating for a theocracy, you're wrong. However, you'll have to wait several chapters before I provide my full thoughts on that issue.

Well, thanks for waiting.

A theocracy is a form of government where top government leaders are religious clerics and the official laws of the land are drawn directly from sacred texts, dictating required religious beliefs. Among Muslim countries, theocracies are still active today, with Iran serving as a prominent example as of 2026.

Since 1979, Iran has been ruled by Shia Muslim clerics who hold both religious and political power, with the Supreme Leader—always a senior Islamic cleric—having authority over all branches of government. There, the ruling clerics use state power to punish religious dissent and compel words and deeds that outwardly confirm state-approved theology. This includes mandatory dress codes such as the hijab, fasting in public during Ramadan, gender segregation rules, legal penalties for proselytizing by non-Muslims or for Muslims converting to other religions, and a state-run education system that promotes Islamic theology.

Similarly, Saudi Arabia, while officially a monarchy, bases its laws directly on the Koran, the Hadith, and fundamentalist Wahhabi Sunni doctrine. Clerics play a strong role in the courts and government and, as in Iran, use state power to enforce speech and behavior that outwardly affirm Islamic orthodoxy. In Afghanistan as well, the Taliban has established a regime that compels a strict interpretation of Sunni Islam derived directly from sacred texts and places religious leaders in top political positions.

In Western history, there have been Catholic theocracies in which the Church held both religious and political power. One clear example is the Papal States, which were ruled by the Pope for over a thousand years until 1870. In these states, the Pope acted as both the head of the Church and the head of government; he held a cross and a sword, the latter serving as a baton to marshal his army. Church law was also the law of the land. In the Middle Ages, the Catholic Church had major influence over the Holy Roman Empire, which stretched across

Europe, and kings often needed the Pope's approval to rule. In late fifteenth-century Spain, during the rule of Ferdinand and Isabella, the Church and government worked closely together, especially during the Inquisition. Bishops sometimes served as government leaders. The Church also controlled the courts and even scientific investigation.

Protestantism, since its beginning in the 1500s, has shown a clear opposition to theocracy—that is, to the direct rule of clergy over the state or the merging of church and government into one authority. This stance arose partly in reaction to the centralized religious and political power of the Catholic Church, particularly in the Papal States, and in monarchies where Catholicism shaped civil law.

The Protestant desire for a nuanced separation of church and state was also rooted in their inclination to try, as much as possible, to adhere to the authority of scripture alone (sola scriptura). They also took seriously Jesus' teaching in Matthew 22:21, "Render unto Caesar the things that are Caesar's, and unto God the things that are God's," interpreting it not as a reason to abandon civic engagement, but as a call to carefully distinguish between temporal and spiritual obligations.

However, some early Protestants—most notably the Anabaptists, ancestors of today's Mennonites and Christian Brethren—took this principle further. They advocated complete separation from governmental authority and rejected any influence of the church on the state, a stance that set them apart from other Reformers. For them, any involvement in politics was forbidden. Even today, among some Anabaptist groups, voting is discouraged. Such a position has caused many of their communities to have little voice or influence in shaping their broader societies. In those cases, they are a people "acted upon," not a people of action. By refusing to advocate publicly for their beliefs, they have often been forced to endure the will of others hostile to their convictions.

Typically, Reformers sought some form of political relationship or leverage. For example, Martin Luther, the founder of the Lutheran Church, advanced a "two kingdoms" doctrine—the claim that God rules through both church and state, each with its own proper sphere. Yet in practice, this doctrine still carried a distinctly Catholic impulse toward theocracy. Luther was, after all, a Catholic priest and Augustinian monk before founding his own movement; old habits die hard. He explicitly called on secular rulers to enforce religious uniformity by endorsing his theological system and punishing those who believed "incorrectly." The result was the creation of government-sanctioned, state-funded churches in Lutheran territories and an enduring alliance between crown and pulpit.

Today, it's theologically liberal Lutherans, such as those in the Evangelical Lutheran Church in America and Canada, who tend to be more politically active—often engaging in advocacy on issues like social justice, environmental care, and economic inequality. Conservative Lutherans, such as those in the Lutheran Church–Missouri Synod, the Wisconsin Evangelical Lutheran Synod, and Lutheran Church Canada, are more cautious about political involvement. This hesitancy stems from a reinterpretation of Martin Luther's "two kingdoms" doctrine that leans starkly away from any type of political engagement (in some conservative Lutheran churches, their attitude now mimics the Anabaptists they once opposed).

To a certain degree, this retreat is a historical reaction against church-state abuses in twentieth-century Europe, which included the Nazification of the German Protestant Church, where some Lutheran church leaders supported or were co-opted by the Nazi regime. Such experiences convinced conservative Lutherans of the dangers of merging church authority with political power, leading them to prioritize the church's spiritual mission over direct political activism. Of course, such a stance of political passivity overlooks the fact that without bold and consistent public engagement, the church's spiritual mission will be hindered and ultimately shut down—even made illegal—by those who *will use* political power to oppose it.

Calvin and His Influence on Traditional Conservatism

In contrast to Martin Luther, John Calvin—the founder of Calvinism and the spiritual father of churches today bearing the Reformed name (for example, Christian Reformed, Presbyterians, and certain Baptist traditions)—drew a sharper line between church and state. Critics are justified in arguing that, in the earliest Calvinist Reformed communities, that dividing line wasn't always as sharp as it needed to be. In fact, like Luther, Calvin himself could lean theocratic. That said, key ideas were introduced early on, and the practical understanding of how to carry them out effectively and judiciously eventually crystallized.

Ideally, the church was to guide spiritual life, applying instruction and discipline to its members in matters of theology and morality, while the state was to maintain public justice, civil order, and support established Christian moral principles for the common good. To solidify this division of powers, Calvin insisted that pastors should not hold political office and that civil magistrates—politicians—should not be accountable to a particular church, but only to God. When he said that political leaders are accountable only to God, Calvin was not advancing support for secularism—banishing God from governance. Rather, he meant that government had a God-given responsibility to carry out its functions in accordance with Christian morality, free from the control of church leaders or institutions.

In short, Protestantism within the Calvinist or Reformed tradition affirmed Christian moral accountability in public life but resisted the fusion of church and state power characteristic of theocracy. The state should protect citizens' right to practice their religion and support public morality based on Christian moral absolutes, but leave matters of doctrinal instruction and moral discipline to the church.

In his division of governing powers, Calvin added a third area: the family. As described briefly in Chapter 6, Calvin maintained that the state, church, and family all had their own separate rights and responsibilities; this doctrine has come to be understood as "sphere sovereignty." The three spheres were to support one another while preventing overlap in their roles. While the role of the state was minimal, the family, and to a lesser extent the religious community, absorbed all other rights to governance. In stark opposition to theocracy, Calvin's model—especially as it was refined over time and as it influences Traditional Conservatism today—does not allow the state to establish churches or compel religious belief. Instead, such formal merging of religious and political authority is expressly forbidden.

Traditional Conservatism owes much to Reformed Protantism. In light of the explanations above, readers can now more clearly understand the declarations in Chapter 1 that Traditional Conservatism "is grounded in British common law and Christianity, in particular, *Reformed Protestantism*" and that "traditional conservatives draw extensively from some of the key principles of *Reformed Protestant theology.*"

While 21st century Traditional Conservatism maps closely to sphere sovereignty, ironically, many contemporary supporters of the philosophy are unaware of the Reformed influence behind this principle. Be that as it may, they intuitively understand and endorse it. For them, they have arrived at a concept approximating sphere sovereignty without direct knowledge of Reformed theology because they are familiar with biblical teaching generally. In particular, traditional conservatives who understand that Christian doctrine should inform their political philosophy can, through scripture alone, reach similar conclusions about the distinct roles of church and state.

For that matter, as Chapter 1 demonstrated, all the principles of Traditional Conservatism can be derived from scripture viewed through a conservative Protestant lens. However, the advantage of engaging with Reformed theology lies in its more comprehensive and systematic framework, which offers a ready-made model for applying these principles. This allows traditional conservatives to quickly reference an established archetype without needing to construct the concept from scratch.

Traditional Conservatism Does Not Advocate Theocracy

Having thoroughly analyzed the defining features of absolute theocracies, as well as the indicators of movements leaning toward theocratic governance, we are now positioned to fully address the question: "Does Traditional Conservatism, in fact, advocate a theocracy?" Of course, the answer is no.

Drawing together the threads of the foregoing discussion, we can see that when Traditional Conservatism asserts the necessity of embedding Christian norms and values within the framework of state governance, it does so with the explicit understanding that such influence is to be exercised in accordance with the Reformed model of sphere sovereignty. The implication is that:

> Guided by Traditional Conservatism, the state supports a Christian ethical position in its statutes but remains institutionally separate from any controlling religious bodies, is not governed by clergy, and does not enact laws that require religious belief. Citizens are free to practice the religion of their choice or no religion; however, religious freedom does not extend to groups advocating violence or revolution against peaceful citizens or the historic norms, values, and culture of the West rooted in the Christian faith. In judicial proceedings, Christians and non-Christian citizens receive the same impartial treatment.

A government informed by theology is not the same as a government that is a theocracy. One involves moral inspiration; the other, direct religious rule. And for those still uncomfortable with the notion of faith guiding civic life, the reality is that, one way or another, some ideological system informs every government. Traditional Conservatism, aligned with sphere sovereignty, accepts the government's role in upholding Christian norms (without compelling belief) because it rejects the notion that a nation's policies and practices can be ideologically or morally neutral. It recognizes that every action of the state—including inaction—provides moral guidance to the population.

Therefore, to foster a unified, harmonious, and prosperous society, it holds that the state must actively support ethical behaviors and customs proven to advance individual and collective well-being. On the basis of historical and empirical evidence from the West, Traditional Conservatism argues that Christian norms and values are uniquely effective in producing these outcomes. In light of this evidence, Christians and non-Christians alike are able to subscribe to Traditional Conservatism not as an act of compelled faith but as a rational choice based on a preponderance of facts. Consequently, supporters of the philosophy hold that it simply makes sense for these singularly potent, faith-derived principles to guide national governance and shape important aspects of public life.

Beyond theory, practical experience itself demonstrates that Traditional Conservatism opposes theocracy rather than endorsing it. From the very founding of America and Canada, until at least World War II and to a certain extent into the 1960s, the norms and values of Christianity *did* inform governance at all levels of the state (this is clearly outlined in Chapter 2). During this time of explicit Christian influence, neither nation was ever described as a theocracy but, instead, repeatedly and accurately celebrated as unique bastions of liberty, harmony, and prosperity the likes of which the world had never seen.

As Chapter 1 clarified, regardless of moniker, "the true measure of Traditional Conservatism is the degree to which a party, politician, or individual aligns with the core principles of the philosophy." To be sure, there were politicians and political parties in the past operating under labels other than "conservative," but, in large measure, they still promoted the tenets of Traditional Conservatism implicitly or explicitly, and freedom and flourishing followed.

North America of the 1800s—Fueled by Theology; Free of Theocracy

As a specific case study, the 1800s are instructive. Those years are described by historians as "The Evangelical Century" because across North America and the UK the influence of devout, traditional, Protestant Christianity was experiencing its greatest impact on all aspects of politics and society.[13] Neither before nor since, in the U.S. or Canada, has the link between Christianity and the state been greater; however, democracy, not theocracy, reigned.

At the height of the Evangelical Century, French political thinker and historian Alexis de Tocqueville traveled to America and studied its people and its governing structures. His observations were expressed in his now famous book *Democracy in America* published in two volumes between 1835 and 1840. Tocqueville argued that the Christian religion, present in all aspects of public life, was not a hindrance but essential to the success of American democracy. He saw it as a stabilizing force that promoted moral behavior and civic virtue, which he considered crucial for maintaining a free society:

> The Americans combine the notions of Christianity and of liberty so intimately in their minds that it is impossible to make them conceive the one without the other...
>
> There is no country in the world where the Christian religion retains a greater influence over the souls of men than in America; and there can be no greater proof of its utility, and of its conformity to human nature, than that

its influence is powerfully felt over the most enlightened and free nation of the earth.[14]

However, among his observations, the most striking are his remarks on the application of sphere sovereignty in the governance of the American nation. While he does not explicitly mention the Reformed model by name—and may not have known its particulars—he saw clearly that the state supported Christian norms and values while retaining independence from any religious organization or clergy. He writes:

> The clergy of all the different sects hold no public appointments; they are not seen in the assemblies of the nation, nor do they mingle in the councils of the state...
>
> Religion in America takes no direct part in the government of society, but it must be regarded as the first of their political institutions; for if it does not impart a taste for freedom, it facilitates the use of it. it directs the customs of the community, and, by regulating domestic life, it regulates the state.[15]
>
> The Americans show, by their practice, that they feel the high necessity of imparting morality to democratic communities by means of religion.[16]

In the 19th century, Canada was equally committed to integrating Christianity into all aspects of public life, though it lacked the strong Reformed Protestant influence that shaped American governance. Instead, it was grounded in British colonial traditions that promoted official state churches, with the Anglican Church dominant in English-speaking regions and the Catholic Church prevailing in Quebec. As a result, when federal and provincial governments sought to embed Christian norms and values throughout governance, they often did so by promoting specific Christian denominations. In some limited cases, they went further, mandating religious beliefs—actions that, from a Reformed theological perspective, overstepped the boundaries of sphere sovereignty. Yet despite this blurred line between church and state, a theocracy never emerged. On the contrary, individual liberties, national unity, and prosperity all increased.

But there were some negative consequences from this governmental overreach, notably the state-compelled attendance of some Indigenous children in religious residential schools. Initially, early tribal chiefs viewed these schools—requested as part of their treaty negotiations—as a way to improve the lives of their people. The schools first enrolled Indigenous children voluntarily, but over time, government policies made attendance compulsory for some. The state, working hand in hand with clerics, granted Catholic and Anglican churches near-exclusive control over the schools, where, in some cases, abusive clergy forced their religious beliefs on students and punished efforts to preserve Indigenous languages and customs. In this regard, Canada serves as a cautionary example showing that, in a properly functioning nation, the state isn't in the "compelling belief business," and parents alone hold full authority over their children.

Sphere Sovereignty—The Sphere of the State

The example above, with its focus on what should fall under the authority of parents, provides a segue to more fully explain the limits of state governance under sphere sovereignty and within the overarching political philosophy of Traditional Conservatism.

We have established that within this framework the state is responsible for ensuring Christian norms and values are reflected in the laws of the land. Furthermore, in keeping with sphere sovereignty, under Traditional Conservatism, the state is mandated to provide a system of national defense to protect citizens from external threats. It also provides laws, police, and courts to enforce justice and maintain public order within the nation. This entails guaranteeing basic legal rights, impartiality, and equality before the law, upholding the validity of contracts, preventing and punishing crime, and protecting the weak or vulnerable from exploitation. With the consent of the governed, there may be some minimal projects of public works initiated by the state. For example, the state may construct a system of main thorough-fares both to facilitate the efficient execution of its duties and to ensure that citizens have reliable access to its outposts.

Most important under sphere sovereignty, however, is what the state must not touch.

Sphere Sovereignty—The Sphere of Family

Apart from the particular mandates given to the state—listed above—all other governing powers flow to the family or church community. The family's governing powers are greatest, with decisions on marriage, procreation, food, shelter, healthcare, education, and the stewardship of household resources decided within the home.

To say that families have authority over marriage requires clarification. It doesn't mean that parents arrange unions, nor that church and state are excluded from involvement. Marriage begins with a man and a woman freely choosing one another and entering into a lifelong covenant; in doing so, they exercise their individual authority to form a new family unit. The church—the local community of like-minded friends and neighbors—doesn't create marriage but blesses and witnesses the union, instructs the couple in their covenantal responsibilities, and calls them to live faithfully within it. When they falter, the church community admonishes and guides them toward reconciliation. For its part, the state doesn't define or invent marriage but publicly recognizes it, securing its legal and civil implications, such as property, inheritance, and custody. Importantly, this role of the state differs from its current function: today, the state claims authority to regulate and define marriage itself (as seen in the legalization of same-sex unions). Under the proposed model, the state's authority is limited to recognizing and protecting what the family and church have already established. Here, the couple establishes the marriage, the church affirms it, and the state records and protects it in law.

More broadly, within the family, parents have the right to guide their children spiritually, morally, culturally, and vocationally, and they are responsible for caring for both children and elderly family members in need. The family doesn't need to provide all these services directly but retains the authority to determine how they are met, whether by choosing a doctor or medical treatment or by selecting a school or alternative form of education. The key point is that the government's role isn't to run these systems or dictate how they operate. Rather, it's to protect the family's freedom to make these decisions. The public education systems of America and Canada provide the strongest testimony against giving the state control of instructing children. Today, they promote scientifically questionable and divisive concepts with curricula emphasizing fraudulent ideas like systemic racism or the notion that gender is a choice and fluid. The history and culture of the West are misrepresented with a primary focus on its shortcomings, such as slavery and the darker aspects of colonialism, while its decisive contributions, including individual liberty, scientific advancement, and democratic institutions, are minimized or ignored. This undermining of shared cultural foundations essential to civic cohesion occurs alongside persistently poor learning outcomes. Every three years, the Organization for Economic Cooperation and Development runs the Programme for International Student Assessment—or PISA for short. It's a massive global test that checks how well 15-year-olds are doing in math, reading, and science, letting countries compare their education systems on an even playing field. The latest results are hard to ignore: North America's scores are slipping, even though we spend more on public education than most of the world.

In the U.S., PISA results show math and reading scores dropping year over year,[17] with today's students registering some of the weakest math performance since PISA started.[18] Canada doesn't fare much better, with scores dropping in similar fashion.[19] This is happening even though U.S. schools spend about $14,347 per student[20] and Canada spends about $15,100[21]—both far above the OECD average of roughly $11,990.[22]

In North America, most of that funding goes to public teachers' salaries.[23] While public school teachers in the U.S. and Canada rank among the best paid in the world,[24] their students tend to perform worse than those educated at home or in private schools—where teachers usually earn less, and resources are often more limited.[25] Studies show homeschooled students regularly score far higher on standardized tests,[26] and private school students consistently outperform their public school peers in both academics and graduation ra tes.[27] Clearly, public education has grown into a bloated system promoting ideology over essential skills, while the most effective teaching increasingly occurs outside the system, on leaner budgets with greater flexibility. It would seem that the greatest lesson taught by public education is that state monopolies in areas beyond their sphere of sovereignty do damage. Without competition, there's no incentive to improve, innovate, or operate efficiently. Employees, shielded by union protections and bureaucratic inertia, face little pressure to excel, and complacency and weak performance become widespread. Meanwhile, taxpayers are forced to bankroll the system regardless of quality, leaving costs to climb unchecked.

In Canada, the inefficiencies and poor results of the public education system are mirrored in the state-run healthcare system. While the country is the highest spender on health care among 30 OECD countries with universal systems, allocating 13.3% of GDP in 2020, it's at the bottom for health outcomes. In terms of resource availability, it is: 28th of 30 for physicians per capita, 23rd of 28 for available care beds, 26th of 29 for MRI machines, and 27th of 30 for CT scanners.[28] It ranks last among universal health-care countries for timely specialist appointments and elective surgeries.[29]

These delays cause significant harm, with an estimated $2.1 billion in lost wages in 2019 rising to $4.1 billion in 2021; there were at least 1,480 deaths in 2018–19 due to waiting for treatment.[30]

Of course, there are problems within the private system of health care found in America, notably the sky-high costs of medications and treatments fueled by corporate greed. Pharmaceutical giants and insurance companies collude to maximize profits, sidelining affordable care for millions. These are issues traditional conservatives would feel duty-bound to tackle head-on.

Sphere Sovereignty—The Sphere of Church

While the sphere of family draws its circle wide, the church's sphere has a smaller circumference. This more limited reach is reflected in its definition within sphere sovereignty and Traditional Conservatism.

Unlike in Catholicism, where the "Church" implies an international organization with a bureaucracy rivalling the world's largest governments, when Traditional Conservatism or sphere sovereignty speaks of powers flowing to the "church," it refers instead to the local, autonomous community exercising spiritual and moral authority within its own distinct social and cultural context. Individuals and families choose to participate in and support their local church community, which operates independently rather than as part of a centralized, compulsory bureaucracy.

As membership is voluntary—respecting personal conscience and local autonomy—citizens who are non-Christian or opposed to religion may choose not to take part. Theoretically, they could create their own version of a church community of likeminded citizens, which would be tasked with the same governing responsibilities, adapted as they saw fit.

As understood by Traditional Conservatism and sphere sovereignty, the church's responsibilities include calling the state to just behavior when it strays, teaching sound doctrine, administering the sacraments, providing pastoral care, fostering moral formation among its members, and disciplining those who persistently breach ethical standards without repentance. Discipline, as practiced by the church, is a loving and orderly process that begins with private admonition, in which a member is gently confronted to encourage repentance; if no remorse is shown, it proceeds to formal reproof by the church's leaders. Should the person continue to resist, the matter is brought before the wider congregation, and if there is still no repentance, the individual may be excluded from fellowship and membership.

The desire is to have the member return to full affiliation, but the integrity of the group won't be compromised for the sake of "inclusivity" and the unapologetic person's feelings. Contrary to what popular television series like *The Handmaid's Tale* suggest, within Traditional Conservatism the most severe forms of church discipline involve social stigma and ostracism for unrepentant ethical violations, not any form of corporal punishment.

In its more "antagonistic" actions, the church's authority is spiritual and persuasive, not coercive, and at its strongest, it's aimed at calling the state to account. When the church urges the state to act justly, it does so through public witness and moral exhortation, not through violence or force. Public protests and rallies are legitimate activities for a church and its leaders; training congregants to make explosives in a church basement is not.

To keep the church at arm's length from the state, clergy generally refrain from holding elected office unless they first step down from church leadership. At the same time, devout Christian members of the congregation are encouraged to exercise their rights as citizens, including seeking public office. Just as progressive politicians deliberately embed the tenets of their doctrine into state policy, elected Christian laity seek to bring the light of Christ into the often-dark halls of political power.

The outward focus of the church, however, is primarily on works of mercy, caring especially for those who lack familial provision, such as orphans, widows, and the poor. These acts of charity and social service may be organized by church leaders, but they are often carried out by members of the congregation or by individuals specifically trained for such work, acting on behalf of the church. In the past, this has taken the form of charity hospitals, foster homes, or free church-run schools. The church's aim is to offer compassionate support, not to replace the family's responsibility; it steps in where families are unable to do so. Like the family, the church is not required to provide every service directly, but it retains the authority to determine how these responsibilities are carried out.

When social services are provided through a church community rather than by the government, care is delivered in the context of ongoing relationships, where needs are known firsthand and help is tailored to the individual's circumstances. This fosters deeper trust and shared accountability—qualities that government programs, by their bureaucratic nature, often struggle to cultivate. Because aid is typically distributed by people who personally know the recipient, resources are less likely to be misallocated or abused. The church community can also provide moral and spiritual encouragement alongside material help, addressing the root causes of hardship, not just the symptoms. Assistance is paired with mentorship, job connections, or skills training to encourage self-reliance, helping recipients move toward independence rather than long-term dependency.

Relying on church communities to provide social support will lead to more efficient use of resources. Churches often leverage volunteer labor, donated goods, and informal networks, reducing reliance on paid staff and complex logistics. In the aggregate, this approach will reduce the tax burden, meaning citizens have more disposable income to give voluntarily. Freed from compulsion through taxation, a more widespread culture of generosity and voluntary action could develop.

Under sphere sovereignty, the church's independence from the state ensures it can govern its internal affairs and public ministries without external interference. For its part, the government safeguards the church's freedom to carry out its divine mandate both within its local community and in the broader public square. However, it provides no funding—and that is a blessing. Contrary to what some may think, by providing no support beyond protecting a church's freedom to operate, the state is doing more, not less, to help. Sociologist of religion Rodney Stark has demonstrated that churches actually do better when the state provides no financial support.[31]

Far from strengthening religion, government funding and formal support tend to produce the opposite: dependency, stagnation, and decline. When churches are cushioned by subsidies, they lose the urgency to evangelize, the discipline to maintain doctrinal integrity, and the accountability that comes from serving real people rather than bureaucratic mandates. Religious leaders begin answering to politicians and state agencies instead of their congregations, hollowing out vitality from within. By contrast, churches that receive no such state aid must compete in the open marketplace of faith. This drives them to be more innovative, responsive, and mission-driven, while also fostering stronger bonds of trust and commitment with their members.[32] In short, what the state withholds in material support gets repaid in spiritual vitality.

Potentially a Forced Choice

Given the current financial situation in the West, sphere sovereignty—or a far worse alternative—may be inevitable. Across North

America, governments at every level are teetering on the brink of financial collapse. National debts are skyrocketing, unfunded liabilities for pensions and entitlements are mounting, and the costs of maintaining sprawling bureaucracies threaten to outstrip the capacity of economies to generate revenue. The primary cause of this impending catastrophe is clear: states have overextended themselves into areas better serviced by family or church, spending trillions on programs unrelated to national defense, courts, police, or the enforcement of rights.

Sphere sovereignty offers a viable path to escape this looming crisis. It proposes that by gradually transferring responsibilities to their proper social spheres—families absorbing duties such as education and churches taking up charitable work—society can maintain order and prosperity without the collapse of the state. Implementing sphere sovereignty now, deliberately and incrementally, would be both the least disruptive and most effective course. Barring some miracle or a return to the right of conquest whereby other nations are plundered to alleviate financial burdens at home, governments will soon be unable to provide even basic social services. Absent this peaceful, structured adoption, the alternatives are grim. We could see a time when desperate individuals turn to lawlessness, guided by the crude rule that might makes right.

How Biblical Principles Should Inform Laws—Soft Theonomy

We've seen that in Traditional Conservatism the family and the church explicitly instruct on religious beliefs and the ethical norms and values that arise from them. We have also determined that, guided by traditional conservative principles, the state does not instruct or compel religious belief. While the laws and policies it creates must align with Christianity's moral code, they need not cite scripture or theology. Instead, appeals to natural law, logic, or empirical evidence—all in support of Christian norms and values—may be the preference of the electorate.

What we have not yet addressed in any substantive way is how, in more concrete forms, a nation's laws should reflect Christian norms and values as revealed in Scripture. Most perplexing of all is this: how should biblical principles, originally given to an ancient Middle Eastern people, be applied to the citizens of modern Western countries?

Ironically, the answer to that question can be answered, at least in part, by looking at any Western nation's laws as they already exist. Even though modern Western legal systems are now largely secular in formulation, many of their foundational principles—prohibitions against murder, theft, and fraud; the protection of property; and the recognition of marriage and family structures—closely mirror moral norms emphasized in the Old and New Testaments. By examining these current laws, one can see how societies that historically drew on Christian moral frameworks have embedded those ethical priorities into public life. In essence, the laws that remain in force today provide a living reflection of which Christian moral principles were considered essential for social order and flourishing.

But our desire is to go deeper and understand exactly how governments practicing Traditional Conservatism have shaped laws in the past—and how they might do so in the future. To gain this deeper understanding, we must turn to some well-established, time-honored guidelines. Perhaps unsurprisingly, these guidelines are shaped by Reformed theology.

For centuries, Reformed theologians have sought to determine which biblical laws remain binding for contemporary society and the manner in which they should be applied. Their conclusions build on previous Christian scholarship showing that the laws of the Old Testament can be divided into ceremonial, moral, and civil categories.

This tripartite division recognizes that many Old Testament laws are no longer binding due to the redemptive work and new understanding brought by Jesus Christ. Specifically, *ceremonial laws* that governed ancient Israel's worship and purity practices, such as animal sacrifices (Leviticus 1-7), dietary and clothing restrictions (Leviticus 11), and the holding of religious festivals like Passover (Exodus 12), are no longer to be followed as national laws.

Conversely, the moral law, exemplified in the Ten Commandments and the biblical ethical teachings that develop directly and organically from them, must be observed. It applies to all people at all times because it expresses God's eternal and unchanging standard of righteousness and moral conduct. These principles are not subject to cultural trends or human opinion—they provide the very foundation for justice and virtue. Accordingly, the laws of the land should reflect and enforce these permanent standards, ensuring society is ordered according to God's unalterable moral truth so that human behavior aligns with the divine vision for a just and flourishing community.

The Ten Commandments themselves, found in Exodus 20:1-17, prohibit idolatry, blasphemy, murder, adultery, theft, lying, and coveting, while commanding exclusive worship of God, Sabbath rest, and honoring parents. While the commands of the Decalogue—the formal name for the Ten Commandments—form the basic framework of all moral law in the Christian tradition, other Old Testament precepts expand and deepen this framework and are likewise understood as moral law.

Simply put, neither the Jews who first received the Ten Commandments nor the Christians who later inherited this legal tradition saw the Decalogue as a complete moral code on its own. Rather, they understood it as establishing the fundamental categories under which more specific ethical requirements and nuanced laws could be organized.

This process of reasoning from the broad commands of the Decalogue to their application in concrete situations is what the tradition calls casuistry. For example, the prohibition against theft—"You shall not steal"—extends not only to outright robbery but also to fraud, unjust wages, or failure to return what is borrowed. Similarly, the prohibition against adultery extends to all forms of sexual activity outside the covenant of marriage (for example, Leviticus 18:22; 20:13). In this way, the Decalogue supplied the essential principles, while casuistry and the additional Old Testament precepts demonstrated how those principles governed the full range of moral life.

Additional moral laws arising from the Ten Commandments include loving one's neighbor (Leviticus 19:18), caring for the vulnerable (Deuteronomy 15:7–11), upholding justice (Leviticus 19:15), and maintaining integrity in business and relationships (Leviticus 19:35–36). Because these Old Testament prohibitions and commands are specifically reaffirmed in the New Testament—for example, practices such as bestiality and homosexual acts are reaffirmed as prohibited, not revoked (see Romans 1:26–27, 1 Corinthians 6:9–11, 1 Timothy 1:9–10)—their status as moral law is regarded as doubly confirmed. The ceremonial and moral laws of the biblical tradition are distinguished from the civil laws. Civil laws in the Old Testament—often referred to as the *Mosaic civil code*—were specific regulations that the people of Israel were to follow in societal and judicial matters. While the moral law defined the behaviors God required or forbade, the civil law prescribed the specific penalties or rewards for obeying or violating those standards, while also addressing other functions necessary to the running of a community. For example, the civil laws gave specific rules and instructions on punishments for crimes, the sale of property, negotiating contracts, resolving disputes, and the governing of the Jewish people. The vast majority of Reformed theologians—and contemporary Christians generally (if they consider the issue at all)—hold that the civil laws of the Old Testament, in their specific instructions, are not binding today. However, they do not dismiss them out of hand.

Typically, the civil law of the Old Testament is the practical application of the moral law. Think of it this way: the moral law says, "Do this," while the civil law explains how to do it or what should happen if it's not done.

It has been long accepted in the Christian tradition that, since the redemptive work of Jesus, humans are not required to follow the civil law of ancient Israel exactly as it was written. However, we are expected to study what those civil laws recommended and let them inform how we address similar situations today. In doing so, we acknowledge that the moral law must be upheld, even if it's not applied in precisely the same manner as in ancient Israel. This process of adaptation is known as the principle of *general equity*.[33] When Christians in government draft new statutes, they are to *translate* the guidance of the Bible's civil laws into forms appropriate for contemporary society, recognizing that specific penalties—such as stoning for certain crimes—are no longer applicable.

Let's recap for a moment. Under this model, clarified by hundreds of years of Reformed theology, ceremonial laws of the Old Testament are *rejected*, moral laws—corroborated by the New Testament—are *respected*, and civil laws are *inspected* for how they might influence modern regulations. Taken together, this can be considered the *soft theonomic* position.[34] The term "theonomy," derived from the Greek words *theos* (God) and *nomos* (law), refers to the incorporation of God's laws into human legal systems.

The soft theonomic position is associated with figures like Abraham Kuyper, the Dutch Reformed theologian, journalist, and Prime Minister of the Netherlands (1901–1905). Kuyper was deeply committed to the idea that all of life should be lived under the influence of Christ, including political life. While he did not explicitly describe his vision in theonomic terms (the term itself gained popularity after his death), he spoke and wrote extensively on the state's calling to promote justice and public morality in ways that aligned with God's moral law, but without insisting on reproducing the penal specifics of the Mosaic civil code. Rather than insisting that governments adopt the full legal structure of ancient Israel, Kuyper believed biblical principles should inform lawmaking in ways that respected each nation's history and needs.

While his writings offer theoretical clarity and a summary of the larger notions, the concept of soft theonomy extends well beyond Abraham Kuyper. Historically—under different names but with the same principles—it shaped legislation in America, Canada, and much of the West from the earliest assemblies through the mid-1900s, and it was viewed, without exaggeration, as the natural or default approach to crafting public policy.

For example, into the modern era every Western country had "blue laws" or "Sabbath laws" meant to enforce the Christian moral statute of "resting" on Sundays. Reflecting the moderation and adaptiveness of soft theonomy, the personal activities of individuals were not regulated or monitored, but organizations and businesses were required to be closed unless they provided lifesaving aid (like police, firefighters, and hospitals).

There's an old saying: "You don't know what you have until it's gone." The widespread removal of Sabbath laws across the West illustrates the truth of that maxim. In an age when family and community bonds are historically weak,[35] the wisdom of reserving a common day with "nothing else to do" but spend time with loved ones and neighbors suddenly makes sense.

Soft theonomy has its rival. Though in the minority, there are those who support the *hard theonomic position*, arguing that the civil law of the Old Testament is not a relic of an ancient culture but a binding expression of God's justice for all nations, at all times. This stance is associated with R.J. Rushdoony, a 20th-century American Presbyterian minister, theologian, and founder of the Christian Reconstruction movement. In his writings, he stated that the penal sanctions found in the Mosaic civil code remain authoritative unless New Testament scripture clearly revokes them.

For him, this meant that capital punishment for crimes such as murder (Exodus 21:12), adultery (Leviticus 20:10), blasphemy (Leviticus 24:16), and certain forms of idolatry (Deuteronomy 13) should still be part of a modern state's legal system. While he allowed for the principle of "general equity" to adapt some case laws to new cultural and technological contexts—for example, taking the Old Testament rule about building a guardrail around a flat roof (Deuteronomy 22:8) and applying its principle to modern building safety laws—he maintained that when it came to moral offenses, the Old Testament's civil penalties should be applied in substance, not merely as moral inspiration.

The Biblical Perspective of Traditional Conservatism

Traditional Conservatism aligns with the soft theonomic position. But it must be clarified what this does, and does not, mean. There will be some who will *want* this to mean that the culturally uncomfortable moral positions of historic Christianity—those that liberal politicians, mainstream media, and most college professors call outdated and intolerant—can be ignored. They will want it to mean that prohibitions against things like homosexual behavior—clearly forbidden in both the Old and New Testaments—are optional, not worth treating as absolute moral commands, and certainly not something that should ever make their way into the laws of the land.

That is not what it means.

Despite what those unsettled by cultural clashes would want, we must not redefine the principle of *general equity* into a device for evading the enforcement of biblical moral law. Nor should we collapse moral law entirely into civil law, treating every Old Testament penalty as merely a judicial provision for an ancient culture and therefore irrelevant today.

Nor must we appeal to "cultural relevance," insisting that because Old Testament laws arose in a vastly different time and place, their moral demands are quaint relics to be applied only when they happen to align with modern sensibilities.

Nor must we adopt the game of liberal theologians who urge us to "take it all as metaphor" by over-spiritualizing the whole. When they play this trick, they assure us that God's moral law is purely symbolic—something to be applied in our hearts, but never in the public square.

We cannot do this, because we've already tried it, and things got worse and worse. Looking at the rise of all these excuses—starting in the mid-1900s and continuing to today—we're able to clearly discern the moral of this story: the more you water down the medicine, the faster you die.

Let's recall the words of C.S. Lewis quoted in Chapter 1: "If you are on the wrong road, progress means doing an about-turn and walking back to the right road, and in that case the man who turns back soonest is the most progressive man..."

We can pinpoint where society veered off course—the road diverged just after World War II, and the accelerating downhill trek began in the 1960s. We need to turn back if we want to move forward. Turning back will require humility, and humility is in very short supply.

We currently have a month where governments across the West mandate that the sin of Pride be celebrated. Conversely, humility gets no public attention. Moreover, if you've been indoctrinated by a school system that told you your country and its Christian heritage are evil, the humility to consider the wisdom of your ancestors will be hard-won. Humility to turn back to laws and customs that openly reflect Christianity will be toughest of all if you are not a person of faith yourself.

If you've lived a life outside of Christian community, you have likely been steeped in the popular narrative from media and academia that "Believers are naïve, ignorant dupes; the smart people reject Christianity." It will require considerable humility to accept that nearly everything you've been told by media, academia, and most politicians about what a society needs to function is false, while Traditional Conservatism's prescription for flourishing is true.

But if you begin by trusting the evidence of your own eyes and are willing to consider the arguments of this book with an open mind, you may find the humility to consider that, in their application of Christian moral principles to law, our forefathers understood something we have forgotten. You may come to see that our past political leaders were not religious tyrants driven to intolerance by blind faith, but men acting in accordance with a body of unique, time-honored wisdom.

If you are truly humble, you may even conclude that wisdom gave them the ability to see that civilization survives on a knife's edge and that changes made under the guise of tolerance and acceptance can destroy it.

But humility is just the start. To share the truth you have discovered, you will need courage too.

Catholic Integralism—Another Christian Approach to Governance

I will close this chapter with the heartening observation that courage is spreading. Traditional Conservatism is not the only political philosophy to call for embedding Christian norms and values into statecraft, nor is its reliance on an established theological system to articulate its political vision unique. Catholic Integralism—a movement growing in popularity thanks in part to academic proponents like Harvard Law Professor Adrian Vermeule—advances the same proposal by employing a comparable process.[36]

Whereas principles of Traditional Conservatism can be derived from scripture viewed through a conservative Protestant lens—with special emphasis on Reformed theological understanding—the principles of Catholic Integralism, as its name suggests, are grounded in Catholic theology, particularly the teachings of St. Thomas Aquinas and his views on natural law, and papal encyclicals (official teaching documents issued by the Pope).[37]

The similarities are many. Central to both philosophies' insistence that Christian truth claims must influence public policy and legal frameworks is the understanding that neither philosophy requires a literal transplantation of Old Testament civil codes into modern society. Rather, both allow for principled adaptation in light of enduring moral truths and contemporary circumstances. Furthermore, neither philosophy accepts the Enlightenment premise of morally neutral governance, arguing that all legal systems necessarily embody particular metaphysical assumptions.

Also, both approaches arise from a shared conviction that secular liberalism, with its emphasis on individual autonomy and purported state neutrality toward religion, fails to adequately order society toward the true, the beautiful, and the good.

Additionally, both philosophies embrace what might be called a "thick" conception of the common good that goes beyond mere procedural fairness or practical calculations. They argue that the state has a responsibility to actively promote human well-being based on a Christian understanding of what makes life flourish, not merely to maintain order or maximize individual preferences. This shared commitment leads both to critique libertarian moral minimalism and progressive statism, though for different reasons and with different alternative visions.[38]

The most significant difference between these approaches lies in their understanding of who gets to be in charge and how much freedom is given to the people being governed. Under Traditional Conservatism, no religious institution holds power over the state. Under Catholic Integralism, the Catholic Church—a specific religious body—is given ultimate authority over the governance of a nation. While bishops would not literally manage government departments or collect taxes, the Church—through the Pope or his appointed proxies—would retain the final say on what is acceptable in public policy, effectively subordinating the state to ecclesiastical oversight. In this hierarchical system, where temporal power must be subordinated to the Church's spiritual power, the state remains functionally separate but must acquiesce to Church direction. Democratic input and majority opinion are insufficient on their own; policies must also conform to Catholic teaching—not just general Christian norms and values—before becoming law.[39]

Traditional Conservatism maintains that the state possesses limited authority. Rather than having the state as supreme overseer, the bulk of governing power falls to the family and to the local church. The state protects the rights of these other spheres but, for the most part, does not intervene in them. Traditional Conservatism favors a bottom-up, organic quality to governance, as it trusts local communities to regulate themselves.

In the Integralist vision, the power of the (Catholic) state is immense and interventionist, and it flows top-down. It has the broad authority to coordinate and direct other institutions in society. Integralists hold that, in pursuit of the common good, the state may legitimately dictate in the affairs of families, businesses, schools, and even individual churches—not merely restraining wrongdoing but actively directing conduct.

This isn't supposed to be a mandate for micromanagement; rather, integralists emphasize the principle of *subsidiarity*—the idea that smaller institutions should govern themselves whenever possible. Yet, when these institutions fail to fulfill their proper functions or drift from their ordained ends, the state has both the right and responsibility to step in and redirect them toward their true purpose. On education, for example, integralists might support government intervention to ensure that schools or curricula serve the common good, even if parents disagree.[40]

Contemporary integralists, following Vermeule's lead, are willing to use assertive legal tactics to advance their agenda without first building broad public support. Traditional conservatives are equally prepared to make vigorous use of existing legal and political mechanisms to advance their goals, but they maintain that proportionate attention must be given to winning hearts and minds alongside the pursuit of political power. This instinct grows out of a conservative Protestant emphasis on evangelism and personal conversion, which prioritizes persuading individuals inwardly rather than assuming outward compliance can be achieved solely through institutional authority. In this respect, Traditional Conservatism might be said to reflect a greater confidence in the ability of ordinary citizens to recognize and embrace Christian principles when they are clearly presented. Finally, as was just implied above, the writings of Catholic integralists suggest that their desire to see Catholic doctrine guiding statecraft is greater than their concerns over personal liberty. Because integralists believe that the Catholic Church possesses "the Truth," they may feel that individual moral autonomy—in many or most cases—is far less important than conformity to ecclesiastical authority. Conversely, traditional conservatives preserve much more room for individual and institutional choice. They take it as a fundamental concern that the state never crosses into the realm of compelling religious belief or dictating matters of conscience.[41] Traditional conservatives insist that diverse worldviews—including secular ones—be allowed to flourish within their appropriate spheres, free from state interference and with impartial judicial protection. This is not a compromise of Christian principles, but because of them.

Traditional Conservatism's greater openness to ideological diversity means it's particularly hospitable to believing Christians of all stripes. To be sure, integralists would be welcomed by traditional conservatives into their movement as full brothers in arms, applauded for their unwavering commitment to the norms and values of Christianity. Conversely, traditional conservatives hoping to join the integralist "club" might themselves be regarded as second-class members—or even inadmissible—if they refused to embrace distinctively Catholic doctrines. Admittedly, Catholic integralism's emphasis on hierarchy and state authority offers a more direct mechanism for achieving its objectives. Yet its apparent willingness to place individual conscience under ecclesiastical authority, together with its view of state power as a vehicle for Catholic doctrine, will understandably trouble those who value democratic accountability. A growing cadre of critics feels the philosophy casts a shadow of authoritarianism and theocracy,[42] echoing the Catholic Church's historical patterns of temporal governance—from medieval Christendom to the Papal States—where doctrinal orthodoxy and institutional dominance routinely outweighed commitments to individual liberty and minority rights.

Nevertheless, when faced with a choice between the progressive theocracy that actually dominates much of the United States and nearly all of Canada and the prospect of a Christian-based nation shaped by Catholic doctrine, even many non-Catholics might prefer the latter.

Happily, another option—Traditional Conservatism—remains.

The next chapter continues our exploration of what that philosophy might look like when put into practice in a nation.

Endnotes for Chapter 2

1. Ernst Troeltsch, *The Social Teaching of the Christian Churches*, vol. 1, trans. Olive Wyon (Chicago: University of Chicago Press, 1931), originally published 1912.

2. H. Richard Niebuhr, *The Social Sources of Denominationalism* (New York: Henry Holt and Company, 1929).

3. For example, Rodney Stark and Roger Finke, *The Churching of America, 1776–2005: Winners and Losers in Our Religious Economy*, 2nd ed. (New Brunswick, NJ: Rutgers University Press, 2005).

4. These works by Stark and Finke provide original evidence and also aggregate studies showing this trend toward progressivism and decline: Rodney Stark and Roger Finke, *Acts of Faith: Explaining the Human Side of Religion* (Berkeley: University of California Press, 2000); Stark and Finke, *The Churching of America*.

5. For example, D. Millard Haskell, Kevin N. Flatt, and Stephanie Burgoyne, "Theology Matters: Comparing the Traits of Growing and Declining Mainline Protestant Church Attendees and Clergy," *Review of Religious Research*

58, no. 4 (2016): 515–41.

6. John Derbyshire, "Conquest's Laws: Robert Conquest's Three Laws of Politics," *National Review*, August 11, 2003, https://www.nationalreview. com/2003/08/con-quests-laws-john-derbyshire/.

7. Ibid.

8. For example, Tertullian, "On Idolatry" 19, in *Ante-Nicene Fathers*, vol. 3, *Latin Christianity: Its Founder, Tertullian*, ed. Alexander Roberts and James Donaldson, trans. S. Thelwall (1885; repr., Peabody, MA: Hendrickson, 1994), 73–74.

9. Quadratus of Athens, *Apology* (fragment preserved in Eusebius, *Historia ecclesiastica* 4.3.1–2), in Eusebius, *The Ecclesiastical History*, vol. 1, ed. and trans. Kirsopp Lake, Loeb Classical Library 153 (Cambridge, MA: Harvard University Press, 1926), 310–13.

10. Justin Martyr, *The First and Second Apologies*, trans. Leslie William Barnard (New York: Paulist Press, 1997), 23–81.

11. Athenagoras, *A Plea for the Christians (Legatio pro Christianis)*, ed. William R. Schoedel, Oxford Early Christian Texts (Oxford: Clarendon Press, 1972).

12. For example: Stephen B. Levine and E. Abbruzzese, "Current Concerns About Gender-Affirming Therapy in Adolescents," *Current Sexual Health Reports* 15, no. 2 (2023): 113–123, https://doi.org/10.1007/s11930-023-00358-x; U.S.

Department of Health and Human Services, *Treatment for Pediatric Gender Dysphoria: Review of Evidence and Best Practices* (Washington, DC: U.S. Department of Health and Human Services, 2025); American Society of Plastic Surgeons, "Position Statement on Gender Surgery for Children and Adolescents" (Arlington Heights, IL: American Society of Plastic Surgeons, 2026), https://www.plasticsurgery.org/documents/health-policy/positions/2026-gender-surgery-children-adolescents.pdf.

13. See David W. Bebbington, *Evangelicalism in Modern Britain: A History from the 1730s to the 1980s* (London: Unwin Hyman, 1989); Mark A. Noll, *A History of Christianity in the United States and Canada* (Grand Rapids, MI: Wm. B. Eerdmans, 1992).

14. Alexis de Tocqueville, *Democracy in America*, vol. 1, pt. 2, ch. 9, trans. Henry Reeve (New York: Bantam Classics, 2000), originally published 1835.

15. Ibid.

16. Ibid., vol. 2, pt. 1, ch. 5, originally published 1840.

17. OECD, *PISA 2022 Results (Volume I): What Students Know and Can Do* (Paris: OECD Publishing, 2023a), https://www.oecd.org/publications/pisa-2022-results-volume-i_53f23881-en.htm; OECD, *PISA 2022 Country Note: United States* (Paris: OECD Publishing, 2023b), https://www.oecd.org/pisa/ publications/PISA-2022-results-country-notes-united-states.pdf.

18. Ibid.

19. Council of Ministers of Education, Canada, *Measuring Up: Canadian Results of the OECD PISA 2022 Study (Highlights)* (Toronto: CMEC, 2023), https:// cmec.ca/docs/pisa2022/ PISA-2022_Highlights_FINAL_EN.pdf.

20. U.S. Census Bureau, "Public School Spending per Pupil Experiences Largest Year-to-Year Increase Since 2008," press release, May 18, 2023, https://www. census.gov/newsroom/press-releases/2023/public-school-spending.html.

21. Fraser Institute, *Education Spending in Public Schools in Canada, 2024 Edition* (Vancouver: Fraser Institute, 2024), https://www.fraserinstitute.org/ sites/default/files/education-spending-in-public-schools-in-canada-2024.pdf.

22. OECD, *Education at a Glance 2023: How Much Is Spent per Student on Educational Institutions?* (Paris: OECD Publishing, 2023c), https://www. oecd.org/education/education-at-a-glance/.

23. U.S. Department of Education, "Public School Expenditures," National Center for Education Statistics, 2021, https://nces.ed.gov/programs/coe/ indicator/cmb; Statistics Canada, "Average and Median Salaries of Full-Time Teachers in Public Elementary and Secondary Schools, by Province," 2023, https://www.statcan.gc.ca/en/subjects/education_training_and_learning.

24. OECD, *Education at a Glance 2023: OECD Indicators* (Paris:

OECD Publishing, 2023), https://doi.org/10.1787/eag-20 23-en.

25. National Center for Education Statistics, *Private School Universe Survey: 2019–20* (U.S. Department of Education, 2020), https://nces.ed.gov/ surveys/pss/; PayScale, "Average Private School Teacher Salary in Canada," 2023, https://www.payscale.com/research/CA/Job=Private_School_Teacher/ Salary; Lawrence M. Rudner, "Scholastic Achievement and Demographic Characteristics of Home School Students in 1998," *Education Policy Analysis Archives* 7, no. 8 (1999), https://doi.org/10.14507/epaa.v7n8.1999; U.S. Bureau of Labor Statistics, "Occupational Employment and Wages: Secondary School Teachers, Except Special and Career/Technical Education," 2023, https://www.bls.gov/ oes/current/oes252031.htm.

26. Brian D. Ray, "Homeschooling Associated with Beneficial Learner and Societal Outcomes but Educators Do Not Promote It," *Peabody Journal of Education* 88, no. 3 (2013): 324–41; see also Rudner, "Scholastic Achievement," 1999.

27. National Center for Education Statistics, *Private School Universe Survey: 2019–20.*

28. Fraser Institute, *Comparing Performance of Universal Health Care Countries, 2021* (Resilient Healthcare, 2023), https://www.resilienthealthcare.ca/ publications/dgb5o0rbj4dlgf9g1gb1uzq8m9gajl.

29. Ibid.

30. Fraser Institute, "Overwhelming Evidence—It's Time to Fix Canadian Health Care," *Montreal Gazette*, September 9, 2022, https://www. fraserinstitute.org/commentary/overw helming-evidence-its-time-fix-canadian-health-care.

31. Stark and Finke, *The Churching of America, 1776–1990.*

32. Ibid.

33. Ligonier Ministries, "Theonomy," *Ligonier.org*, https://lea rn.ligonier.org/ guides/theonomy.

34. See Ligonier Ministries, "Theonomy."

35. For example, Robert D. Putnam, *Bowling Alone: The Collapse and Revival of American Community* (New York: Simon & Schuster, 2000).

36. Adrian Vermeule, *Common Good Constitutionalism: Recovering the Classical Legal Tradition* (Medford, MA: Polity Press, 2022); Adrian Vermeule, "Beyond Originalism," *The Atlantic*, March 31, 2020, https://www.theatlantic.c om/ ideas/archive/2020/03/common-good-constitutional- ism/609037/.

37. Ibid.

38. Ibid.

39. Charles Camosy, "What Is Integralism, Anyway?" *The Pillar*, April 14, 2022, https://www.pillarcatholic.com/p/wha t-is-integralism-anyway; Steven P. Millies, "What Is Catholic Integralism?" *U.S. Catholic*, October 14, 2019, https://usca

tholic.org/articles/201910/what-is-catholic-integralism/.

40. Ibid.

41. Ibid.

42. For example: Jonathan Ingersoll, "The Theocratic Blueprint of Christian Nationalism, Reconstructionism, and Catholic Integralism Behind Trump's Agenda," *European Centre for Populism Studies*, March 4, 2025, https://www.populismstudies.org/professor-ingersoll-the-theocratic-blueprint-of-christian-nationalism-reconstructionism-and-catholic-integralism-behind-trumps-agenda/; Samuel Moyn, "Nudging Toward Theocracy: Adrian Vermeule's War on Liberalism," *Dissent*, December 23, 2020, https://www.dissentmagazine.org/article/nudging-towards-theocracy/; Micah J. Schwartzman, "The Unreasonableness of Catholic Integralism," University of Virginia School of Law, September 18, 2024, https://www.law.virginia.edu/scholarship/publication/micah-j-schwartzman/789536.

3

Traditional Conservatism: History as Blueprint

Trend Setter: King Alfred the Great

The only British king in history to be given the honorific "the Great" is King Alfred. Born in 849 and dying in 899, Alfred was given this title by later generations in recognition of his exceptional contributions to Anglo-Saxon England. He successfully defended against Viking invasions, promoted education and literacy across the land, and laid the foundations for a unified country—a task his son and grandson would make a reality.

A unified country was made possible primarily through the legal reforms that Alfred brought about. His reforms ensured justice and peace but, more importantly, created a common moral identity for his people. Of his codified reforms, Alfred proclaimed: "Let every man, high and low, know these judgments and keep them, that we may live in peace and righteousness under God's protection."[1] Following the admonition of their king, people across England came to understand: "this is what we stand for"; "this is who we are." Alfred collected his legal reforms into a single text called the *Domboc*, or *Doom Book*. The name comes from the Anglo-Saxon word *dom*, meaning "judgment," so it can be understood as the "Book of Judgments." This text was unique in Western history, as it marked the first systematic attempt by the English state to align its laws explicitly with biblical principles. If we were to ask: "When did theonomy—the incorporation of Christianity's laws into human legal systems—begin in the English legal tradition?" we would have a very clear answer.

For over a thousand years, this model established by Alfred would carry through to all legal systems in the Anglosphere—from the UK to the US, Canada, Australia, and New Zealand. From the 800s to the 1960s, mixing Christianity and governance was uncontroversially accepted as the natural state of affairs and the most effective way of ensuring justice and prosperity. In the Introduction to the *Domboc*, Alfred explained that the laws of a nation must "be grounded in the wisdom and justice of God's commandments" because they "are eternal and true" and not based on impulsive desires of men.[2] Humbly acknowledging his—and all humans'—limited reasoning and inclination to confuse evil for good, he stated: "I have not presumed to set down many of my own laws in writing, for I did not know what would please those who come after us."[3] He cautioned that unless laws are based on Christianity's time-tested, moral absolutes, they are destined to collapse into corruption and cruelty.

To ensure that God's ideas—not his own—would take precedence, Alfred prefaced the *Domboc* with a near-verbatim translation of Exodus chapters 20 through 23. He began with the Ten Commandments and moved into what is commonly known as the Book of the Covenant, a grouping of Old Testament cases and examples illustrating how the principles of the Ten Commandments are to be applied. The biblical content was accompanied, point for point, by Alfred's own commentary in which he explained how the application of Old Testament civil law principles should be modified for life in medieval England.[4] These Old Testament provisions needed adaptation, he noted, for two reasons. First, adaptation was necessary because Jesus had brought mercy and grace to balance the Old Testament law. He wrote: "Jesus Christ has fulfilled and perfected these laws, teaching us to love God and our neighbor... This commandment, which our Lord gave, sums up the justice and mercy we are to show one another, and it guides the laws I set forth for our people."[5] This didn't mean that what the Old Testament code deemed immoral suddenly became righteous; it meant only that there was latitude in *how* violations of the code might be addressed.

Secondly, Alfred explained that the Old Testament civil code—essentially the application of the moral law in ancient Israel—though instructive and valuable for guidance, could not simply be transplanted wholesale into Anglo-Saxon society without adaptation. He rightly pointed out that its detailed regulations were crafted for the historical circumstances of a pre-Christian people in the Middle East rather than for the social structures, customs, and needs of his own society. Summarizing his method, he stated: "These divine laws, both from the Old Law given to Moses and the New Law given by Christ, I have set as the foundation of our judgments. To these I have added our own customs that accord with right reason and the needs of our realm."[6] As discussed in the previous chapter, *theonomy* is the principle that a state should align its laws with biblical standards. *Soft theonomy* represents a moderated form of this approach, permitting rulers to adapt Old Testament legal provisions so that they speak more directly to the circumstances of their own time. In his application of balance—holding firmly to biblical moral convictions while tempering them with the grace of Christ and the practical realities of governance—King Alfred stands as a model of soft theonomy and arguably the earliest architect of what would become Traditional Conservatism. His *Domboc* functions not merely as a law book but as a recipe book, providing the necessary ingredients for governance that leads to a flourishing nation.

Faith-Informed Laws: Soft Theonomy in Modern Practice

In the example above, I offered an early instance from the Western tradition where Christian norms and values shaped governance. I will provide additional illustrations from more modern times. Yet, limitations of space and my own intellectual constraints necessarily restrict how fully this book can describe what a future legal order might look like under Traditional Conservatism with its application of soft theonomy. Of course, as noted earlier, a defining feature of governance under this vision would be a significant reduction in the overall number of statutes, as the state's role becomes smaller. The aim of the philosophy is largely to leave people free to order their own lives. And while the number of laws would contract as the state withdraws from many areas, some laws would remain unchanged. In fact, many existing laws would require little alteration, since the enduring Christian heritage of the West has already shaped them in ways consistent with biblical moral teaching.

But in other cases, clear differences would emerge. Under a Traditional Conservative government, laws set aside after the Second World War under the influence of the Post-War Consensus would likely be restored, including those addressing the Christian Sabbath, blasphemy, obscenity, abortion, homosexuality, and other moral concerns. In the sections that follow, I will examine several of these key areas in greater detail and offer an outline of how a nation's laws might align with Traditional Conservatism on these matters. My comments will be an overview; I leave the work of translating these principles into detailed legislation to future elected officials.

As a final preparatory notion, let me reiterate where there is room to maneuver and where there is not. While soft theonomy and, by extension, Traditional Conservatism insist that the moral code of Christianity—including the parts deemed politically incorrect by some—must be embedded in the laws of the state, they allow room to adapt as the will of the electorate is discerned and honored. But adaptation must never mean abrogation; God's laws cannot be canceled.

The guiding principle remains:

At a minimum, within Traditional Conservatism there can be no circumstance in which the state's laws regard actions prohibited by Christian morality as acceptable or praiseworthy. In fact, under the philosophy, some actions that the state currently treats with ethical indifference or even celebration would no longer be greeted with neutrality or favor.

As will become clear, my discussion of laws leaves some moral concerns unaddressed. But these omissions need not create confusion. If you find yourself wondering, "Where would Traditional Conservatism stand on this issue?" simply return to the guiding maxim set out above, consult the historic witness of Christianity, and the answer will almost certainly follow.

On the topic of shortcuts, a handy heuristic—or investigative shortcut—for comprehending what soft theonomy looks like in practice on a full slate of issues is to examine the statutes of the United States and Canada (or almost any Western nation) before the propaganda of the Post-War Consensus convinced legislators to remove every vestige of the Christian faith from the laws of the land. This means looking especially at the period before the sweeping secular reforms of the 1960s.

I'm aware that some detractors will scrutinize this book—especially this chapter—searching for reasons to label its ideas as bigotry. While it would be impossible to anticipate and rebut every false claim (as the philosopher Taylor Swift has noted, "Haters gonna hate"), I will state plainly that when I commend statutes from before the 1960s, I'm not endorsing those that enforced racial inequality.

To be sure, laws prior to the 1960s that privileged White citizens and denied impartial treatment to others directly contradicted the core tenets of Traditional Conservatism, which insists on the equal dignity of all under the moral law promoted by Christianity. In short, past laws enforcing racism are at odds with Traditional Conservatism, not aligned with it. Those injustices serve as reminders that fidelity to conservative principles requires discernment; we are not called to resurrect the past wholesale, but to draw from it wisely. The moral absolutes of biblical Christianity applied in the West over eighty generations—not 50 or even 150 years—are to be the measure.

Traditional Conservative Laws—Revising Criminal Law

Before examining how a traditional conservative government could approach the niche areas of Sabbath observance, blasphemy, obscenity, abortion, or homosexuality, let's first consider the broader changes it might bring to criminal law as a whole.

Over the past several decades, the criminal justice systems of North America have moved away from strict accountability and effective deterrence toward leniency and offender-focused protections. A traditional conservative government, reflecting its reliance on scriptural models for direction, would seek to reverse that trend by restoring laws that truly deter crime and deliver justice. To see what has been lost, it helps to remember how judicial punishment was historically understood. Today, short jail sentences are increasingly common, yet for much of American and Canadian history, incarceration by itself was never considered sufficient to restrain wrongdoing. Corporal and capital punishment were important, additional options.

Today in the U.S., the death penalty—at one time ubiquitous—has been banned in 23 states.[7] In the past it was applied for murder, treason, and rape, but now—where it's allowed—it's reserved only for the most heinous of homicides. Canada, by contrast, has no capital punishment today, despite the majority of the population supporting it;[8] Parliament abolished the practice in 1976.[9]

In America, corporal punishment—typically flogging the offender across the back with a leather whip or long strap—was a legally sanctioned part of the criminal justice system well into the mid-20th century. Delaware was the last holdout, recording the final judicial whipping in 1952 for a conviction of robbery and wife beating.[10] Canada followed a similar pattern, with floggings administered with a leather strap for offenses such as robbery with violence, sexual assault, or mutiny within prisons. Flogging sentences were almost always accompanied by imprisonment. Notable cases include a 1914 Toronto man convicted of sexually assaulting a child, who received 10 lashes plus two years in prison. The last recorded judicial whipping in Canada was in 1967.[11] The shift from corporal punishment to incarceration alone arose from humanitarian concerns and doubts about physical punishment's effectiveness. Research shows those doubts were ill-informed: the countries that have made corporal punishment a formal, near-scientific process within their legal systems have seen exceptional results.

In Singapore, where caning—flogging with a springy wooden

stick—has been a standard penalty since the mid-20th century, crime rates are among the lowest in the world and have steadily declined decade after decade. Singapore's overall crime rate, at approximately 0.10 per 100,000 people,[12] is dramatically lower than that of the United States, where violent crimes alone occur at roughly 370 per 100,000 and property crimes at about 1,760 per 100,000.[13] Malaysia and Brunei, which also use caning for violent and drug-related offenses, also have some of the lowest rates worldwide. By comparison, Malaysia's overall crime rate is about 50% lower than America's,[14] and Brunei's is more than 90% lower.[15] Furthermore, all three of these Asian nations have recidivism (re-offense) rates around 20% or less,[16] compared with about 82% in America.[17]

Singapore, Malaysia, and Brunei stand out as premier models for administering judicial caning in a controlled and responsible way. It's carried out by trained officers under strict court supervision, with clear limits on the number of strokes. Medical checks are required before and after each sentence, and the aim is deterrence, not spectacle. As a result, the practice rarely causes lasting injury and is widely credited with helping keep violent-crime rates extremely low in these countries.

In North America, our justice system is moving further away from any kind of physical discipline, opting for increasingly mellow therapeutic approaches. Although programs that encourage Christian belief and practice have shown notable success in reducing criminal behavior,[18] those that focus solely on emotions, empathy-building, or "therapeutic dialogue"—the very approaches that dominate our criminal justice system today—tend to produce weak or inconsistent effects on reoffending.[19]

The laws themselves are growing softer too. In Canada, legislation in the early 2020s removed mandatory minimum sentences for serious crimes like armed robbery, weapons trafficking, and major drug offenses, leaving judges free to impose lighter sentences.[20] In the United States, bail reform measures in states like New York and Illinois in the late 2010s and early 2020s have allowed violent repeat offenders back on the streets within hours of their arrest. These states have seen dramatic increases in rearrest rates for violent crimes, including assaults, robberies, and homicides.[21]

Illustrating the far-reaching consequences of insufficient penalties, California reduced property theft under $950 to a misdemeanor punishable only by a fine in the late 2010s. The change was followed by a surge of "smash-and-grab" thefts in San Francisco, where offenders, facing minimal consequences, looted stores in broad daylight and forced many retail chains to close.[22]

This climate of reform has tilted the system against victims. Families shattered by violent crime in both the U.S. and Canada are forced to watch perpetrators receive reduced sentences, early parole, or no meaningful punishment, while their own suffering is sidelined. The focus on offender rights often overshadows closure for those harmed, eroding faith in the rule of law. Most troubling is the rise of a two-tiered justice system, in which conservatives face harsher penalties while violent offenders and others receive leniency.

In Canada, Pastor Tim Stephens was jailed in the early 2020s for holding church services during COVID restrictions,[23] and Freedom Convoy leader Tamara Lich faced aggressive prosecution, repeated bail denials, and jail for charges related to peaceful protest.[24] In the United States, pro-life activist Mark Houck endured an FBI raid and federal prosecution over a minor altercation.[25] By contrast, in both countries, violent offenders are often released on bail hours after being arrested, only to reoffend within days.[26] It has repeatedly been the case that rioters and looters—whether affiliated with Antifa, Black Lives Matter, or pro-Palestinian protests—have shut down major highways or caused millions in damage while police "protect" their right to protest and decline to hold perpetrators accountable.[27]

In a striking example of asymmetrical legal treatment, a U.S . court portrayed Christianity itself as psychologically harmful when it stripped a Christian mother of the right to take her daughter to church, deeming her faith made her an unfit parent and labeling ordinary evangelical practices—such as expository Bible teaching and baptism—as cult-like.[28] By contrast, the courts treat the identity claims of transgender offenders with deference. This was made starkly evident in 2024 in *People v. Tremaine Carroll*, where a California judge required prosecutors, witnesses, and even the female victims of a male rapist to use she/her pronouns for him. Under threat of removal from the courtroom, the victims were forced to affirm their male attacker's *chosen* female identity, while their dignity and mental well-being were disregarded.[29] These examples reflect a court system where certain groups receive preferred treatment. Applying a biblical definition of justice that allows no partiality, a traditional conservative government would reject a two-tiered system and restore equality under the law.

Furthermore, a traditional conservative government would view broader use of the death penalty as a necessary instrument of justice, and applying it to crimes involving deliberate physical or sexual harm to children would be considered both reasonable and just. Similarly, other cases of extreme sexual violence, such as brutal rape, would also warrant capital punishment.

Informed by the Mosaic civil code and English common law, a traditional conservative government might more generally shift the focus away from costly, ineffective mass incarceration and toward swift, restorative penalties that hold offenders accountable and put victims first. Where there is endless imprisonment that wastes lives and drains the public purse, there could be multiple-fold restitution for theft and property crimes.

For example, in line with biblical principles, offenders in some cases could be required to repay and restore their victims with added interest. Where financial repayment was impossible, temporary indentured servitude under government oversight until the debt was cleared could be imposed. In more aggravated cases, corporal punishment using a flexible wooden cane or leather strap could also be applied as a swift and unforgettable deterrent for lesser offenses like assault, perjury, or fraud.

While such reforms would shrink the prison system, save taxpayers billions, and, most importantly, restore public trust by ensuring justice is both equal and effective, many will reject them under the guise of empathy. In fact, many critics will falsely claim that Christianity itself stands against these needed reforms, but such claims reveal ignorance of history and Christian theology. With current Western nations providing the only exception, majority Christian countries have historically seen it as ethically imperative to include capital and corporal punishment among their methods of applied justice.

Corporal Punishment and Christianity

From the time of the early Church until the social upheavals of the 1960s, most Christians—because they read all of Scripture rather than cherry-picking convenient verses—understood the crucial distinction between Christ's commands for personal conduct and the God-ordained duties of civil government. Jesus' call to "turn the other cheek"

(Matthew 5:39) and "love your enemies" (Matthew 5:44) governs how believers are to treat others in their private lives, not how the state must respond to crime. The individual Christian is commanded to forgive, but civil authorities are commanded to punish wrongdoing in proportion to the offense, even to the point of execution for deliberate murder. Scripture makes clear that leniency in sentencing is itself a form of injustice.

Allow me to use a recent public memorial ceremony to illustrate the theological principle that forgiveness is a personal matter, while the state retains a fixed duty to protect citizens and administer just punishment to wrongdoers. On a Sunday in mid-September 2025, people across North America watched a memorial tribute to conservative pundit Charlie Kirk, who had been assassinated the previous week by a young man reportedly driven to murderous intent by his interpretation of transgender ideology. Approaching the close of the event, Kirk's wife, Erika, stood before the crowd and said: "My husband, Charlie, he wanted to save young men just like the one who took his life ... That man, that young man — I forgive him. I forgive him because it was what Christ did, and it is what Charlie would do."[30]

Immediately following Erika Kirk's words, President Donald Trump took the podium. He began by praising her faith and calling her forgiveness a powerful testimony. But as President—as the head of state—he emphasized justice and retribution, saying: "I hate my opponents, and I don't want the best for them."[31]

Left-wing media rushed to condemn the President's words as vindictive and divisive. They saw why he was wrong, yet missed why he was right. Few grasped that the role of a ruler is enforcement, not empathy. Traditional conservatives, by contrast, understand that "turning the other *cheek*" can only become a widespread virtue if citizens can trust the state to wield the *fist* against the worst offenders. Individual mercy can only flourish where public justice is swift and certain.

To a large extent, the media's reaction reflected progressive sensibilities in general and helps explain why communities governed by those sensibilities so often deteriorate into lawless hellholes. When rulers prize empathy over enforcement, predators strut fearlessly through the streets while honest citizens cower behind locked doors.

Christian scripture is unambiguous in its support for capital and corporal punishment by the state. Romans 13:1–4 tells us that the governing authority "does not bear the sword in vain" but is "God's servant to execute wrath on the wrongdoer." The "sword" is not a metaphor for a counseling session. It is a weapon of death, authorizing the state to use force, even lethal force, against criminals.

Even Christ sanctions such punishments. In Matthew 18:6, Jesus warns that those who harm children deserve to have a millstone tied around their neck and to be drowned in the sea. If Jesus considered that image an appropriate warning, it's dishonest to suggest he opposed severe punishment. In his parables too, such as Matthew 18:34, he describes as a natural consequence that a criminal act would result in corporal punishment (flogging) from the authorities. Similarly, the New Testament records several instances in which Jesus' disciples were flogged by civil authorities for preaching the Gospel (for example, Acts 5:40; 16:22–23; 2 Corinthians 11:24–25). A review of these passages indicates that the objection lies not in corporal punishment itself, but in its unjust application to the innocent. By implication, this affirms the legitimacy of flogging when it is *justly* administered.

The biblical foundation for corporal punishment runs deep. Proverbs 13:24 teaches that the "rod" is a tool of correction, applied not out of cruelty but out of concern for the offender's ultimate good.

Deuteronomy 25:2–3 prescribes flogging for certain crimes, setting limits to ensure fairness and restraint, thereby affirming the practice as both just and measured.

The early church fathers understood this. In the fourth century, Augustine taught that while Christians must forgive personal wrongs, magistrates could and must impose punishments, even executions, to protect society.[32] In the thirteenth century, Thomas Aquinas sharpened the point, writing that charity means willing the good of the larger community, and sometimes the good of the community requires cutting off a diseased limb—removing the criminal—so that the body politic may live.[33]

Again, to reiterate, a traditional conservative government referencing these and other precedents would maintain that the reinstatement of capital and corporal punishment is not cruelty; it is justice ordered to the common good.

Reviving the Defunct Laws—Models for Consideration

As we turn our attention to more specific laws guiding a wide range of moral and social concerns, keep in mind that a future government following traditional conservative principles is not obliged to reproduce earlier laws in exact detail. Its responsibility is to legislate in continuity with timeless truths while adapting them wisely to present circumstances. The pre-1960s examples related to the Christian Sabbath, blasphemy, obscenity, abortion, and homosexuality that are offered here serve as models from the past, not necessarily a word-for-word mandate for the future.

As models, it's worth remembering that the statutes of this earlier era, while unashamed in expressing Christian moral absolutes, did not attempt to replicate the penalties of the Old Testament civil code. For example, stoning was never considered a viable option. Instead, lawmakers employed alternative deterrents that nonetheless unmistakably signaled that certain behaviors were destructive to society's flourishing. Though adapted to a modern context, their approach resisted any drift toward sentimentality or undue leniency.

Appropriate punishment of wrongdoing was seen not only as essential for the common good but also for the offender's own good, since his actions revealed a corrupt state of character. For the legislator of the past, withholding the necessary discipline to turn him from depravity was regarded as an act of hatred rather than compassion.

Also notable, apart from abortion, these now-defunct laws of the recent past focused on regulating what was happening in public forums, not in private. That is to say, in the mid-1900s someone had almost no chance of punishment for breaking the Sabbath, blasphemy, obscenity, or laws against homosexuality unless they were exceedingly public in their actions or their behavior was connected to children.[34] In my opinion, that is a wise prescription for any traditional conservative government to carry forward: avoid regulating the private lives of citizens, in keeping with the philosophy's strong insistence on personal freedom and its belief that the spheres of family and church have their own important roles to play in regulating society.

Another factor shapes Traditional Conservatism's reluctance to press for radical reforms today that would apply biblical law more literally than seemed appropriate in the mid-twentieth century. Unlike progressivism, which—consistent with its Marxist roots—readily advances sweeping mandates through raw political power or even coercion, Traditional Conservatism seeks majority support by cultivating understanding and securing the willing consent of citizens.

Of course, Traditional Conservatism's measured temperament—its preference for gradual and peaceful cultural change—is not without limits. That goodwill can be withdrawn. Its patience depends on a political environment in which its people and ideas are free to compete on fair terms. The biblical and Christian moral framework underlying this philosophy teaches that when a government abandons the rule of law, enforces it unjustly, denies equal protection, or uses its authority to oppress rather than uphold justice, it forfeits any claim to unconditional obedience (chapter 12 addresses this issue in detail). For the traditional conservative, "when tyranny becomes law, rebellion becomes duty."[35]

Sabbath Laws

The social benefits that flowed from Sunday rest laws, or *blue laws*, which restricted business activity, labor, and alcohol sales on Sundays, have already been noted several times. In the United States, laws restricting work on the Sabbath began to fall in the 1960s, starting with Washington State's repeal in 1966 and followed by gradual rollbacks elsewhere, including Massachusetts and Pennsylvania.[36] In Canada, the federal Lord's Day Act of 1906 set nationwide restrictions, but the Supreme Court struck it down in 1985 in the Crown versus Big M Drug Mart case. The Jewish owners of the pharmacy retailer said that being forced to close their store on Sundays violated their freedom of religion under the Charter, and the court agreed.[37] After that decision, provinces moved quickly to deregulate Sunday shopping, and by the 1990s blue laws had largely disappeared across Canada.

In the future, applying traditional conservative principles, the state would revive Sunday as a day of rest. Personal activities of individuals would not be regulated or monitored, and neither religious worship nor any form of spiritual exercise would be compelled. However, organizations, businesses, and large-scale amusements would be required to close on Sundays unless they provided essential services. With this change, overwork would be recognized as a public injustice, while collective rest—supporting family bonds, community engagement, and social unity—would be regarded as a public good.

Designating a single day of the week for observance, rather than allowing variation, reduces fragmentation caused by disparate schedules. Sunday is the natural choice, reflecting the cultural and demographic realities of the United States and Canada, where Christian values shaped society and the majority continue to identify with a Christian heritage. Finally, this approach aligns with the widely accepted and conventional markers of national time still provided by Christian holidays. Even today, Christmas and Easter continue to structure winter and spring breaks, while Thanksgiving, rooted in Christian traditions of gratitude and harvest, serves as a nationwide marker for fall. Virtually all major holidays in North America trace back to Christian origins, so reinstating a weekly unified Sabbath is not an innovation but a restoration of the cultural and chronological rhythm that has long sustained communal life.

Blasphemy Laws

In the United States, blasphemy laws—typically defined as laws preventing the malicious ridicule of God or Christian doctrine—remained on the books in various states into the mid-20th century. However, a 1952 Supreme Court decision ruled them incompatible with free speech in America, so they were basically unenforceable from that point onward. In Canada, blasphemous libel was a crime under section 296 of the Criminal Code, a provision dating back to the 19th century. Though prosecutions were virtually unheard of after the 1950s, the law remained on the books until 2018, when Parliament repealed it as part of a broader effort to modernize the Criminal Code. Until then, Canada technically maintained one of the last active blasphemy statutes in the Western world.

Today, many people are puzzled that blasphemy laws ever existed in the United States—of all places. Unlike Canada—which has a long record of limiting personal liberty for relatively weak reasons—America is known to have treated freedom of expression as sacred and inalienable from its founding, through the First Amendment. Most people assume this freedom has always meant the right to say anything, in any manner, about any subject, provided it does not explicitly incite violence. Viewed through that lens, it seems impossible to imagine how the United States at one time enforced laws against hateful insults or contempt directed at the God of the Bible or Christianity. Such laws look like obvious violations of free speech.

But this modern understanding is very different from how freedom of expression was interpreted before the 1950s. I'll continue with the American example, but know that the same pre-1950s understanding applies similarly to Canada. From the framers of the First Amendment to every judge deciding free-speech cases up to mid-century, no one believed the right to free expression was an unlimited license for all speech. Lawmakers, courts, and citizens alike understood free expression as a qualified right, not an absolute one. In fact, across all North America and the West generally, freedom of expression was interpreted narrowly: it protected morally decent speech or writing that contributed to rational discourse, opinion formation, or temperate debate. On the other hand, it excluded speech or publications considered harmful or devoid of value to the public good. While no particular subject was off-limits, the manner of expression mattered.[38]

Free-speech absolutists today look at the criteria our forefathers used to justify their *qualified* view of free expression and roll their eyes. They argue that excluding speech because it's "harmful or devoid of value to the public good" is nonsensical—after all, how can anyone decide what is good? Of course, such a reaction would have had our forefathers rolling *their* eyes. They had a ready answer: "God is good. And He has given us His norms and values so that we may pursue the good in society."

In other words, for most of North America's history, determining what forms of expression were good—and therefore legitimate and protected under law—did not depend on subjective judgment, but on an objective appeal to Holy Scripture.

The "anything goes" outlook of today's free-speech absolutists did not emerge because new wisdom was gained but because old wisdom was abandoned. That is, in the 1950s society did not suddenly gain deeper insight into human freedom; there was no brilliant revelation that unrestricted speech would somehow strengthen the public square. To be sure, simple observation shows that it usually does not. Rather, under the influence of the Post-War Consensus, there was the forfeiture of Christian norms and values for the weak pap of pluralism, and with it the loss of the ability to make meaningful distinctions between right and wrong.

Citizens' earlier framework for judging whether certain speech strengthened or damaged the public good was pushed to the side, so the only principle left standing was maximal permissiveness. To be more specific, lacking a common standard of the good, people—including judges and legislators—adopted the only position left to them: if no moral judgment can be agreed upon, then no judgment will be made at all. It was a conclusion reached by default.

When we remember that North American society once held a shared standard for what strengthened or harmed the public good—including in matters of expression—blasphemy laws become understandable. Within that framework, restrictions on blasphemy were viewed not as punishments for private belief but as penalties for something closer to libel or a breach of the peace; each was understood as a form of expression capable of causing social disruption or moral decline.

These laws of limitation and restraint rested on the conviction that Christianity was not just a personal creed but the foundation of civilized life. Because Christian teaching shaped the core of Western ethics, protecting God and Jesus from public insult—though generally not policing private conversations or actions—was seen as a way to maintain society's moral underpinnings. Yes, theologically, these laws aimed to defend God's honor, but from the state's perspective, safeguarding the sacredness of God and Christ in public was effectively the same as elevating and protecting the values and behaviors needed to sustain civilization. In short, if God was undermined, the moral absolutes that He commanded—which were the foundations of the nation's laws—were equally weakened.

Blasphemy Laws Revived—Considerations

Based on the sociological considerations just outlined, together with theological reasons, some traditional conservatives will want the state to restore blasphemy laws. Were that to happen, in keeping with outcomes from the recent past, public writing, speaking, broadcasting, or other means of broad transmission that exposed God, Jesus, or the Holy Spirit to "scurrility, vilification, ridicule, and contempt" would be punishable, typically by a fine.[39] The area where society at large might see the greatest change is in the products of popular culture; films, television, books, and music would suddenly have to curb their use of "God" and "Jesus" as standalone expletives or, more often, in combination with the f-bomb.

It must be emphasized that across the U.S. states and Canada, when they were in effect, blasphemy laws took no issue with biblical or theological criticisms of Christianity—publicly rejecting one doctrine or another was fair game. Rather, it was primarily the public, malicious reviling of the *name* of the Father, Son, and Holy Spirit that led to legal trouble.[40] In contrast to the moderate restrictions put on individuals, the state itself was held to a stricter standard: it was not allowed to promote ideas contrary to the Christian faith. While citizens could exercise freedom of conscience and expression to advance contrary religious ideas under this model, the state could not.

Traditional conservatives who seek to limit blasphemy without strangling free expression could argue that there is wisdom in a balanced approach that ensures the state encourages debate and allows truth to prevail in the clash of ideas but does not actively contradict Christian teaching. They would not want to mimic blasphemy laws in Muslim countries such as Pakistan, Saudi Arabia, and Iran, where any critique of the Koran or Islamic teaching is branded a crime, intent is irrelevant, and the result is intellectual suffocation under the weight of enforced orthodoxy.

As a historical observation, I would note that the impulse to prevent the abuse of God's name reflects a cultural instinct that was once strong in the West. People understood that love and loyalty required defending the honor—the name—of those persons and things most cherished. It was not uncommon for men to risk their very lives in duels, or at least come to blows, to force a scoundrel to retract slander against a father, mother, or wife. While a slander against one's own person might be met with "turning the other cheek," the commandment to "honor your mother and your father" or "love your wife as Christ loves the church" added a complex theological dimension to libels against family. I'm not calling for a return to dueling, but I do think men should regain a stronger sense of protecting the name or honor of those people and things they hold in highest regard.

In essence, laws against blasphemy were an extension of that same sense of duty to kin. The logic was straightforward: if one would defend the reputation of one's family, how much more should one defend the holy name of the Heavenly Father? Far from reflecting insecurity, such laws expressed the conviction that God's name, like one's family name, must be guarded not only for the sake of truth but also as a profound act of loyalty toward those most loved. In earlier generations, the impulse to defend core values and core relationships hadn't been systematically beaten out of men by a school system and government propaganda; our forefathers would have regarded the idea that each person could have "their own truth" as complete nonsense.

Not all traditional conservatives will accept the model I've outlined. Some will judge it too timid. They will applaud prevention of blasphemy by the state (that is, preventing the state from undermining Christian norms and values) and the prevention of public expression that degrades God, Jesus, and the Holy Spirit, but they will want more restrictions. They will argue that blasphemy—and its traveling companion heresy, defined as the promotion of beliefs incompatible with Christianity—should not be given any opportunity to run rampant in the public square under the banner of freedom of expression, conscience, or religion.

If these hardliners are well-versed in Christian theology, to bolster their case, they might appeal to the classic Protestant view, represented in writings like the Belgic Confession.[41] Written in 1561, a portion asserts that it is the role of the state to prevent the spread of false religion and worship practices that lead people away from Christianity, meaning any unorthodox Christian belief or non-Christian religious expression would be banned in public. I think such a position goes too far and shows too little confidence in the truth of orthodox Christian belief. Others have observed that Christian truth is like a lion: you don't need to defend it; you simply need to let it loose. On that latter point, I would add that it must be kept free from the deliberate snares of government. With those conditions secured, nothing further is required.

With some irony, I wonder whether traditional conservatives who wish to impose this hardline Protestant view on society would accept a compromise regarding their censorship of non-Christian religious expression. Taking demographic realities in the United States and Canada into account, would they support restricting Islam, Hinduism, Judaism, and other faiths—but only to the same degree that Christianity is restricted in countries such as Saudi Arabia, India, or Israel?

For example, public and, to a large extent, even private expression of Christian belief is prohibited in Muslim-majority countries like Saudi Arabia (it's even illegal to build a church).[42] Similarly, in India, Christian aid organizations are banned from operation,[43] and in many of its states, basic Christian practices—including church services—are criminalized.[44] Even in Israel, Christian speech used to convince others of the goodness of Jesus faces several legal restrictions.[45] If reciprocity is the standard, perhaps such an approach could be justified.

There is also a third position. Some traditional conservatives will find *any* reinstatement of *state*-enforced blasphemy laws too strong a prescription. They might argue that regulating irreverence toward God belongs within the spheres of the church and family, not the civil magistrate. They could make their case by pointing to Reformed politicians of the past who sought to distinguish between the "first table" of the Ten Commandments—the first five commandments governing duties toward God (such as worship and reverence to His name)—and the "second table," which governs duties toward one's neighbor (such as prohibitions against murder and theft).[46] For them, the state's role is limited to upholding the second table, while the first is left to the church's moral authority and the family's instruction.

Beyond theological reasoning, some will oppose blasphemy laws because they are free-speech absolutists who—channeling the mindset of the Post-War Consensus—maintain that the state should not use the norms and values of Christianity to evaluate whether expression is harmful or devoid of value to the public good. They might further contend that such laws are simply impractical in the current society because the vast majority of modern people would *simply never follow them*.

Of course, to rebut anyone making that last claim, one need only ask when they last heard a White person utter the n-word—and I mean even in a neutral or academic context—or when a mainstream politician, journalist, or professor dared to refer to a transgender individual by the pronoun that matched their biological sex. Given that such benign actions are not even entertained at the level of thought, let alone speech, those who argue the public would never fall in line with blasphemy laws are willfully ignoring the reality that blasphemy codes already rule our culture and most people do follow them willingly.

Have we reached a moment when a legal code that treats God as sacred, rather than elevating skin color or the sexual confusions of humans, might represent a change in the right direction?

A Diversion into Restricting "Free Speech" More Generally

This tension between curbing speech that undermines essential norms and protecting free expression echoes Karl Popper's "paradox of tolerance."[47] Popper, an Austrian-British philosopher who died in 1994, proposed that a society that extends unlimited tolerance to individuals and groups that are intolerant will inevitably be enslaved by them.

This adage rings true in today's Western pluralistic democracies, where authoritarian movements—whether Islamist, Marxist-progressive, or other illiberal factions—exploit the very freedoms of speech, assembly, and political participation to gain power, only to strip away those same liberties and shut down democratic access once their authority is secured. Blinded by propaganda that preaches diversity and inclusion for anything but Christian norms and values, Western democracies have allowed *entryism*—the infiltration of institutions by ideologues hostile to Christian principles (which are Western principles)—to erode societal foundations.

An objective assessment of the major institutions of the U.S. and Canada establishes that a slow-motion coup against the core values of individual liberty, rule of law, and cultural cohesion has been underway since the 1960s. Freedom, absent the balance provided by Traditional Conservatism's insistence on protecting the common good, has left us in a precarious position. In such circumstances, only bold intervention may suffice. Unyielding legislative measures to cut off these threats at their roots are necessary to prevent a collapse into tyranny.

Because traditional conservatives are political realists and recognize that the choice is to finesse now or forfeit forever, they argue that certain rights must be carefully applied if they are to endure, and they therefore assert the following principle:

> Freedoms of expression, association, and religion *must not extend* to individuals or groups that advocate violence, revolution, or the dismantling of the West's historic, Christian-based norms, values, and culture, nor to those who seek to delegitimize or weaken the communities and institutions that embody and sustain them.

Traditional conservative statesmen of the near future must put flesh on the bones of this principle. When they do, their new law should draw clear boundaries supported by explicit, concrete examples rather than abstract formulations. Those boundaries must identify when freedom of expression moves from good-faith criticism—even criticism of the West's historic, Christian-based norms, values, and culture—into advocacy for violence or revolution against those norms, values and cultural foundations. Such a framework must balance the widest possible scope for free expression with the prohibition of speech and action aimed at undermining Western civilization.

As a starting point for consideration—though not to be taken as the law itself—it may be reasonable, for the preservation of Western society, to classify certain ideologies—such as communism and political Islam (the doctrine that Islam should extend into governance and law)—as "inherently subversive" to Western democratic norms. Members of Antifa, some *Black Lives Matter* chapter leaders, and some organizers of pro-Palestinian protest groups are examples of these ideologies at work in North American society. Their doctrines often call for overthrowing the constitutional order and Christianity itself. Those advancing these ideologies should face penalties and for non-citizens, deportation. This should not be a witch-hunt: courts would need to apply strict scrutiny, requiring clear evidence of intent to subvert, thus preserving free speech for non-violent discourse.

There may be those who feel that direct restrictions on the free expression of proven bad-faith actors are not enough. Within traditional conservative circles, there is also growing discussion about repealing certain other rights. Specifically, some are advancing arguments for voting reforms that would restrict participation to those who make a net financial contribution to society. The concern is that individuals whose primary income comes from government benefits are especially susceptible to authoritarian leaders who secure votes by promising more power or by redistributing the resources of others. From this perspective, restricting the vote is viewed as a safeguard against creating a voting bloc of the dependent class inclined toward policies that erode stability and undermine the common good.

Critics may decry these measures against authoritarianism as authoritarian themselves. But inaction invites far greater tyranny, as evidenced by the erosion of freedoms in illiberal regimes like Soviet Russia and Maoist China. Proactively legislating against subversion is the only way that the U.S. and Canada, or any democracy, can ensure that their commitment to tolerance extends only to those who reciprocate it.

Obscenity Laws

Similar to the limits that blasphemy laws placed on public speech or writing that maliciously reviled God, Jesus, or the Christian faith, obscenity laws of the past also imposed restrictions on free expression. Obscene material—typically cultural products depicting sexual acts or themes in a grossly graphic manner—was banned outright. What may seem surprising, before the propaganda of the Post-War Consensus, this was something almost everyone accepted as necessary to preserve civilization. Moreover, because the government reinforced—and the population generally embraced—Christian norms and values, there was little confusion about what "obscenity" meant. Again, as highlighted in the previous discussion of blasphemy, the contemporary claim that one simply cannot know what materials are "harmful or devoid of value to the public good" would have been deemed the height of ignorance and ridiculousness by those born before the Second World War. The driving motivation behind obscenity laws was not sexual prudishness but, as noted above, the preservation of civilization. Earlier generations believed that banning obscenity was one practical means of sustaining a functioning society, since civilization can endure only if it maintains a high level of innocence—an intentional freedom from moral corruption. The opposite of innocence is depravity, which by its nature undermines order and civic stability. Obscene materials were therefore seen as fostering depravity and eroding the moral foundations on which social order depends.

To be banned as obscene, it was not enough that material was sexual; it had to be likely to mislead and corrupt impressionable or vulnerable minds. Expressed as a simple test, if Christian parents would not permit their children or teenagers to view it because of its graphic nature, the law regarded it as obscene. We should not misunderstand this child-and-youth test—it was never really about age. The chronological standard simply made the issue clearer: we shield children not merely because they are young, but because what harms them also harms the moral sensibilities that sustain a civilization.[48] This test, applied in the realm of children, works because it taps into a hardwired reflex that's difficult to suppress. At a basic level, we all sense the harm obscenity can cause, but that instinct can be dulled by seductive cultural messages. What is far harder to suppress is our natural drive to protect children. When obscenity is linked to that deeper, more unshakable instinct, our moral sense awakens again. We see this in the near-universal impulse adults have to shield children from curse words and graphic images. Of course, even that "universal impulse" can be deadened through repeated exposure to the right kind of propaganda. If you've ever wondered why the LGBT community invests so much effort in promoting "Drag Queen Story Hour" in schools, public libraries, and community centers, I've just given you the explanation.

It's difficult to imagine an era when obscenity laws were strictly enforced, especially now that children are routinely exposed to men dressed as hyper-sexualized, scantily clad women during special drag events at their elementary schools. Moreover, nudity and simulated sex acts at Gay Pride parades are promoted as family entertainment, and pornography is available on every smartphone, with more than 70% of teenagers viewing it weekly or more.[49] Yet only half a century ago, across the United States and Canada, the public display of genitals—especially "genitals doing their work"—whether in person or in photographic form, was illegal. Narrative pornographic accounts were equally forbidden. Because Christian norms and values permeated society, it was simply understood that sexual organs and sexual acts were not for commodification or distribution.

Christian society recognized that sexuality was not shameful or "bad," but so profoundly good that it should not be reduced to a product to be bought and sold. Within this vision, sexual intimacy was seen as the crown of human bonding—the act by which a man and a woman formed the deepest attachment, stronger than any contract or social obligation. Beyond this, there was a truth that contemporary popular culture often forgets: from that union flows the highest calling of human beings—the creation and nurturing of new life. As the bond that held couples together and the life-giving act that brought children into the world, sexual intimacy was understood by lawmakers of the past to demand respect, restraint, and protection—not public display or trivialization. When they crafted laws against obscenity, aside from safe-guarding civilizational innocence, they recognized that an act so central to human connection and generational continuity should never be reduced to entertainment or spectacle. To do so, they believed, would risk undermining the stability of intimate, lifelong unions. Trivialize sex, and you trivialize relationships, children's lives, and the formation of families; in short, you get North America today.

The trivialization, commodification, and distribution of sex—in the form of obscene materials and acts—began in America in the 1960s as First Amendment jurisprudence significantly narrowed the scope of public decency laws.[50] Canada saw parallel developments under the Charter of Rights and Freedoms, with courts gradually limiting the reach of obscenity and indecency prosecutions.[51]

Thanks to modern research, we now know that obscene material has dire effects far beyond the destruction of innocence and the civilizational harms identified by our forefathers. Graphic sexual images, videos, and writing rewire the brain toward addiction and objectification, fuel sex trafficking, are a gateway to sexual violence, and erode marital fidelity. More than ever, it's clear that such material poses a serious threat to the common good.

A government guided by traditional conservative principles would therefore prohibit all forms of obscenity. This would include any visual or narrative depictions that display or describe genitalia in the context of sexual activity for the sake of entertainment. Not only would hardcore pornography be prohibited, but much of today's mainstream television and streaming content would likewise be required to adopt more modest standards of presentation. Many popular series on Netflix or other services now contain more explicit sexual material than the X-rated films that were illegal in the 1950s and 1960s. Outside the mainstream, I would propose that the production of child sexual abuse material or trafficking-related content incur the death penalty, while those distributing it face flogging and incarceration. Those found in possession of such material should likewise face severe criminal penalties, including imprisonment and corporal punishment proportionate to their involvement. To effectively prohibit obscene material, a government would need to take coordinated legal, technological, and regulatory steps across all forms of media. Online, this could mean requiring internet providers to block access to sites that display or describe genitalia for sexual entertainment, enforce strict age verification, and hold producers or distributors accountable under law.

In films and television, content boards could prohibit the production or public distribution of sexually explicit material, requiring streaming services and broadcasters to remove or edit such content and impose fines or criminal penalties for violations. For books and printed media, laws could ban the production, sale, or import of works with explicit sexual content, with publishers, bookstores, and libraries monitored to ensure compliance.

Similar measures already exist in other parts of the world, and the United States and Canada once strictly regulated films, television, and books. For example, before the 1960s, the U.S. Post Office (under the Comstock Act of 1873), the Customs Service, the Department of Justice, and even Hollywood itself—through industry guidelines known as the Hays Code—took it upon themselves to protect public morals and shield families from corrupting content in books and movies.

A traditional conservative government would not only prohibit pornographic material made with human actors but also extend that ban to so-called "artificial" pornography generated by AI. Some will argue that, since no real people are directly exploited in its creation, such materials should be treated differently. It's true that protecting the dignity of those who would otherwise be reduced to objects of sexual gratification is essential—but that is only part of the issue.

The traditional conservative holds that the deeper problem with pornography, whether involving real persons or digital fabrications, is that it deforms the mind and heart of the user. It undermines their ability to build authentic relationships, warps their vision of human worth, and fosters habits of depersonalization that can bleed into real life, at times even feeding impulses toward sexual violence.[52] For these reasons, banning AI-generated pornography is no less necessary than banning the traditional kind.

Abortion Laws

Abortion bans were once universal, with both the United States and

Canada criminalizing the practice before the mid-20th century under laws that, reflecting Christian doctrine, viewed unborn life as sacred. In the U.S., *Roe v. Wade* (1973) invalidated state bans, legalizing abortion nationwide.[53] Under President Trump, abortion law shifted dramatically when, in 2022, his Supreme Court appointments secured the majority that overturned federal protections for abortion, returning authority over abortion legislation to individual states. In practice, this meant that each state could now set its own abortion laws, leading some to impose strict bans while others moved to expand access.

In Canada, Parliament allowed limited liberalization of abortion in 1969, but all restrictions were struck down in 1988 by the Supreme Court in the *Crown v. Morgentaler* case. The abortionist on trial, Morgentaler, was the son of Jewish Holocaust survivors. Given his family history, one might have expected him to be repelled by the taking of innocent life. That was not the case. Since his 1988 court decision, Canada has had no laws restricting abortion.[54]

While Canada hides or obscures the statistics, U.S. records show that nearly one-third (28.6%) of all children conceived in America are now killed by their mothers through abortion.[55] This is a testament to the barbarity a population can achieve when a government abandons the moral absolutes of Christianity. It also speaks to a dark irony: this butchery of the unborn occurs as Leftist politicians scream about needing millions more immigrants to "fix" perilous population decline.

There's an even darker, crueler irony. In North America, couples now wanting to adopt have so few opportunities that many must search outside the continent to find a child to love as their own. In the U.S., about 1 million parents a year are ready and willing but unable to find an infant to adopt.[56] In Canada, domestic infant adoptions are even scarcer than in the U.S.[57] For example, in the entire province of British Columbia, only 20 to 30 babies are placed annually through licensed agencies, with infants and toddlers virtually unavailable from government care.[58] The number of willing parents in North America who are unable to secure a domestic adoption is virtually equal to the number of unborn children killed domestically.

When over one million mothers choose to kill their own child annually,[59] what is the response of most North Americans? Instead of recoiling in horror, they have been conditioned to applaud. Those familiar with the Bible understand that this is not a new moral development, but a return to one of humanity's oldest and darkest sins—a pattern that reappears whenever a nation's laws cease to reflect God's moral standards.

The Bible repeatedly recounts[60] how the Canaanites and other tribes at odds with the one true God engaged in child sacrifice.[61] Without the modern instruments we use today to butcher infants in the womb, they waited until after birth to carry out their killing. The difference was only one of timing; the motivation was the same. They slaughtered their children—slitting throats or casting them into fire—to bring a better life for themselves. More rain, richer harvests, greater political stability—these were the rewards they believed they would secure by sacrificing their most precious treasures to their gods .[62] The natural inclination of any sane human is to protect their young at all costs, but the doctrines of a perverse faith—enabled by powerful self-interest—can rewire the deepest moral instincts.

Today, the parallels are chilling. Women who kill their babies in the womb are similar to the Baal and Molech worshippers of old. The dominant motivation is the same: they think that the death of their child will make their life easier. Today they do not claim their child's death will bring rain or crops or peace, but they do insist it will secure them more time, more freedom, and more money. Surveys show that three-quarters of women seeking abortion in North America do it to avoid personal inconvenience—not because of health or sexual trauma.[63] Contemporary women openly say their child in the womb must die because giving birth would interfere with work, school, or their lifestyle. While the ancients sacrificed their children for better harvests, the modern woman sacrifices hers for freer evenings and weekends, a slimmer figure, or extra cash to buy designer brands. If anything, this leads us to conclude that today's baby killers are worse because their perceived gains are so pitifully small.

Another thing that suggests that our generation's baby exterminators are even more depraved than the ancients is the intellectual dishonesty that cloaks their actions. The idolaters of old did not deny what they were doing. They openly admitted: "We are killing our children for Baal so that the rains might come and the harvest be fruitful." Today's abortion advocates, by contrast, hide behind the slogan "It's my body, my choice," as if repeating that mantra can erase the reality that another body—a baby's body—is being slaughtered in the process.

And, worst of all, they deny any responsibility for the choices that led to conception in the first place. In nearly 100 percent of cases, no one forced the woman to have sex. That was her body; that was her choice. But when that choice results in a new life, she decides her baby must die for it. Nowhere else in Western society do we apply such twisted reasoning. If a man gets drunk, drives recklessly, and smashes into another car, he cannot stand before a judge and chant, "My body, my choice." He is held accountable. If someone gambles away her life savings, she cannot demand that society erase the consequences. Yet when it comes to sex and pregnancy, accountability is thrown out the window, and the child is killed to cover the mother's irresponsibility and selfishness.

This is why abortion is not just a private matter but a public crime that the state must stop. Just as the Israelites were commanded to end child sacrifice, we must see abortion as the deliberate killing of children for selfish reasons and work to end it.

A government shaped by traditional conservative principles would call for a near-total ban on abortion, allowing an exception only when the mother's physical life is clearly in danger due to serious medical complications. This reflects the core pro-life belief that life begins at conception and that every unborn child has the same dignity and right to legal protection as any other human being. This position exposes exceptions for rape or incest as morally flawed: when the mother suffers a terrible injustice, taking the life of an innocent child for a crime they did not commit only compounds the injustice. Rather than facilitating or financing the destruction of unborn life, the state—alongside the church and family—would provide meaningful assistance to mothers who are themselves victims. Women who have suffered rape would receive substantial support, including counseling, financial aid, prenatal care, and accessible adoption pathways. Guided by Christian principles, the state recognizes that, within the framework of sphere sovereignty, it has a proper—though limited—role in protecting infants who face hardship through no fault of their own or their mothers. In this way, the state serves as a safeguard, addressing necessary gaps while encouraging families and church communities to take primary responsibility for ongoing care and support.

A key element of a traditional conservative government's legal reversal on abortion would be communication strategies and public educational campaigns that refuse to describe the intentional murder of children inside their mother's womb as "termination of a pregnancy" or other euphemistic labels meant to hide the brutality and immorality of this practice. Organizations attempting to sanitize the language to dull the horror would face penalties. Currently, in North America, laws make it a serious crime to promote genocide of an identifiable group; similar laws could be enacted that make promoting the killing of unborn children an equally serious offense.

Finally, those performing abortions would be guaranteed to face the same legal punishments as others who commit murder.

Sodomy Laws

Christian moral teaching prohibiting homosexual acts found support in the laws of every nation across the West up until the 1960s. The statutes, termed "sodomy laws," were named after the biblical city of Sodom, whose male inhabitants were condemned for their same-sex acts. Despite their biblical pedigree, sodomy laws in most countries drew on reasoning beyond scripture to justify their enforcement.

In fact, from the dawn of recorded history, most societies have discouraged homosexuality primarily to preserve civility rather than on theological grounds. The earliest legal codes in Mesopotamia (c. 2000–1000 BC) already punished male-on-male intercourse; similarly, the Middle Assyrian Laws prescribed castration, while ancient China's Confucian writers condemned it as a form of moral disorder. Pre-Islamic Arabia and pre-colonial kingdoms in sub-Saharan Africa likewise prohibited it. Most familiar to Western audiences, the Hebrew Bible provides a primarily theological rationale and prescribes capital punishment for homosexual acts. Across every inhabited continent, the overwhelming majority of recorded societies treated homosexual behavior as a serious violation requiring prohibition.[64]

Limited and highly regulated exceptions to the general disapproval of homosexuality did exist in specific contexts, such as Greek pederasty or Roman dominance-based relationships. The former was most prominent during the Classical period of the fifth and fourth centuries BC, while the latter were prevalent from roughly the third century BC to the third century AD. Even so, these cases were outliers, surrounded by far broader and often harsher prohibitions that shaped legal, religious, and social practice in most major civilizations from antiquity to the modern era. The historical pattern is difficult to ignore: for at least the past four millennia, most human societies, regardless of region or period, have discouraged or punished homosexual behavior rather than embraced it.[65]

When justifying the prohibition of homosexual acts, religious doctrines might be cited, but, as I've noted, rationalizations were as much sociological as theological. Ancient—and not so ancient—peoples regarded homosexual behavior as deeply corrosive to the foundations of civilization for several enduring reasons. Previous critics of the practice argued that it threatens society's long-term stability by weakening the link between sex, marriage, and childbearing. They maintained that sexual activity between a man and a woman within marriage channels a powerful human drive toward socially constructive ends. Recognizing the immense destructive potential of sex without norms and boundaries, they viewed marriage—a union uniquely capable of producing and raising children—as the most effective means of containing sexual desire for the benefit of the partners, their offspring, and society.

They believed that elevating non-procreative relationships—often framed around personal fulfillment or companionship—as equal or superior to marriage shifts cultural norms, diminishes the perceived importance of procreation, and contributes to delayed marriage or fewer marriages, as children come to be seen as optional. By devaluing the procreative purpose of sex, such trends risk prioritizing individual choice over generational continuity, increasing the likelihood of population decline and demographic instability.

As demonstrated in Chapter 6, for good or ill, the vast majority of the population follows the cues its culture provides. If cultural norms signal that procreation is optional or secondary, behavior will adjust accordingly. The West's current demographic freefall, with native citizens unwilling or unable to meet replacement rates, suggests that this implicit message—recognized by the ancients—has been received loud and clear by modern society.

No less seriously, past thought leaders who opposed homosexuality maintained that it normalizes the ideal of a submissive or weaker male. They argued that by presenting the effeminate man as a legitimate and even celebrated alternative, it introduces a competing model of manhood—one that values yielding, ornamentation, or passivity over the traditional traits of strength, protectiveness, assertiveness, and self-mastery.

History shows repeatedly that when a society loses a unified and uncompromising image of male strength, its capacity for collective defense and internal order declines. Men who are taught that softness, submission, or feminine traits are equally valid expressions of manhood are far less likely to develop the physical courage, willingness to sacrifice, and hierarchical clarity needed for military cohesion, family authority, and civic resilience.[66] This is why virtually every martial, expansionist, or long-lived culture—from Sparta to republican Rome, from medieval Christendom to Confucian China—treated the normalization of male submissiveness and feminization with deep suspicion or outright prohibition. They understood, long before modern sociology, that a civilization's survival depends on its men aspiring, almost without exception, to the archetype of the strong protector rather than embracing a sanctioned alternative built around the feminized man.[67]

In recent years, the effects of feminization within various social systems and institutions have drawn increasing scholarly attention. In the legal system, feminization has been associated with more emotionally driven decisions, in which empathy—often extended toward offenders—can outweigh impartiality and precedent.[68] In medicine, this shift has been linked to a lower tolerance for risk and a greater sensitivity to emotional and psychological concerns, leading to more diagnoses and the treatment of ordinary life challenges as medical problems.[69] For example, reluctance to complete homework may be labeled "ADHD," pre-exam nerves become "anxiety," and ordinary stress is treated with accommodations or medication. As a result, normal experiences are pathologized, while resilience, rational judgment, and high standards are weakened.

Some researchers argue that the sharp decline of men—and the near erasure of traditionally masculine traits and values—from universities has hindered the advancement of knowledge. They contend that norms suited to mothering within the home have been imported into campus policy and culture, and that harm-avoidance has replaced intellectual risk, equity has supplanted excellence, and social conformity has overtaken truth-seeking. This feminized emphasis has transformed universities into therapeutic and regulatory spaces where speech is managed, standards are softened, disagreement is treated as harm, and ordinary male characteristics are increasingly labeled "toxic."[70] Relatedly, there has been the suggestion that the surge in violent campus protests is closely associated with female administrators who place the emotional validation of protesters—often from various minority groups—above maintaining order and safeguarding the broader educational experience.[71]

Returning to historical arguments against homosexual practice, a final common claim was that it defied natural impulses and violated the natural order. The union of man and woman, it was argued, is self-evidently natural because of the complementary design of male and female bodies, enabling life-giving and physically safe intercourse. However, the natural union of a man and woman stands in sharp contrast to the anal intercourse associated with homosexuality, which even modern medicine recognizes as carrying higher risks of trauma, infection, and long-term damage to the rectum and colon.

By openly defying this evident natural design—arguably the most important natural design of humans—it's been claimed that homosexual practice sets a precedent for overturning other long-established, normal behaviors. Its celebrated exercise is seen to make possible the rejection of all manner of previously revered sexual, familial, and social customs. If the most basic biological realities can be treated as optional or a matter of personal preference, then any norm can be challenged and replaced.

What It Takes to Reverse a Natural Impulse

Let us briefly consider the claim that homosexuality violates instinct, not in terms of reproduction or social norms, but from the standpoint of emotional reaction. A body of research suggests that, outside of homosexual individuals themselves, much of the global population is predisposed to experience a disgust response toward homosexual behavior.[72] In other words, many people appear hardwired from birth to feel discomfort when exposed to homosexual acts—whether through sight, sound, or written description. For example, some modern studies using MRI scans have measured neural activation patterns and found that heterosexual participants—particularly men exposed to male-male erotic stimuli—show elevated markers associated with disgust.[73] Notably, even participants from countries where homosexuality is widely affirmed were not entirely immune to this response.[74]

Recognizing that a natural impulse of repulsion toward acts of homosexuality exists, some liberal researchers—seeking to prevent this reaction from casting homosexuality in a negative light—have argued that such disgust is simply a misfiring of an outdated purity response. This alternative explanation gained popular expression in the Moral Foundations Theory of social psychologist Jonathan Haidt. Summarizing the dominant scholarly narrative, he contends that the "purity" foundation of moral reasoning evolved to protect humans from pathogens and contamination but was later inappropriately extended into broader social and moral domains—like a security system calibrated for armed intruders that begins sounding alarms at every passing shadow. On this account, behaviors historically labeled "impure," including homosexuality in many cultures, can thus trigger this system. The resulting moral disgust, in this view, is neither rational nor necessary but a vestige of an evolutionary mechanism operating outside its original context.[75]

Of course, this explanation from Haidt's theory is speculative rather than fact-based and serves a broader progressive agenda. Specifically, it portrays left-leaning supporters of homosexuality and other non-traditional sexual behaviors as having wisely moved beyond a mistaken way of thinking; conversely, conservatives are depicted as foolishly focused on seeing certain behaviors as "impure," despite the fact that they pose no real threat of harm. But if speculation is allowed, why could it not be that conservatives are the insightful ones in this scenario?

I propose that when conservatives feel an innate revulsion against homo-sexual acts—or other sexual behaviors that fall outside traditional norms—they are not triggering an antiquated purity response rooted in false ideas about contamination. Instead, they are activating a protective response attuned to societal decline. Unlike those with progressive sensibilities, conservatives possess an almost prescient ability—a kind of sixth sense—that allows them to perceive which behaviors, if left unchecked and normalized, will ultimately undermine the stability of civilization. In my scenario, progressives get to enjoy the prospect of defective moral functioning.

Regardless of what cognitively underpins the negative response, it's not conjecture to say that the vast majority of humans are not instinctively tolerant of homosexual activity but have an innate revulsion toward it. Such a hard-wired response has posed a monumental challenge to the social engineers of the West, who are determined to make homosexual behavior acceptable. If you will permit the analogy, sausage serves as a metaphor for their public relations success.

Before refrigeration, storing and eating meat—especially from large animals like pigs and cows that could not be consumed all at once—was a serious challenge. Humans are naturally repulsed by rancid meat, and our sense of smell is highly sensitive to even slight spoilage. In fact, it's so sensitive that sometimes we will recoil from meat that is still safe to eat but no longer fresh to our sense of smell. Because spoiled meat can cause illness, this strong detection system is a necessary and useful adaptation.

It's easy to understand why we recoil from truly rotten food—our lives can depend on it. But what about meat that smells slightly off yet remains edible? Our ancestors faced that problem regularly. For them, meat was valuable and often scarce, so it couldn't be wasted. When large amounts of pork or beef couldn't be frozen and risked rejection at the first whiff of staleness, a practical solution was required. Sausage provided the remedy. Meat that was no longer appealing but not yet dangerous to eat could be ground, heavily seasoned, and reshaped. With generous amounts of salt, pepper, garlic, and other aromatic spices, sausage transformed involuntary gagging into involuntary mouth-watering. If cured over a fire for a few days, its taste was completely altered, and the risk of spoilage was reduced for months.

In the West, parties, parades, flags, and costumes saturated in rainbow colors function much like the heavy seasoning of sausage, serving as the salt, pepper, and garlic applied to a phenomenon from which many would instinctively recoil if left unadorned. By wrapping it in the visual language of childhood, festivity, and harmless play, and infusing it with the familiar notes of joy and pride, activists don't eliminate the underlying reaction so much as overpower it. This bold combination of sweetness and spectacle overcomes what research suggests is a natural reflex of avoidance, turning it into an almost automatic response of approval and attraction. Hung for years in the smoke of relentless public affirmation—including state-mandated Pride Months, Pride Flags, and Pride Parades—the phenomenon not only loses its sharp edge but takes on an indefinite shelf life in the public square.

Sadly, I must conclude this section not with a whimsical allusion to sausage but with a sober recognition of our present era. We live in a moment when advancing philosophical arguments, citing empirical research, or even employing pointed analogies (about sausage, no less) can provoke serious consequences if they challenge prevailing progressive orthodoxies. Such traditional academic practices no longer provide adequate protection from lawsuits, professional reprisals, reputational attacks, or even threats to persons or property. Given the charged and punitive climate that now surrounds public disagreement—and given that many on the Left dedicate themselves to targeting conservatives with whom they disagree—it's necessary to make the following point explicit. I offer this clarification not out of fear, but out of a certain sympathy for my ideological opponents, whose preferred tools of academic engagement now too often appear to be censorship, intimidation, and strategic litigation rather than open scholarly debate.

To acknowledge that scientific research indicates many people experience a measurable, instinctive aversion to homosexual behavior doesn't diminish the obligation to treat others with compassion. While involuntary emotional reactions may lie outside conscious control, the choice to act with fairness, restraint, and basic respect remains within it. The purpose of presenting this evidence is to advance a political and philosophical argument about social order and civilizational stability, not to incite hostility toward LGBT persons. Describing observable patterns of human response is not the same as endorsing mistreatment of any individual. I therefore expect that disagreement over moral norms should never be used to justify physical aggression.

Respect for Our Forefathers' Insights

Our great-grandfathers didn't have MRI scans to measure neural activity, yet in forming a response to homosexual acts they relied on what they considered the most credible evidence available in their time and in the historical record. Lawmakers in modern Europe and North America frequently drew on arguments reaching back to ancient Greece and Rome, as well as the Enlightenment, to justify prohibitions in their own era. In doing so, they noted that Greek philosophers such as Plato and Aristotle described homosexual acts as "against nature," arguing that sexual behavior should serve procreation, reinforce clear distinctions between the sexes, and sustain the social structures necessary for civilizational flourishing.[76]

Plato, in particular, proved to be a significant source because—in the spirit of a true man of reason—he revised his views over time. You may recall that in the Introduction of this book I noted that a rational human being is someone who adopts a new position when presented with better evidence. So it was with Plato, the greatest of the Greek philosophers.

His treatment of same-sex relationships is one of the most striking reversals in the history of Western philosophy. In his early and middle-period dialogues—such as *Lysis, Charmides, Symposium* and *Phaedrus*—he presents homosexual attraction and acts as philosophically noble, whereas in his final works, especially the *Laws*, he condemns them and declares they should be punishable by law. He proposes escalating penalties: first private admonition and loss of certain civic rights, then public disgrace, and (in extreme or repeated cases) exile or death. This isn't a softening of earlier views; it's a total repudiation.

The most influential modern explanation for the complete turnabout in Plato's ethical judgment—promoted by scholars like Leo Strauss[77]—is that he came to see institutionalized homosexuality as both a symptom and accelerator of the moral and political degeneration destroying his home city of Athens and threatening city-states elsewhere.

Aside from the most esteemed Greek philosophers, works from ancient Rome argued against homosexual behavior as well. For example, the *Lex Scantinia* (circa 149 BC)—a law penalizing men who engaged in certain homosexual acts—demonstrated that the vitality of the state was linked to the preservation of social hierarchies and gender norms.[78]

Thousands of years later, the works of Enlightenment thinkers like Immanuel Kant could be referenced to argue that homosexual acts violated human dignity by objectifying the body and frustrating its proper capacities.[79] Aligned with this unbroken historical trend, sodomy laws were in force in the United States and Canada well into the 20th century. Change came earlier in Canada, where the Criminal Law Amendment Act of 1969 decriminalized consensual homosexual acts in private, though full legalization took longer to secure.[80] In the U.S., Illinois was the first state to repeal its law in 1961, but nationwide invalidation didn't come until the Supreme Court's 2003 ruling in *Lawrence v. Texas*.[81]

Same-sex marriage became legal in Canada on July 20, 2005, with the passage of the Civil Marriage Act, and in the United States on June 26, 2015, following the Supreme Court's decision in *Obergefell v. Hodges*.

As a starting point, a government directed by traditional conservative principles would restore marriage to its historic definition as the monogamous union of a man and a woman, thereby abolishing the legal recognition of same-sex marriage. Beyond this, for the sake of the common good, it would also seek ways to counter the promotion of homosexuality in the public sphere. Because this issue will likely be the most contested argument in this book, the next chapter is devoted entirely to exploring it.

Christianity or Homosexuality—The Incompatibility Conundrum

Some readers will read the last paragraph, above, and be convinced that they've found all the reason they need to dismiss this book altogether. After all, doesn't such a stance reveal Traditional Conservatism to be nothing more than a totalitarian project, hostile to peaceful coexistence with the gay community?

Others will roll their eyes at what they feel is the childishness of the philosophy's stand. Like a mother dealing with squabbling children, they will scold, "Why can't we all just get along?"

Let me explain why, in fact, we cannot *all* get along. In the 1980s, as the campaign for full acceptance of homosexuality gained momentum, activists often assured practicing Christians that gays and lesbians sought nothing more than peaceful coexistence. Pamphlets, speeches, and editorials repeated some version of the pledge: "We will leave you alone if you leave us alone."

Nearly forty years on, the unworkability of that promise has become evident. There is only one public square, and within it, the rights of Christians to advance their beliefs collide directly with the rights of homosexuals to advance theirs. This tension has been underscored by countless court rulings, government policies, educational directives, and media portrayals, nearly all of which conclude that the two sets of rights cannot fully coexist. In these official determinations, Christian freedoms are treated as the ones that must be revoked. The earlier chapters of this book expose, case after case, how Christians are being trampled and stripped of their rights, all to guarantee that homosexuals feel comfortable and affirmed in society.

By the mid-twentieth century, it had become clear that Jim Crow laws—state and local rules enforcing racial segregation and limiting African Americans' access to public spaces, education, and voting—were incompatible with the full protection of the rights of Black citizens. It made no sense to say to Black Americans: "You have rights but can't exercise them *here, here, and here.*" In the same way, the modern pluralist framework shows that Christianity cannot be fully and freely exercised where homosexuality is institutionally affirmed and openly endorsed.

The expansion of homosexual rights, therefore, is not simply a neutral matter of "live and let live." It results in the revocation of Christian freedoms, leaving believers vulnerable to penalties or discrimination. This can take the form of anti-discrimination lawsuits against faith-based organizations, restrictions on preaching labeled "hateful," reduced parental authority for Christian families, or disciplinary action against Christian public employees found deficient in their celebration of Pride events.[82]

The next chapter examines a series of significant cases in which, under the banner of protecting the rights of homosexuals, the rights of Christians have been removed. These cases build on earlier examples discussed in other chapters—instances in which courts barred Christians from praying in spaces where Pride events were permitted, blocked Christian schools from opening, or forced businesses to close because they would not affirm LGBT lifestyles. Even so, before moving on to the additional cases, I want to share one more personal example that illustrates the same pattern.

Until recently, I helped run youth leadership camps during the summer as part of a broader Christian camping ministry. Adults like me volunteered our time, while university students were hired as counselors. Their wages were paid through donations and camp fees, along with federal grants designed to help young adults gain work experience and strengthen their résumés.

In the spring of 2018, the Liberal government under Justin Trudeau introduced new eligibility requirements for organizations seeking access to the federal summer jobs grant. To receive funding, applicants were required to sign an attestation stating that their organization supported abortion (framed as "reproductive rights") and affirmed LGBT lifestyles (expressed as non-discrimination based on sexual orientation or gender identity).

For the first time in Canadian history, a legally protected religious belief became a barrier to receiving public funds—funds drawn from the taxes of all Canadians and intended to benefit citizens across the country. Like many Christian organizations, we refused to sign the attestation and lost the grant. For us, among other consequences, it meant we had to shuffle finances and could not offer as many free spots to kids in need. Across the country, thousands of camps, food banks, soup kitchens, and other Christian charities likewise scaled back their services that summer because the federal government chose to penalize them for holding traditional Christian convictions.

Most of these charities were too small and financially vulnerable to challenge the federal government in court—and they later saw that such a fight would have failed in any case. The Right to Life Association of Toronto Area, one of the country's larger conservative Christian organizations, did bring a lawsuit after being denied Canada Summer Jobs funding. It argued that being required to sign an attestation affirming abortion and LGBT rights directly violated its core religious convictions and freedom of conscience. The case went before the Federal Court, which has jurisdiction over such matters, and in October 2021, their challenge was rejected completely.[83]

In its ruling, the court acknowledged that the attestation requirement *did interfere* with the conscience and religious freedom of conservative Christians, including those at Toronto Right to Life, by compelling them to endorse positions contrary to their sincere pro-life and pro-traditional marriage beliefs. The court accepted that this amounted to compelled speech. However, echoing a pattern seen in numerous prior cases—where Christian claims have been given less weight when they conflict with prevailing progressive norms—the court nevertheless concluded that the infringement was justified.[84]

Under Canadian constitutional law, it held that the government's objectives—specifically, ensuring the distribution of public funds aligned with its interpretation of Charter values—outweighed any hardship the pro-life Christian claimants faced. Their loss of funding was deemed acceptable—"a reasonable limit on their rights"—because their organization remained free to operate and promote its views *without* the grant. In other words, they were free to enjoy their second-class status.

This cultural onslaught has no signs of stopping. As the rights of homosexuals expand, the rights of Christians to live and act according to their religious convictions without penalty are correspondingly diminished.

To recognize that one set of rights must give way is not to desire oppression but to acknowledge an unavoidable conflict of visions. History and empirical evidence demonstrate that a Christian moral order has been foundational to Western peace and prosperity. If that legacy is to revive and endure, Christianity must be allowed its full public exercise, which will require a legal reversal restoring moral clarity and protecting its values.

One vision must govern public life. There is no sustainable path in which the values of Christianity and those of homosexuality hold equal sway under public law. Citizens must choose which will yield. As a starting point for their deliberations, they should acknowledge that many of their thoughts are likely not their own: they have been exposed to a deliberate propaganda campaign throughout their lives, designed to censor opposing narratives. Next, they should evaluate the evidence to determine which vision, when celebrated in the public sphere, has produced the greatest good.

Endnotes for Chapter 3

1. Jay Gates, "Prologue to the Laws of King Alfred: An Edition and Translation for Students," *Journal of Early Medieval Northwestern Europe* 18 (2018), https://jemne.org/issues/18/gates.php.

2. Ibid.

3. Ibid.

4. Ibid.

5. Ibid.

6. Ibid.

7. Death Penalty Information Center, "State by State," https://deathpenaltyinfo.org/state-and-federal-info/state-by-state.

8. Research Co., "Most Canadians Support Death Penalty for Murder," April 3, 2024, https://researchco.ca/2024/04/03/death-penalty-canada-2024/.

9. World Corporal Punishment Research, "Country Files: Canada," https:// www.corpun.com/canada.htm.

10. Harry Themal, "The End of Delaware's Infamous Whipping Post," *The News Journal*, June 30, 2017, https://www.delawareonline.com/story/opinion/columnists/harry-themal/2017/06/30/end-delawares-infamous-whipping-post/443020001/.

11. World Corporal Punishment Research, "Country Files: Canada," https:// www.corpun.com/canada.htm.

12. Singapore Ministry of Law, "Handout on Law and Order Statistics," https:// www.mlaw.gov.sg/files/news/press-releases/2024/handout on_law_and_ order_statistics.pdf.

13. Macrotrends, "Singapore Crime Rate & Statistics | Historical Chart & Data," 2021, https://www.macrotrends.net/global-metrics/countries/sgp/ singapore/crime-rate-statistics; USAFacts, "What Is the Crime Rate in the U.S.?," 2024, https://usafacts.org/answers/what-is-the-crime-rate-in-the-us/ country/united-states.

14. Department of Statistics Malaysia, *Crime Statistics, Malaysia, 2023* (Putrajaya: Department of Statistics Malaysia, November 2, 2023), https://www.dosm. gov.my/portal-main/release-content/crime-statistics-malaysia-2023; see also Macrotrends, "Malaysia Crime Rate & Statistics | Historical Chart & Data," 2021, https://www.macrotrends.net/global-metrics/countries/mys/malaysia/ crime-rate-statistics.

15. World Bank, "Intentional Homicides (per 100,000 People)—Brunei Darussalam," *DataBank*, https://data.world

bank.org/indicator/VC.IHR.PSRC. P5?locations=BN; see also Macrotrends, "Brunei Crime Rate & Statistics | Historical Chart & Data," 2012, https://www.macrotrends.net/global-metrics/ countries/brn/brunei/crime-rate-statistics.

16. "Fewer Malaysian Convicts Return to Life of Crime Compared to Global Average, Says Prisons Dept.," *The Star*, September 3, 2025, https://www.thestar.com.my/news/nation/2025/09/03/rate-of-repeat-offences-by-former-inmates-below-global-benchmark-at-just-16; Lisa Mundia, "A Descriptive Profile of Selected Brunei Convicts: Viewpoint," *Journal of Public Administration and Governance* 10, no. 3 (2020): 6–25, https://doi.org/10.5296/jpag.v10i3.17357.

17. B. C. Hutchinson, A. Parascandola, and T. Wintle, "Does the United States Have High Recidivism Rates? New Data Provides Insights," *SSRN*, 2024, https://papers.ssrn.com/sol3/papers.cfm?abstract_id=5029176.

18. For example, Byron R. Johnson, *More God, Less Crime: Why Faith Matters and How It Could Matter More* (West Conshohocken, PA: Templeton Press, 2011).

19. Geneviève Beaudry et al., "Effectiveness of Psychological Interventions in Prison to Reduce Recidivism: A Systematic Review and Meta-Analysis of Randomised Controlled Trials," *The Lancet Psychiatry* 8, no. 9 (September 2021): 759–73, https://doi.org/10.1016/S2215-0366(21)00170-X.

20. Government of Canada, "Bill C-5: Mandatory Minimum Penalties to Be Repealed," December 7, 2021, https://www.canada.ca/en/department-justice/news/2021/12/mandatory-minimum-penalties-to-be-repealed.html.

21. Stephen Koppel and René Ropac, "Examining the Effects of New York's Bail Law on Pretrial Recidivism: A Controlled-Interrupted Time Series Analysis," *Criminal Justice Policy Review*, published online August 29, 2025, https://doi.org/10.1177/08874034251363835.

22. H. E. Myers, "Not Taking Crime Seriously: California's Prop 47 Exacerbated Crime and Drug Abuse," *Manhattan Institute*, October 17, 2024, https://manhattan.institute/article/not-taking-crime-seriously-californias-prop-47-exacerbated-crime-and-drug-abuse.

23. Stephanie Warren, "Canadian Pastor Acquitted after Pandemic Police Hunted Him and His Church with a Helicopter," *Christian Broadcasting Network*, November 2, 2022, https://cbn.com/news/world/canadian-pastor-acquitted-after-pandemic-police-hunted-him-and-his-church-helicopter.

24. Canadian Press, "'Freedom Convoy' Organizer Tamara Lich Denied Bail, Will Remain in Jail Pending Trial," *Lethbridge News Now*, July 8, 2022, https://lethbridgenewsnow.com/2022/07/08/freedom-convoy-organizer-tamara-lich-denied-bail-will-remain-in-jail-pending-trial/.

25. Joe Bukuras, "Acquitted Pro-Life Activist Mark Houck Reveals Details of 'Reckless' FBI Raid; Will Press Charges," *Catholic News Agency*, February 1, 2023, https://www.catholicnewsagency.com/news/253523/acquit ted-pro-life-activist-mark-houck-reveals-details-of-fbi-raid -will-press-charges.

26. For example, in Toronto, Randall McKenzie, 28, was arrested for assaulting a 13-year-old girl but released on bail the same day, only to fatally stab a 16-year-old girl less than 24 hours later. Similarly, in Ottawa, Sami Awad, 22, was arrested for domestic assault in 2022, released on bail immediately, and murdered the same woman two days afterward.

27. Kristen Hult and Paul Walsh, "Few Face Criminal Charges from Minneapolis Protests; Most Arrests Were for Minor Offenses," *Star Tribune*, June 19, 2020, https://www.startribune.com/few-face-criminal-charges-fro m-minneapolis-protests-most-arrests-were-for-minor-offens es/571385172/; Rochelle Raveendran, "Toronto Police Spent $19.5M on Response to Israel-Gaza War Protests Last Year: Report," *CBC News*, April 4, 2025, https://www. cbc.ca/news/canada/toronto/toronto-police-israel-gaza-pro tests-policing-report-1.7502044; Mirna Alsharif and Corky Siemaszko, "As Pro-Israeli and Pro-Palestinian Protests Sweep U.S., Police Worry About Clashes," *NBC News*, October 14, 2023, https://www.nbcnews.com/news/-palestinian-israeli-protes ts-sweep-us-police-worry-clashes-rcna119599.

28. Christina Grube, "Maine Court Removes Mother's Right to Bring Child to Church," *WORLD Magazine*, May 1, 2025, https://wng.org/roundups/maine-court-removes-mothers-right-to-bring-child-to-church-1746129135.

29. Brianna Willis, "Pronoun Use at Center of Rape Case Involving Former Chowchilla Prisoner," *ABC30*, December 20, 2024, https://abc30.com/post/ pronoun-use-center-rape-case-involving-former-chowchilla-prisoner/15684307/.

30. Jake Offenhartz et al., "Trump Praises Charlie Kirk, Says: 'I Hate My Opponent, and I Don't Want the Best for Them,'" *Associated Press*, September 21, 2025, https://apnews.com/article/b5469086954908b162f464da966cf238.

31. Ibid.

32. Augustine, *City of God*, book 19, chap. 6, trans. Henry Bettenson (New York: Penguin Books, 2003), original work ca. 413–426 CE; Augustine, *Letter 153*, trans. Roland Teske, in *The Works of Saint Augustine: A Translation for the 21st Century: Letters 100–155*, vol. II/2, ed. John E. Rotelle (Hyde Park, NY: New City Press, 2001), 406–421.

33. Thomas Aquinas, *Summa Theologica*, II-II, q. 64, art. 2, trans. Fathers of the English Dominican Province (New York: Benziger Bros., 1947), original work ca. 1265–1274.

34. William N. Eskridge Jr., *Dishonorable Passions: Sodomy Laws in America, 1861–2003* (New York: Viking, 2008); David

Nash, "The Fall and Rise of Blasphemy in the West," in *The Fall and Rise of Blasphemy Law*, ed. Paul Cliteur and Tommy J. Herrenberg (Leiden: Leiden University Press, 2016), 31–50; David Nash, "From Scurrilous Periodical to the Public Platform: Policing Blasphemers and Anti-Social Behaviour—Constructing the Public Peace Then and Now," in *Anti-Social Behaviour in Britain: Victorian and Contemporary Perspectives*, ed. Anne-Marie Kilday and David Nash (London: Palgrave Macmillan, 2014), chap. 5.

35. Often attributed to Thomas Jefferson, it is actually a paraphrase from a statement in his "A Summary View of the Rights of British America" (1774): "When a long train of abuses and usurpations, pursuing invariably the same Object evinces a design to reduce them under absolute Despotism, it is their right, it is their duty, to throw off such Government, and to provide new Guards for their future security."

36. William Crowley, "Blue Laws—Washington State," *History Link.org*, June 20, 2009, https://www.historylink.org/File/9057.

37. Supreme Court of Canada, *R. v. Big M Drug Mart Ltd.*, [1985] 1 S.C.R. 295, https://decisions.scc-csc.ca/scc-csc/scc-csc/en/item/43/index.do.

38. Note, "Blasphemy and the Original Meaning of the First Amendment," *Harvard Law Review* 135, no. 2 (December 2021): 689–750, https:// harvardlawreview.org/print/vol-135/blasphemy-and-the-original-meaning-of-the-first-amendment/.

39. *Criminal Code*, R.S.C. 1985, c. C-46, s. 296 (repealed 2018) (Canada, 1892).

40. In some states very public denials of core doctrines—for instance, denying God's existence or saying that Christian scriptures were "mostly lies"—if deemed purposely malicious could result in charges. See: *Updegraph v. Commonwealth* (1824, Pennsylvania) or the 1926 prosecution of Anthony Bimba in Massachusetts for atheistic statements.

41. Guy de Brès, *Belgic Confession* (1561), https://www.prca.org/bc_index.html.

42. U.S. Commission on International Religious Freedom, *Annual Report 2012: Saudi Arabia* (Washington, DC: USCIRF, 2012), quoted in "State Harassment of Private Worship and Restrictions on Religious Materials," https://www.refworld.org/reference/annualreport/uscirf/2012/en/85611.

43. "FCRA Overhaul: Major Blow for Christian NGOs; 70% Religious NGOs 'Deemed to Have Ceased' Aligned to Christian Programmes," *The CSR Universe*, January 2, 2022, https://thecsruniverse.com/articles/fcra-overhaul-major-blow-for-christian-ngos-70-religious-ngos-deemed-to-have-ceased-aligned-to-christian-programmes-.

44. For example, Open Doors UK & Ireland, "Persecution Increases in Uttar Pradesh under Harsher Anti-Conversion Laws," October 31, 2024, https://www.opendoorsuk.org/news/latest-news/persecution-incre

ases-in-uttar-pradesh-under-harsher-anti-conversion-laws/.

45. U.S. Department of State, "2018 Report on International Religious Freedom: Israel, West Bank and Gaza," Report (2018), 24–25, https://en.idi. org.il/media/12979/israel-2018-international-religious-freedom-report.pdf.

46. For a summary of the debate see Homer Hanko, "The State's Relation to the Law of God," *Protestant Reformed Theological Journal* 37, no. 2 (2004): 11–30.

47. Karl Popper, *The Open Society and Its Enemies*, vol. 1, *The Spell of Plato* (London: Routledge & Kegan Paul, 1945), 265n4.

48. Bret Boyce, "Obscenity and Community Standards," *Yale Journal of International Law* 33, no. 2 (2008): 299–368, https://openyls.law.yale.edu/ server/api/core/bitstreams/39ee06c9-7e56-480b-b772-0090d9ef1f3f/content.

49. Thomas Lickona, "New Report Finds Most Teens Watch Online Pornography," *Psychology Today*, June 1, 2023, https://www.psychologytoday. com/us/blog/raising-kind-kids/202305/new-report-finds-most-teens-watch-online-pornography; Melissa B. Robb and Sarah Mann, "Teens and Pornography," *Common Sense Media*, January 10, 2023, https://www. commonsensemedia.org/research/teens-and-pornography.

50. Richard F. Hixson, *Pornography and the Justices: The Supreme Court and the Intractable Obscenity Problem* (Car-

bondale: Southern Illinois University Press, 1996); John E. Semonche, *Censoring Sex: A Historical Journey through American Media* (Lanham, MD: Rowman & Littlefield, 2007).

51. Richard Moon, "Obscenity Law and the Canadian Charter of Rights and Freedoms," in *The Constitutional Protection of Freedom of Expression* (Toronto: University of Toronto Press, 2000), 97–124.

52. William M. Struthers, *Wired for Intimacy: How Pornography Hijacks the Male Brain* (Downers Grove, IL: IVP Books, 2009); Paul J. Wright, Robert S. Tokunaga, and Ashley Kraus, "A Meta-Analysis of Pornography Consumption and Actual Acts of Sexual Aggression in General Population Studies," *Journal of Communication* 66, no. 1 (February 2016): 183–205, https://doi.org/10.1111/jcom.12201.

53. David J. Garrow, *Liberty and Sexuality: The Right to Privacy and the Making of Roe v. Wade* (New York: Macmillan, 1994).

54. Raymond Tatalovich, *The Politics of Abortion in the United States and Canada: A Comparative Study* (Armonk, NY: M .E. Sharpe, 1997).

55. Isaac Maddow-Zimet and Kimya Forouzan, "Stability in the Number of Abortions from 2023 to 2024 in US States without Total Bans Masks Major Shifts in Access" (New York: Guttmacher Institute, 2025), https://www. guttmacher.org/report/stability-number-abortions-2023-20

24-us-states-without-total-bans-masks-major-shifts-access.

56. National Council for Adoption, "Adoption by the Numbers: A New Report from the National Council for Adoption," August 7, 2025, https:// showhope.org/stories/adoption-by-the-numbers-a -new-report-from-the-national-council-for-adoption/.

57. Evert Pieterman and Peter J. Mitchell, "Adoption Policies across Canada" (Cardus, August 2024), https://www.cardu s.ca/wp-content/uploads/2024/08/ Adoption-Policies-Acr oss-Canada-1.pdf.

58. Ibid.

59. Abortion Rights Coalition of Canada, "Statistics—Abortion Rights Coalition of Canada," June 19, 2025, http://www.arcc-cdac.ca/ media/2020/07/statistics-abortion-in-canada.pdf; Guttmacher Institute, "Medication Abortion Accounted for 63% of All US Abortions in 2023—an Increase from 53% in 2020," March 19, 2024, https://www.guttmacher.org/2024/03/medication-abortio n-accounted-63-all-us-abortions-2023-increase-53-2020; Selena Simmons-Duffin, "Despite Bans in Some States, More Than a Million Abortions Were Provided in 2023," NPR, March 19, 2024, https://www.npr.org/sections/health-shots/2024/03/19/1 238293143/ abortion-data-how-many-us-2023.

60. For example, Leviticus 18:2; Leviticus 20:2–5; Deuteronomy

12:31; Deuteronomy 18:10; 2 Kings 17:17; Jeremiah 7:31; Jeremiah 19:5; Ezekiel 16:20–21.

61. Heath D. Dewrell, "Child Sacrifice in Ancient Israel," *The Ancient Near East Today*, December 2017, https://www.as or.org/anetoday/2017/12/child-sacrifice-ancient-israel.

62. Ibid.

63. M. Antonia Biggs, Heather Gould, and Diana G. Foster, "Understanding Why Women Seek Abortions in the US," *BMC Women's Health* 13 (2013): 29, https://pmc.ncbi.nlm.nih.gov/articles/PMC3729671/; Lawrence B. Finer et al., "Reasons U.S. Women Have Abortions: Quantitative and Qualitative Perspectives," *Perspectives on Sexual and Reproductive Health* 37, no. 3 (2005): 110–118, https://www.guttmacher.org/journa ls/psrh/2005/ reasons-us-women-have-abortions-quantita tive-and-qualitative-perspectives.

64. Donald J. Wold, *Out of Order: Homosexuality in the Bible and the Ancient Near East* (Peabody, MA: Hendrickson Publish ers, 1998).

65. Louis Crompton, *Homosexuality and Civilization* (Cam bridge, MA: Belknap Press of Harvard University Press, 2003).

66. For example: Camille Paglia, *Free Women, Free Men: Sex, Gender, Feminism* (New York: Pantheon Books, 2017); Camille Paglia, "Camille Paglia: A Feminist Defense of Mas-

culine Virtues," interview by Bari Weiss, *Wall Street Journal*, December 28, 2013, https://www.wsj.com/articles/SB1000 1424052702303997604579240022857012920.

67. Ibid.

68. For example, Helen Andrews, "The Great Feminization," *Compact*, October 16, 2025, https://www.compactmag.co m/article/the-great-feminization/.

69. For example, Shelby Ross, "The Feminization of Medicine," *AMA Journal of Ethics* 5, no. 9 (September 2003): 398–400, https://doi.org/10.1001/ virtualmentor.2003.5.9.msoc1-0 309.

70. Cory Clark and Bo Winegard, "Sex and the Academy," *Quillette*, October 8, 2022, https://quillette.com/2022/10/08/ sex-and-the-academy/; Cory Jane Clark, "From Worriers to Warriors: The Cultural Rise of Women," *Journal of Controversial Ideas* 5, no. 2 (2025): 6, https://doi.org/10.63466/ jci05020006.

71. Anemona Hartocollis, "A Year Ago, Women Were the Majority Among Ivy League Presidents. Now Most of Them Have Quit," *Chronicle of Higher Education*, August 20, 2024, https://www.chronicle.com/article/a-year-ago-women-were -the-majority-among-ivy-league-presidents-now-most-of-th em-have-quit; Hilary Burns, "Three-Quarters of Ivy League Presidents Were Women. Then the Israel-Hamas Protests Rocked Campuses," *Boston Globe*, August 24, 2024,

https://www.bostonglobe.com/2024/08/24/metro/ivy-league-presidents-israel-hamas-protests/.

72. Minming Zhang et al., "Neural Circuits of Disgust Induced by Sexual Stimuli in Homosexual and Heterosexual Men: An fMRI Study," *European Journal of Radiology* 80, no. 2 (November 2011): 418–25, https://doi.org/10.1016/j. ejrad.2010.05.021; S. H. Hu et al., "Patterns of Brain Activation during Visually Evoked Sexual Arousal Differ between Homosexual and Heterosexual Men," *American Journal of Neuroradiology* 29, no. 10 (November 2008): 1890–96, https://doi.org/10.3174/ajnr.A1260; Tim Paul et al., "Brain Response to Visual Sexual Stimuli in Heterosexual and Homosexual Males," *Human Brain Mapping* 29, no. 6 (June 2008): 726–35, https://doi. org/10.1002/hbm.20435; Adam Safron et al., "Neural Correlates of Sexual Arousal in Homosexual and Heterosexual Men," *Behavioral Neuroscience* 121, no. 2 (April 2007): 237–48, https://doi.org/10.1037/0735-7044.121.2.237; Jorge Ponseti et al., "A Functional Endophenotype for Sexual Orientation in Humans," *NeuroImage* 33, no. 3 (November 2006): 825–33, https:// doi.org/10.1016/j.neuroimage.2006.08.0 02; Sabine Kagerer et al., "Neural Activation toward Erotic Stimuli in Homosexual and Heterosexual Males," *Journal of Sexual Medicine* 8, no. 11 (November 2011): 3132–43, https://doi. org/10.1111/j.1743-6109.2011.02449.x; Mark J. Kiss, Melanie A. Morrison, and Todd G. Morrison, "A Meta-Analytic Review of the Association Between Disgust and Prejudice Toward Gay Men," *Journal of Homosexuality* 67, no. 5 (2020): 674–96, https://doi.org/10.1080/009183

69.2018.1553349.

73. Ibid.

74. For example, Zhang et al., "Neural Circuits of Disgust."

75. Jonathan Haidt, *The Righteous Mind: Why Good People Are Divided by Politics and Religion* (New York: Pantheon Books, 2012), 125–26, 149.

76. John M. Finnis, "Law, Morality, and 'Sexual Orientation,'" *Notre Dame Journal of Law, Ethics & Public Policy* 9, no. 1 (1994): 11–40, https://www. princeton.edu/~anscombe/a rticles/finnisorientation.pdf; Adrienne Pick, "Homosexuality," in *The Stanford Encyclopedia of Philosophy*, ed. Edward N. Zalta and Uri Nodelman, Summer 2023 ed., https://pla to.stanford.edu/ entries/homosexuality/.

77. Leo Strauss, *The Argument and the Action of Plato's "Laws"* (Chicago: University of Chicago Press, 1975), 3–5, 142–45.

78. See Craig A. Williams, *Roman Homosexuality*, 2nd ed. (Oxford: Oxford University Press, 2010).

79. Pauline Kleingeld, "The Case against Different-Sex Marriage in Kant," *Kantian Review* 25, no. 3 (2020): 441–464.

80. See Tom Warner, *Never Going Back: A History of Queer Activism in Canada* (Toronto: University of Toronto Press, 2002).

81. *Lawrence v. Texas*, 539 U.S. 558 (2003), https://supreme .justia.com/cases/ federal/us/539/558/; see Marc Stein, ed.,

Encyclopedia of Lesbian, Gay, Bisexual, and Transgender History in America, 3 vols. (New York: Charles Scribner's Sons, 2004).

82. For example, Élie Cantin-Nantel, "Ontario Teacher Berated Muslim Students for Skipping 'Pride Day,'" *True North*, July 19, 2023, https://tnc. news/2023/07/19/teacher-berated-muslim-students-pride-day/; Tristin Hopper, "Ontario Town Fined $10,000 for Refusing to Celebrate Pride Month," *National Post*, November 27, 2024, https://nationalpost.com/news/canada/ontario-town-fined-for-not-celebrating-pride-month.

83. The Canadian Press. "Canada Summer Jobs Change Barring Anti-Abortion Groups Was 'Reasonable': Federal Court." *Global News*, October 25, 2021. https://globalnews.ca/news/8323742/canada-summer-jobs-anti-abortion-groups/.

84. Ibid.

4

Restricting Homosexuality: Humility Over Pride

The Hump to Get Over

For many, soft theonomy's—and, correspondingly, Traditional Conservatism's—support for laws restricting homosexuality goes too far. In my experience, most self-described secular and left-leaning people are willing to calmly consider arguments regarding the regulation of Sunday rest or an end to public defamation of Christianity, public obscenity, or even abortion without losing their temper. But mention laws restricting homosexuality, and they not only stop listening—they start attacking.

The propaganda of the Post-War Consensus taught generations that the highest virtue is blind acceptance of all customs, cultures, and lifestyles. Combined with a multi-million-dollar marketing campaign employed by gay-rights groups since the 1980s,[1] this has brought us to an era in which challenging LGBT positions can result in job loss, fines, or even jail.[2]

In the previous chapter I mentioned that blasphemy laws to preserve the honor of Christianity were largely phased out by the 1960s in America and Canada. Since the 2000s, de facto LGBT blasphemy laws have emerged in their place. These are enforced with the full weight of the state and applied not only to public declarations but even to private communications.

How extreme is this official taboo? In the U.S., a person can burn his nation's flag without judicial consequence, but burning the Gay Pride flag will get you charged with a hate crime.[3] In Canada, there is tolerance for many forms of protests—except those that intersect with homosexuality. Black Lives Matter protestors can block city streets and snarl traffic for hours without being arrested;[4] Indigenous activists can block rail lines, causing millions in economic losses, and not be arrested;[5] pro-Palestinian demonstrators can storm the Art Gallery of Ontario during a prime ministerial fundraiser—chanting slogans, blocking entrances, and forcing the event's cancellation—and still not be arrested.[6]

Yet a Christian pastor who voices objections at a Drag Queen Story Hour at the Calgary Public Library is arrested. In addition to being charged with criminal harassment and sentenced to 12 months of house arrest with two years of probation, Derek Reimer was later jailed for refusing to comply with a court-ordered apology letter.[7]

The LGBT taboo that grips North America offers no grace or forgiveness to dissenters, and I know firsthand about this new orthodoxy. In the not-so-distant past, I was on the inside looking out; I was among those who accepted—and even helped reinforce—the very taboo I now seek to dismantle.

The Tale of a Reluctant Convert

At several points in these pages, I've described my journey from an à la carte Christianity—picking only politically acceptable doctrines—to a traditionalist commitment, trusting that all of God's Word is essential for life. For me, the most difficult part of that process was accepting the faith's historical moral position on homosexuality. I was one of those people who believed that laws restricting homosexuality were antiquated relics fit only for the trash bin of history.

My advocacy against the traditional Christian position was ferocious. I participated in public debates with conservative seminary professors, arguing that today's faith must abandon its outdated prohibitions. In my public writing, I let it be known where I stood. For example, in the Preface to my 2009 book on media bias against Christians, I admitted:

> ...many of my evangelical friends say I'm too liberal for their comfort. For example, while I think that sexual orientation is irrelevant to a person's Christianity, a great number of my evangelical brothers and sisters believe I am wrong. Interestingly, we all back up our opinions with verses from the same Bible. So it goes. We have amicably agreed to disagree.[8]

Today, I continue to insist, unequivocally, that same-sex attracted individuals, conducting themselves peacefully and observing societal proprieties, should be fully protected from any physical harm or violence by the state or any third parties. Moreover, I hold that Christians—and, indeed, everyone—have a duty to treat homosexuals as individuals with inherent human dignity, avoiding hatred, since all humans are made in the image of God.

But on homosexuality's place in the public square, I've changed. It was not a Damascus Road experience of instant clarity like that visited upon the Apostle Paul. No, my change in attitude came gradually over time and was the result of a process akin to causal chain analysis.

Causal chain analysis is an analytical method used to trace a sequence of events, causes, or decisions leading to an outcome or problem, where each step contributes to or influences the next. It seeks to clarify how an initial cause ("A") sets in motion subsequent effects ("B," "C," and so on). It demonstrates the logical or empirical connections along the chain while identifying root causes.

People sometimes confuse causal chain analysis with the discredited slippery slope fallacy. They may look similar at first, but they are not. Slippery slope arguments usually look to *the future* and predict doom without filling in the gaps or offering evidence. Causal chain analysis, by contrast, looks to *the past* and gathers the facts: it traces how events really unfolded, step by step, to show the connections. One is speculation; the other is explanation. As will become clear, the removal of all restrictions against homosexuality—including those on same-sex marriage—has produced a mounting cascade of developments unfolding at an accelerating pace, many of them neither anticipated nor intended.

It's Not Like the Civil Rights Movement

In Canada, consensual same-sex activity between adults was decriminalized nationwide in 1969. In America, Illinois became the first state to legalize it in 1962, and about half the states followed over the next forty years. However, in America, the decisive legal shift came in 2003, when the U.S. Supreme Court struck down all remaining state sodomy laws.

However, the modern gay-rights movement in the United States and Canada is not generally said to have sprung from its first court victories. It's usually traced to the Stonewall riots, which began in the early hours of June 28, 1969, at the Stonewall Inn, a mafia-run gay bar in New York City's Greenwich Village.

Police raids on gay bars were common, but that night a multiracial crowd of drag queens, street youth, lesbians, and bar patrons fought back for hours and continued protesting for five more nights. Widespread press coverage quickly turned the riots into a symbol. A previously cautious gay-rights lobby transformed into an aggressive, confrontational liberation movement. Within weeks, the Gay Liberation Front was formed in New York City, and its chapters spread quickly across the U.S.; the first pride marches were planned, and the Stonewall energy crossed the border. Inspired by the American events, Canadian activists formed new militant groups in 1970 and held Canada's first major gay-rights protest on Parliament Hill in August 1971.[9]

From the 1970s, it took only a few decades for North American society's opposition to homosexual activity to crumble and for tacit acceptance to become the norm. This moral prohibition, which had endured for roughly 4,000 years in written form and was upheld across nations and cultures as essential to social order, was not only abandoned but also recast as harmful and unjust. Many high-level academics across the West, who had long argued that restrictions on homosexuality were unnecessary holdovers from an ignorant, pre-Enlightenment era, became even louder and more public in their calls to end these bans.

Prominent Hollywood figures soon joined them, using their platforms to amplify the push for change. The Playboy Foundation—an organization that used money from the sale of *Playboy* magazine to fund causes opposing traditional values—provided grants to the movement, while wealthy gay professionals quietly wrote personal checks to bankroll the effort.[10]

Apart from receiving high-level support, the campaign for acceptance of homosexuality was so successful because it was framed as a civil rights issue akin to the struggle of Black Americans against racial discrimination, and it rode the momentum of the Civil Rights Movement.

The Civil Rights Movement was a broad campaign—driven primarily by Black Americans but strongly supported by many Whites—to dismantle the "Jim Crow" system of segregation, a set of laws and customs that kept Black citizens politically weak, socially separated, and economically disadvantaged. The struggle for legal and political equality reached its height from the mid-1950s to the mid-1960s, culminating in landmark legislation that ended racial segregation, outlawed discrimination, and secured equal rights for Black Americans.

As the gay-rights movement advanced, activists frequently drew on this history of racial injustice. They argued that denying homosexuals the right to have sex as they pleased was equivalent to the denials of equal treatment, dignity, and basic freedoms Blacks had endured under the law. This was a powerful tool of persuasion for an emotionally vulnerable population. In the aftermath of the Civil Rights era, many Americans were still grappling with guilt and moral reflection over past racial wrongs. The emotional exhaustion left by that earlier national reckoning made many more susceptible to the idea that nearly any legal restriction on personal behavior risked repeating a similar injustice.

In his book, *It's Not Like Being Black: How Sexual Activists Hijacked the Civil Rights Movement*, scholar and pastor Voddie Baucham contends that equating the LGBT movement with the Black civil rights struggle is a false comparison.[11] He argues that race is an unchangeable trait with no element of choice; how one presents racially to the world cannot change. Conversely, he states that sexuality is not simply about unchangeable traits but involves behaviors and choices; how one presents sexually to the world can change.

Hoping the reader will keep in mind the no choice/choice dichotomy he has proposed, Baucham urges readers to recognize the distinct historical and moral foundations of these two struggles. Historically, because Blacks are identifiable on sight, discrimination against them has been immediate and inescapable. Homosexuals, by contrast, have always been able to pass without detection if they chose not to identify themselves. This difference in visibility meant that Blacks endured significant and relentless systemic oppression, while homosexuals faced only occasional and isolated punishments.

On the question of morality and theological grounding, he stresses that Christianity affirms equality across races but not equality for homosexuality. Furthermore, he wants us to consider why that might be. He implicitly petitions his audience to consider whether it's reasonable to believe that the Christian faith— which gets everything else absolutely right when it comes to social flourishing—could be entirely mistaken in this one area. His answer is no.[12] Because the work of Professor Baucham fully addresses the false equivalence between the civil rights movement and the LGBTQ movement, I will not pursue the same arguments here but simply commend readers to examine his book.

Pride in Their Propaganda

In their campaign to make homosexuality acceptable, activists used advanced public relations techniques. In addition to comparing the plight of homosexuals to that of Blacks before the end of Jim Crow, gay-rights activists deliberately leveraged the AIDS crisis of the 1980s and early 1990s to generate public sympathy and support. The strategy was laid out in detail by gay advertising psychologist Marshall Kirk and public relations consultant Hunter Madsen in their widely read book *After the Ball: How America Will Conquer Its Fear and Hatred of Gays in the '90s.*[13]

In *After the Ball,* the authors openly acknowledge that their book is a sophisticated media and public relations tool for promoting gay rights, explicitly describing it as "propaganda" aimed at reshaping public opinion. To achieve success, they stress avoiding any connection between AIDS and gay "lifestyle" behaviors—such as sex with multiple men in bathhouses.[14] Instead, they caution that focus must be on narratives of *undeserved* suffering. The authors explain the power of victimhood, stating: "As cynical as it may seem, AIDS gives us a chance, however brief, to establish ourselves as a victimized minority legitimately deserving of America's special protection and care."[15]

Aiding the victimhood narrative was the repeated claim that prudish *straight* society—not personal agency—was to blame for the decimation of the gay population ravaged by AIDS. The argument was advanced that if homosexuals could "come out of the closet," the perceived need for risky promiscuity would decline.[16] Research has not borne that out. For example, U.S. General Social Survey data from 2008–2018—a period of broad public acceptance—showed that gay men were not moderating their behavior in response to changing attitudes. Instead of settling down, they reported a median of 10 lifetime sexual partners, with nearly 50% reporting 10 or more, about 30% reporting 20 or more, roughly 15% reporting 50 or more, and just over 7% claiming 100 or more sexual partners. By comparison, heterosexual men reported a median of about four lifetime partners.[17]

As Kirk and Madsen had emphasized in their book, a key to popular acceptance of homosexuality rested on misdirection. Like a magician who gets the audience to look "here" but not "there," the propagandists of the gay-rights movement used all their skills and connections to turn the focus away from homosexuals' actual behaviors to homosexuals' idealized behaviors. Their connections in Hollywood assisted immensely by producing films and TV series featuring homosexual lovers with moderate lifestyles more closely mirroring 1950s married couples than bathhouse or gay bar philanderers. While media messaging was of great help, the legalization of same-sex marriage was the most decisive tipping point in normalizing homosexuality for the broader society.

Marriage as the Key Moral Signal

In America, same-sex marriage first became legal at the state level, starting in Massachusetts in 2004, when the state's Supreme Judicial Court ruled that banning it violated the state constitution. Over the next eleven years, more states followed through court rulings, legislation, or voter referendums, and by early 2015, thirty-six states plus the District of Columbia allowed same-sex marriage. On June 26, 2015, the U.S. Supreme Court resolved the issue nationwide in *Obergefell v. Hodges*, ruling 5–4 that all states must license and recognize marriages between two people of the same sex.

In Canada, same-sex marriage was legalized nationwide on July 20, 2005, when the federal Civil Marriage Act received royal assent, defining marriage as the lawful union of two people. This followed a series of provincial court decisions starting in 2003 in Ontario, British Columbia, and Quebec, which struck down limits to opposite-sex marriage and led Parliament to pass a uniform law for the whole country.

In the wake of approving court decisions, the population at large came to accept that marriage was fundamentally redefined. Other government legislation affirming the equal worth and legitimacy of homosexual relationships—with titles like the "All Families are Equal Act"[18]—sent a strong moral signal to the public, who were primed to accept that their traditional views of marriage needed to be replaced. Again, we recall that when people have no preexisting ethical code—as we find in secular society today—the ability of the courts and government to define or impose what is right or wrong is immense. Once marriage was no longer promoted as a God-ordained, child-centered covenant between a man and a woman, it became vulnerable to being reframed as a state-licensed "love contract" between any two consenting adults.

This legal and legislative shift not only stripped marriage and the family of their traditional meanings, it crushed their status as the gold standard of social respectability. If marriage could be anything, many concluded, it was nothing, or at least nothing special. Cohabitation, with its high levels of infidelity and low levels of stability, has risen sharply since the legislative triumph of gay marriage. About 70% of first unions among young adults in the U.S. are now cohabiting couples, with only around 30% of 18–34-year-olds marrying.[19]

The decline of spousal permanence that comes with cohabitation is reflected in the growth of single-parent households. According to the U.S. Census Bureau, roughly two-thirds of Black families, half of Hispanic families, and one-third of White families with children under 18 are headed by a single parent.[20] Children in these households face higher risks of abuse, poverty, and worse overall outcomes.[21]

Contributing to the devaluation of traditional marriage and family, we now see law, media, and education treat the mother-father household as merely one option among many, ignoring the unique relational, economic, and child-rearing benefits that only the traditional family structure provides.[22]

From Acceptance to Celebration Requires Silencing Critics

With the traditional concepts of marriage and family stripped of their status and authority, society became open to a broader push to normalize homosexuality in every aspect of life and insist on its celebration. It became clear that marriage "equality" was never the endpoint; it was the decisive breach in the wall that would allow a total sexual free-for-all to flood through unchallenged. Instrumental to this change—moving from calls for coexistence to demands for cultural dominance—was the silencing of ideological opponents.

If homosexuality were to be celebrated as an unqualified good, it would require censorship of competing messages. Within the academy, research showing any negative effects related to homosexuality—if it could even find a publisher—came under attack, with calls for retraction and the firing of faculty. For example, psychiatrist Robert Spitzer published a study suggesting some gays and lesbians could change orientation through therapy,[23] but after backlash from activist pressure, he publicly recanted. Although he personally denounced his study, leading some to question its findings, the journal was satisfied with its rigor and validity and never retracted it. Similarly, when sociologist Mark Regnerus published his *New Family Structures Study* showing worse outcomes for children of parents in same-sex relationships, activists called for his firing and launched a petition for retraction of the research.[24] The journal subjected the work to a re-evaluation, and it was cleared; however, it's still denounced as unsound by pro-homosexual academic organizations (which is basically all academic organizations). Like Regnerus, Paul Sullins published two studies showing negative outcomes for children of same-sex parents.[25] These too drew activist calls for retraction, though none has been formally removed.

In Canada, Douglas Allen, an economics professor at Simon Fraser University, has examined reams of government data to assess the outcomes of same-sex parenting on children. Analyzing measures such as graduation rates, he concluded that "children living in both gay and lesbian households struggle compared to children from opposite-sex married households." His research found that the children of same-sex households were "65% as likely" to graduate as those from heterosexual households.[26] Addressing why many other studies report "no difference" in outcomes between children raised by homosexual parents and those raised by heterosexual parents, Allen—author of more than 100 peer-reviewed articles—attributes those findings to what he describes as "weak designs, biased samples, and low-powered tests."[27]

In her study, Lisa Littman found that the sudden rise in transgender identification among teens—especially girls—was driven by social contagion rooted in peer influence and learned, mirrored behavior, rather than biology or gender distress going back to childhood. She termed this pattern Rapid Onset Gender Dysphoria (ROGD). Her article was rabidly attacked by LGBT activists, prompting the publishing journal, *PLOS ONE*, to temporarily remove it. When impartial investigation proved it credible, it was republished. Activists were just as aggressive in trying to remove J. Michael Bailey and Suzanna Diaz's large parent-survey study on ROGD, which supported Littman's findings. They were partly successful: although the paper passed peer review and was published online in *Archives of Sexual Behavior*, the journal later caved to activist pressure and retracted it, prompting Bailey to accuse the journal of censorship and republish the study elsewhere.[28]

Perhaps reflective of this larger censorship trend, research from the 1980s and before that showed higher rates of child-adult molestation among the homosexual population has come to be spoken of as "discredited" owing to an official redefinition of pedophilia.

Around the 1990s, major psychological and psychiatric organizations—such as the American Psychological Association (APA)—began arguing for researchers to ignore sexual orientation when studying pedophilia. They claimed that the *sexual orientation* of a male-on-boy molester is not a useful or valid factor for classifying or explaining pedophilia. In place of that framework, they emphasized that child sexual abuse is better understood as driven primarily by power and control dynamics, opportunity, and the offender's ability to overcome internal and external inhibitions.[29] Using these new criteria, these organizations claim that previous scholarship finding that gay men are disproportionately likely to molest children has been discredited.

The impact of this new understanding on past research has been significant. With the new definition in place, a well-known 1988 peer-reviewed study reporting that 86% of convicted child molesters called themselves homosexual or bisexual[30] was discarded as definitionally flawed. It's no longer cited in university classrooms or new peer-reviewed papers. Receiving the same treatment was research by Paul Cameron and colleagues that showed "those who practice homosexual acts are at least 12 times more apt to molest a child sexually, and with suitable corrections for bisexuals (who molest both genders), probably at least 16 times more apt to molest a child."[31] Several other studies have likewise been suppressed for their "antiquated" definition suggesting sexual orientation *could* relate to rates of pedophilia.[32]

I have no desire to refute the new criteria the American Psychological Association and other major organizations use to explain pedophilia. Perhaps they are right. However, skeptics might note that the APA's credibility is questionable when it comes to setting accurate criteria and defining what is scientifically valid. This is the same organization that continues to insist that gender transitioning confused, dysphoric youth is legitimate, even as international reviews debunk it as junk science[33] and leading practitioners in the field admit that they were "making things up as they went along."[34]

While conscientious medical professionals around the world are warning, "Stop gender transitioning children and youth because there is no scientific justification," the APA continues to maintain that prevailing gender-affirming models of care are evidence-based and clinically necessary. Remarkably, it claims that surgeries removing healthy body parts from distressed teens do not constitute child abuse, that puberty blockers with sterilizing effects are safe and reversible, that these interventions—known as gender-affirming care—improve mental health outcomes, and that social influences are not driving the rise in gender dysphoria. Given what critics observe as a consistent pattern of advancing a progressive agenda over prioritizing children's welfare, one might be forgiven for questioning the APA's judgments about other contentious issues.

The Homosexual Agenda Hits the Schools

Let's return our focus to the march of the homosexual agenda. Beyond governments, courts, and elite professional bodies—where new definitions were being formed and established understandings of "truth" were being revised—secondary and elementary schools quickly became a primary arena for promoting the celebration of homosexuality.

School anti-bullying campaigns and clubs focused solely on the advancement of LGBT-related ideas suddenly began to appear in the early 2000s. These campaigns and clubs did not grow naturally out of student concerns but were imported into schools by powerful outside organizations. Groups like the Gay, Lesbian & Straight Education Network (GLSEN), the Human Rights Campaign (HRC), and the Gay-Straight Alliance (GSA) Network provided funding, resources, and policy pressure.[35]

Though anti-bullying programs were advertised as addressing all forms of bullying, in practice they zeroed in on advancing homosexual causes. The same was true for the Gay-Straight Alliances, which presented themselves as clubs promoting "safety" and "inclusion." In reality, their aim was to insert more and more homosexual content throughout school life while actively seeking to remove any vestige of Christian teaching or heritage.[36] These efforts and others have led to a school system where Christian concerts and Christmas trees are banned, yet Pride parades are welcomed, Pride month is celebrated, and the Pride flag is flown year-round.

Thanks to pressure from these advocacy groups—backed by activist judges and school boards eager to silence anyone who questioned their version of "inclusivity"—the new priority in schools became a child's supposed "right" to explore and affirm any emerging sexual or gender identity. At the forefront of this shift was the transgender movement, which grew out of the broader homosexual rights movement of the late 20th century. While the original movement sought uncompromising acceptance for gay and lesbian individuals, the transgender movement pushed the boundaries further, challenging the very notion of fixed gender.

The new movement's central message was gender fluidity: the idea that anyone could define—or redefine—their gender at will. In schools, this translated into programs and policies that encouraged children to question their biological sex, experiment with pronouns, and assert self-defined identities. What began as a conversation about sexual orientation evolved into a full-scale cultural effort to reshape how society, and particularly children, understand gender itself. The radical appeal to personal choice and self-invented identity used to justify children "choosing" a new gender should ring familiar; it's the same logic that was first used to tear down and redefine marriage as "anything you want it to be."

With children's autonomy exalted and their sexual identity treated as central to personhood and crucial to development, schools expanded opportunities to teach and celebrate homosexual behavior generally, doing so increasingly without parental consent. School board policies were written that specifically instructed teachers not to tell parents if their son or daughter was now identifying as the opposite sex; they were to lie if asked directly.[37] Teachers and school officials actively promoted a rise in "cultural programs" like drag queen story hours and transgender breast-binding workshops[38]—held in libraries, community spaces, or directly on school grounds[39]—using their authority to encourage children to participate.

In some cases, parents who sought to shield their children from such instruction faced legal censure, highlighting the expanding reach of the state into areas traditionally governed by parental oversight.[40]

And while parents seeking protection for their children from teachers pushing an LGBT agenda get little satisfaction, LGBT teachers who request "protection" from the children of conservative families find their complaints treated with full seriousness—a twist emblematic of the strange era in which we live. This dynamic was on display in Tumwater, Washington, where a fifth-grade gender-nonbinary teacher refused to teach the 10-year-old son of a conservative school board member, claiming the child posed a "safety" concern. The teacher, TJ Thornton, went so far as to request that the school create a formal policy to "help mitigate the placement of students in their class who come from families that do not support LGBTQIA+ identities ."[41] If a White teacher had asked her employer to keep Black students out of her class for fear-related reasons, she would not only be fired but brought up on charges—yet when segregation for conservatives is proposed by a member of the "protected class," administrators treat it as routine. Pundits argue that this nonstop messaging—essentially, "to be LGBT is to be the most special of all"—has contributed to the surge in young people identifying as some variant of homosexual.[42] They point out that nearly a quarter of those aged 18–30 now identify as LGBT, representing a 20 percent jump over the past decade. They propose that this is rooted in cultural pressures and social contagion rather than mere biological inevitability.[43]

What is not debatable is that the rejection of conventional ideas about sex and the active promotion of homosexuality have spread from schools into nearly every facet of daily life. Children now encounter hypersexualized messaging through rainbow-themed marketing, book and online content featuring sexualized material, and TV series designed to include a proliferation of homosexual characters and storylines.[44]

A recent study found that 41% of children's programming on Netflix contains LGBT content.[45] Meanwhile, even while openly showcasing adult nudity, Pride events are promoted as family-friendly, signaling that sexual identity is now a public spectacle. Universities and other formerly "serious" institutions also reinforce these trends with kink festivals, sex toy events, and explicit programming, saturating public spaces with eroticized LGBT imagery. Paradoxically, the message that all of society—but especially children—receives 24/7 is that sexuality *is nothing* if you are being exposed to a stranger's genitals, but *is everything* if you are defining your core identity.

LGBT activists are open about their goal of exposing children to some of the most provocative aspects of homosexual culture. In academic work such as the 2021 *Curriculum Inquiry* article "Drag Pedagogy: The Playful Practice of Queer Imagination in Early Childhood,"[46] they state plainly that the purpose of child-focused events is to introduce kids to "queer ways of knowing and being."[47] They describe activities like "playfully 'reading' each other to filth" as tools for encouraging queer imagination in young children and for undermining traditional ideas about gender and sexuality.[48]

Similarly, a 2025 article in the *International Journal of Qualitative Studies in Education* by pro-queer academics from the University of California's College of Education admonishes "aspiring teachers, counselors, and school leaders" to include drag-focused activities from kindergarten through high school.[49] To ensure that male homosexual men dressed as women will "trans-form school environments' relationship to sexuality and gender expression," the authors offer a "framework" for the "centraliz[ation]" and "celebration" of drag pedagogy.[50] The stated purpose of incorporating "queer content" into "coursework, discussions and assessments" is to have children "embrac[ing] fluidity and 'messiness' in the process of social transformation" and rejecting the idea that gender is binary.[51]

To an unindoctrinated child—one who is not routinely subjected to homosexual men acting as highly sexualized women—drag-type materials would typically trigger confusion, fear, or instinctive discomfort. However, with repeat exposure, such materials function like a distorted form of cognitive behavioral therapy. Slowly, both parents and children are trained to accept what they would otherwise reject as inappropriate and unnatural. What once would have seemed shocking—strange men talking directly to children about sex—gradually comes to feel normal.

Apart from deadening the natural defenses of children against future sexual predators, this hyper-sexualization in the name of LGBT acceptance is unhealthy in other ways. These calls to reject biological markers and be "who you really are"—which inevitably means some kind of LGBT identification—may be taking a psychological toll. A recent U.S. study of almost 34,000 LGBT youth ages 13 to 24 found that 42% had seriously thought about suicide in the past year. Rates were even higher among transgender and nonbinary youth, with more than half reporting suicidal thoughts.[52] With a suicidal ideation rate double that of heterosexual youth,[53] one might reckon that pushing youth toward an identity founded in sexual orientation is more prone to grief than glee.

From Gay Rights to Trans Rights: Following the Same Trail

Earlier, I touched on transgenderism as an element of the LGBT juggernaut, but it must be discussed in detail as an entity unto itself. In 2005, the belief that someone could change their sex and that gender identity should override biological reality in law, medicine, language, and policy was considered fringe—even within most LGBT groups. Today, it has become a moral litmus test enforced by governments, corporations, universities, and professional organizations across the Western world and beyond.

The speed at which this group within the homosexual community has bent institutions to its will suggests that the LGBT movement as a whole has learned what strategies work best for gaining acceptance most quickly. Thus, these strategies, which produced such accelerated success, deserve to be studied with slow scrutiny. Among other things, this rapid success shows that with the right marketing campaign, even a mental disorder (the official diagnosis of gender confusion before 2013) can be rebranded as positive.

In my last comment, I'm not trying to mock or slander. For decades, the medical world treated gender confusion—intense distress over one's biological sex—as a mental disorder that needed psychological intervention. That was the standard view until the early 2010s, when activist pressure and intense public homage for homosexuality helped push through a radical shift in cultural and medical norms. The turning point came in 2013 with the release of the *Diagnostic and Statistical Manual of Mental Disorders*, Fifth Edition, or DSM-5. The text is the American Psychiatric Association's go-to manual for classifying mental health conditions. In DSM-5, what was previously called "Gender Identity Disorder"—which framed a patient's mismatch between perceived gender and biological sex as a psychiatric problem—was rebranded as "Gender Dysphoria." Under this new understanding, the primary goal of treatment was no longer to get the patient to accept their biological gender as correct, but to help them feel comfortable and happy, which could involve affirming their chosen gender and offering hormones and surgery to modify their physical appearance.

Critics argued at the time that this switch was not based on solid science, but on ideological pressure that recast a mental health concern as a celebrated diversity marker.[54] More and more research would accumulate to prove the critics right. However, despite the best evidence finally seeing the light of day, in many states and virtually all of Canada, there is little movement away from the faulty narratives and practices. The unsupported claims are nearly invincible; they have been blessed by the leading professional associations and baptized into law by naive or complicit politicians. In this, we see the power of capturing the institutions that define social reality. This is a lesson the LGBT movement has mastered.

Whether it's marriage or gender, once you control how something is officially defined, you can punish those who spread "misinformation" contrary to the approved narrative. The LGBT movement learned that the penalty for misinformation must be swift and severe. During their campaign for general homosexual acceptance, they tested the use of public stigma and punishment—methods that have since been employed to perfection by the transgender lobby. Now, even minor irreverence toward transgender people invites heavy penalties.

A string of school shootings, combined with the recent assassination of Christian conservative commentator Charlie Kirk, starkly illustrates the sometimes-lethal hostility that can be directed at those who publicly challenge transgender ideology.[55] While these examples are rarer and more extreme, it's common that refusing a transgender person's demand to use their new pronouns or self-chosen name can end your career. Take the recent cases of Nicholas Meriwether, Peter Vlaming, and John Kluge—American educators who faced firings or forced resignations simply for refusing to use transgender individuals' preferred pronouns, something their devout Christian faith would not permit.[56] Because the U.S. Constitution still stands as a safeguard for Christians, they took their battles to court and won significant monetary victories.

Another blessing that America has, envied by those on the wrong side of the border, is Republican governors who have enacted laws to curb gender ideology in schools. States like Florida, Texas, Alabama, Oklahoma, and Tennessee have passed legislation preventing teachings like "a man can wish himself into being a woman."

In Canada—always the cautionary tale—those unwilling to bow to the "god of transgenderism" have no political heroes and no legal standing thanks to Bill C-16. When Bill C-16 passed in 2017, gender identity was protected under the law. Saying that its only aim was to protect transgender Canadians from discrimination and hate speech, officials assured the public it would not force anyone to speak against their beliefs. They lied. Furthermore, thanks to legislation passed in 2022, it's now illegal in Canada for any doctor, counselor, teacher, or pastor to suggest that a person with gender dysphoria might pursue talk therapy aimed at exploring or addressing their feelings about gender instead of immediately pursuing drugs or surgery.[57]

While self-censorship has been the main fallout of these laws, in just the last couple of years the news has reported on a father in British Columbia who, while embroiled in a legal battle to stop his teenage daughter's gender transition, was jailed for contempt for refusing to call his daughter "he."[58] Similarly, employees at a tractor service business in Ontario who persisted in using a transgender colleague's birth name and pronouns, citing their Christian beliefs, were ordered to pay $18,000 in damages.[59] Religious convictions gave no protection. At a restaurant in British Columbia, a bar manager who misgendered a non-binary employee was fined $30,000 and forced to revise policies and undergo training.[60] In February 2026, a retired school board trustee in British Columbia was fined $750,000 for comments he posted on Facebook and other platforms. In those posts, he described his board's mandated teaching resources on sexual orientation and gender ideology as "biologically absurd" and "propaganda."[61] In Canada, to not believe in gender ideology can bankrupt you.

Early on, as the transgender agenda was gaining momentum, the first targets of the activists' life-destroying public punishments were medical professionals who had previously been at the forefront of caring for gender-confused patients. These experts made the mistake of challenging the affirmation-only approach to transgenderism promoted by the DSM-5. For their academic honesty, they faced open hostility and were accused of bigotry or being out of step with the times, even when presenting evidence-based concerns. Some were fired, blacklisted, or pressured into silence for pointing out that rushing children into medical transitions without addressing underlying psychological issues could be harmful.

A striking example is Dr. Ken Zucker, who ran Toronto's Centre for Addiction and Mental Health (CAMH) gender clinic for over 30 years. Zucker favored a "watchful waiting" approach, exploring factors like trauma or autism before moving toward medical interventions—a method backed by research showing many kids outgrow dysphoria on their own. In 2015, transgender activists began a campaign of slander, labeling his work "conversion therapy."[62] In doing so, they deliberately invoked associations with extreme, abusive practices from the past—methods that inflicted physical pain on homosexuals to force a change in sexual orientation. In stark contrast, Zucker's approach involved careful, thoughtful questioning and guidance, aimed at understanding and supporting his patients rather than punishing them. The misrepresentation of his work could not have been more extreme.

Zucker's employer, CAMH, abruptly closed down his clinic and fired him after an external review that *ignored* scientific best practices in the name of affirming trans rights.[63] The process was so flawed and egregious that the hospital later was forced to apologize and settle with Zucker for $586,000 in 2018. However, the episode made it clear: dissent wasn't tolerated in the rush to normalize what a mountain of research proves is unscientific doctrine.[64]

What Mastering Propaganda Can Accomplish—A Summary

When we inspect the rapid and near-universal triumph of transgender activists, we see what the tools of propaganda set out in the early homosexual rights movement can accomplish when applied in heightened form: Victimhood is refined and amplified; institutional and legislative capture is refined and amplified; cooperation with elite media and academia is refined and amplified; stigmatization and punishment for ideological dissenters is refined and amplified.

We can observe that the major wins for homosexual acceptance paved the way and became the template for transgender acceptance. Let's follow the path:

1. Once same-sex practice was declared a fundamental human right, the public internalized the deeper principle that personal identity, desire, and self-definition must override any prior notion of what is normal or natural for male and female sexuality.

2. Accepting that marriage was no longer rooted in the complementary union of male and female, but merely in the roman-

tic feelings of any two adults, further eroded confidence in the objective meaning and public purpose of sexual difference itself.

3. These shifts, taken together, left society with no coherent intellectual or moral defense when the next claim arrived: that biological sex itself is fluid, exists on a spectrum, and must yield to individual self-identification rather than to the enduring male-female reality.

Both the homosexual and transgender rights movements rest on the same revolutionary idea: the physical differences between men and women have no built-in moral or social meaning. Therefore, they argue that any institution or space that recognizes or enforces traditional male-female distinctions is inherently discriminatory; individual self-identification is the only legitimate distinction. Once that logic was established through the celebration of homosexual acts and the opening of the definition of marriage, transgender ideology didn't have to overcome a resistant public; it simply presented itself as the inevitable next step in the same march toward celebrating self-identification and inclusivity.

In keeping with the new logic, in the last few years policies have been passed forcing sports leagues, rape-crisis shelters, and single-sex spaces like sororities to open to biological males identifying as women. Examples such as gays being barred from military service—a restriction later condemned as unjust—were invoked as precedents to argue that transgender individuals should not be excluded from any arena. Female safety, privacy, and opportunity were simultaneously erased in the name of LGBT solidarity. Perhaps most horrific of all, male rapists claiming "female gender identity" were let loose in women's prisons, able to prey on their captive victims like a fox in a henhouse. We can look to specific instances. With the passage of its Senate Bill 132, *The Transgender Respect Act*, which allows prison inmates to be placed based on their gender identity rather than biological sex, California became a leader in the rights of transgender prisoners (if not the rights of women). As of 2023, about 50 biological males claiming to be women have been transferred into women's prisons. Nearly half of those male inmates identifying as female have sex convictions, compared to under 12% in the general male prison population.[65]

In Canada, Policy Bulletin 685 allows inmates to be housed according to their self-declared gender identity, regardless of their anatomy. A 2022 Correctional Service Canada study found that between 2017 and 2022, 20 male inmates identifying as transgender were housed in federal women's prisons—accounting for one-third of all trans-identified male inmates during that period. The study also revealed that most transgender and gender-diverse prisoners in Canada are biologically male serving long sentences, with 90% convicted of violent crimes, including sexual offenses and homicide. A separate report on gender identity and offending patterns in Canada found that nearly all inmates with prior sexual offense histories committed them before identifying as transgender or non-binary.[66]

The consequences of this magical thinking by activists and politicians have been stark. Incidents of sexual assault have been repeatedly documented. For example, in California, Tremaine Carroll, a biologically male inmate identifying as transgender, allegedly raped multiple female inmates after being transferred under the 2021 *Transgender Respect Act*.[67] In Illinois, Janiah Monroe, a convicted killer from a men's prison, was accused of raping a female inmate on his first night in a women's facility.[68] In Washington state, a former female inmate is suing the Department of Corrections, alleging that it failed to protect her from sexual assault by a biological male cellmate known for his history of violent offenses.[69]

Canada has faced similar crises. At the Grand Valley Institution for Women in Kitchener, Ontario, a biological male formerly known as Steve Mehlenbacher but now identifying as Samantha repeatedly sexually assaulted a female inmate over several months, a pattern confirmed in a 2020 Parole Board decision.[70] Likewise, a serial sex offender and pedophile who previously identified as Matthew Harks, but now identifies as a woman, was housed in multiple women's prisons under self-identification policies, terrorizing female inmates through harassment, threats, and assaults. Harks' repeat offenses while behind bars triggered lawsuits against the prison for its failure to protect vulnerable women.[71]

At the risk of coming across as too "meta" (as in breaking the fourth wall between audience and writer), I want to stop and draw your attention to something extraordinary. Some of you will have just read the two paragraphs above about female prisoners being subjected to rape by biological male predators and felt revulsion and outrage over what those females have been forced to endure. If that is you, you lean traditional conservative.

However, some of you will have just read those same paragraphs and felt revulsion and outrage because I "deadnamed" the rapists—that is, I mentioned the male name they were given at birth. If that's you, you lean morally compromised, and by extension, progressive.

The Next Step Along the LGBT Trail

I believe it was the British, Christian apologist G.K. Chesterton who once warned: "Don't remove a fence until you understand why it was built." His point was that something might look useless, but it could actually be protecting us from dangers we don't see. Today, as we witness women's rights and safety being compromised in the push to advance the trans agenda, we should recall that this erosion began when the homosexual movement dismantled the historic boundaries that once clearly separated male from female. Only now, following the causal chain backward, are we beginning to understand what the "fence"—laws restricting homosexuality's presence in the public sphere—kept in check. And make no mistake, the wall is still being chipped away, brick by brick, with the aim of lowering it so far that even the innocence and safety of children may no longer be shielded.

The most troubling cascade effect of the public veneration of homosexuality is the push to ease restrictions on sexual relationships between adults and children. The argument of proponents of adult-child sex goes like this: just as homosexuality was once seen as deviant but later accepted, intergenerational sex could also be rethought and normalized.

They frame both homosexuality and pedophilic attraction as "oppressed sexualities" unfairly held down by power structures, and they justify loosening restrictions by pointing to ideas like agency (which they claim children have), consent (which they claim children can give), and new theories of child development.

Some conservative commentators have identified that this once-fringe conversation is now moving mainstream, and they warn that they see a disturbing pattern. It's already the case that pre-teen children are being told they can "consent" to gender transitions—often against the wishes of their own parents. In their view, this radical shift, made possible by the incremental advancement of the LGBT agenda, is building respectability for the darker idea. Specifically, if children can supposedly consent to changing their sex, why could they not consent to sex with adults?[72]

Of course, this so-called "agency and consent" of children is nothing of the sort. What it truly amounts to is impressionable, vulnerable kids parroting the wishes of the adults who most heavily influence them. These are life-altering decisions they simply cannot understand.

Skeptics might dismiss these warnings as sheer conjecture, more slippery slope than credible causal chain. Yet such dismissal becomes more difficult given that some of the most esteemed voices in modern cultural theory—figures like Michel Foucault and other celebrated academics—have already floated these very ideas. In their writings and activism, they explicitly draw parallels between the decriminalization of homosexuality and the proposed "liberation" of adult-child relations. What naysayers insist we must dismiss as alarmist speculation is, in fact, rooted in a documented intellectual tradition.

Michel Foucault

For most academics, the ideas that Michel Foucault endorses become unquestionable fixtures—assumptions to be inherited rather than examined. Foucault (1926–1984) was a French philosopher, historian, and social theorist. Openly homosexual, he was the subject of serious allegations that, during his travels in developing countries, he raped underage boys—though he was never formally investigated or prosecuted.[73]

Foucault died in 1984 from complications related to AIDS. The core of his intellectual project was to dismantle traditional Christian norms by portraying them not as moral truths but as instruments of oppressive power. He insisted that what Christianity had long labeled "good" or "normal" was never inherently so—it only appeared that way because Christian institutions and broader culture had the power to enforce those judgments. By this same logic, behaviors historically condemned as deviant—including sex with minors—were not inherently wrong or abnormal, but had simply been suppressed by dominant institutions. For Foucault, the task was to unmask this power dynamic and to argue that so-called "deviance" could be reclaimed as natural, legitimate, and even liberating once freed from the weight of Christian moral authority.[74]

In the late 1970s, Michel Foucault engaged in public debates and petitions, pushing for the decriminalization of consensual sexual relations between adults and minors under 15. In a May 1977 petition to the French Parliament, he and a circle of leading intellectuals demanded a full review and potential overhaul of age-of-consent laws.[75] Considering the reports of his sexual activities with pre-teen boys in developing countries, it's worth asking whether his advocacy was driven by a desire to indulge in predatory behaviors closer to home.

Soon after launching his petition, on a national France Culture broadcast in 1978, Foucault defended it and directly challenged conventional under-standings of consent, calling it a mere "contractual notion" incapable of truly measuring harm. He insisted it was intolerable to automatically assume that a minor could not give meaningful consent and argued that judges must seriously consider the opinions of the children themselves.[76]

I'll underscore again: For most academics today, the words of Michel Foucault are their Gospel Truth. That is, among the intellectual elite of the West, and North America in particular, Foucault's ideas are by far the most influential. This is not an exaggeration.

A recent analysis of university syllabi worldwide, conducted through the Open Syllabus project, reveals that Foucault is the most frequently assigned theorist for student reading, outranking even classical philosophers such as Plato and Aristotle in citations and course appearances.[77] His ideas are not fringe; they dominate.

Given his unparalleled influence, Foucault's ideas alone have the power to distort norms in ways that can excuse sexual harm against children. But he has had no shortage of willing allies. By the 1990s, a notable circle of academics had taken up the task of advancing arguments aligned with his views, arguing that the growing social and legal acceptance of adult homosexual relationships should serve as precedent and permission to destigmatize adult-child sexual relations.

Team Foucault—Other Academic Advocates for Sex with Children

In Europe, Theo Sandfort, formerly Professor of Clinical Psychology at Utrecht University, maintained that if society recognized the legitimacy of consensual homosexual relations among adults, it could not logically continue to criminalize analogous relationships involving adults and youth.[78] Similarly, Gert Hekma, Associate Professor of Gay Studies at the University of Amsterdam, argued that once adult homosexual relationships were accepted, it was inconsistent to deny boys under sixteen their sexual autonomy and felt progressive sexual ethics required respecting their consent to have sex with adults.[79] Not to be outdone, Dutch jurist and former Labor Party Senator Edward Brongersma likewise contended that modern recognition of adult homosexuality challenged the idea that sexual activity under age sixteen should be automatically considered non-consensual.[80] Brongersma died in 1998 while under renewed investigation for possession of child-abuse pornography.

Around the same time, across the Atlantic, North American scholars engaged with comparable reasoning. In her essay "Thinking Sex," anthropologist and queer theorist Gayle Rubin drew a bold parallel: just as society once stigmatized homosexuality but later embraced it, she argued, so-called "cross-generational" relationships could be reconsidered. To Rubin, that adult homosexuals gained civil liberties while those involved in intergenerational sex remained criminalized was an egregious double-standard that had to be rectified.[81]

In 1995, using the same language of civil rights, historian Hubert Kennedy, then at Providence College and later at California State University, argued that the acceptance of adult homosexual relations necessitated a re-examination of age-of-consent laws to prevent creating new inequalities across generations of homosexuals.[82]

Making a psychological appeal, Bruce Rind of Temple University argued that the same reasoning that removed homosexuality from the DSM-III (recall that this is the manual psychologists use to define what counts as normal or abnormal behavior) should also apply to consensual sexual relationships between adults and youth.[83]

Writing in the late 1990s, anthropologist Gilbert Herdt suggested that the reframing of homosexuality from a pathology to a natural variation within the human species should serve as a model for thinking about adult-youth sexual relations. Appealing to his expertise with remote cultures, he argued that in certain non-Western societies, adult-adolescent sexual acts are considered developmentally beneficial and that Westerners—in their continued embrace of natural variation and rejection of cultural supremacy—should abandon their strict prohibitions on man-boy sexual activity.[84]

In his 2021 book *A Long, Dark Shadow*, published by the prestigious University of California Press, Allyn Walker, at the time an Assistant Professor of Sociology and Criminal Justice, sought to end the stigma against adults desiring (though not acting on) sex with minors. Applying the euphemism "minor-attracted persons (MAPs)" to those with pedophilic inclinations, Walker stated they should not be stigmatized for attractions they did not choose. In his call for tolerance and compassion for those who cannot control "the way they are born," Walker directly appealed to society's newfound inclusivity toward homosexuality and insisted it must be extended to other kinds of involuntary sexual orientations.[85]

Current legal scholarship also argues that the decriminalization of homosexuality can serve as a precedent for rethinking age-of-consent laws. In his 2023 law review article, Prem Vinod Parwani points to a seminal case in India which struck down colonial-era anti-homosexuality laws. He suggests that just as society has come to accept homosexuality as an innate orientation, the innate qualities of children (such as their intellectual maturity despite a young age) should be considered when assessing whether they might be capable of consenting to sexual relations with an adult. He states that a competence-based standard—rather than a fixed age—could allow emotionally-mature minors greater agency to consent to sexual relationships with adults.[86]

Building on this same reasoning, in their 2023 paper, philosophers Melissa Rees and Jonathan Ichikawa argue that automatically denying children agency for sex with adults is both a theoretical and moral error. They say that just as homosexual individuals gained recognition of their autonomy, by logical extension, the autonomy of children should at least be considered.[87]

In 2025, public money and scholarly authority converged in a

Canadian study that blurred moral boundaries and advanced the notion that pedophilia is just another identity worth "understanding." Conducted at the University of Ottawa and funded with $20,000 in taxpayer dollars, the research surveyed self-identified pedophiles and asked them to rate their sexual attraction not only to adolescents but also to babies as young as eleven months.[88] Several aspects show that this was not objective research, but an effort to move pedophilia toward acceptance while pretending to promote understanding of all sexual orientations.

The study was promoted through an activist group openly working to destigmatize "minor-attracted persons," and its author, doctoral student Lucas Walters, withheld crucial details from the Social Sciences and Humanities Research Council (SSHRC), the federal body that supplied his funding and is responsible for safeguarding academic standards. When pressed by reporters, SSHRC officials admitted that "nowhere in SSHRC's records, or in Mr. Walters' own research proposal, is it indicated" that the survey would ask pedophiles about their sexual attraction to infants and toddlers. In other words, Walters concealed the true scope of his project, misleading both SSHRC and the public.[89] When the study was published, it hid its focus on pedophilia behind neutral-sounding academic language, calling these behaviors "chronophilias," a term for sexual attractions to certain age groups. By listing "nepiophilia" (attraction to infants and toddlers) next to "gerontophilia" (attraction to the elderly), it made abuse of children seem like just another variation of human sexuality. This rhetorical sleight of hand was viewed not as academic precision but as a calculated effort to launder the unspeakable through scholarly respectability—turning the abuse of society's most vulnerable into just another "preference" worthy of acceptance.[90]

Another recently released paper was more forthcoming in its explicit goals. The 2025 peer-reviewed article in *Sex & Sexualities* titled "Childhood Sexualities: On Pleasure and Meaning from the Margins" calls for dismantling the notion of childhood sexual innocence and overturning the ethical taboos against children engaging in sexual activity.[91] The arguments set the stage for removing age-of-consent protections, paving the way for adult-child sex. The appeals of the authors hit very familiar notes, as they call ideas about normal sexual behavior *artificial constructs* imposed to oppress minorities. They make the case that civil rights and social justice are in peril if this sexual minority—children—is not allowed autonomy and consent. They employ the same persuasive techniques that achieved celebration of homosexuality and transgenderism.

On specifics, the authors contend that children are inherently sexual and that "the notion of childhood sexual innocence is not a natural construct" but rather "a colonial fiction" enforced by oppressive power structures.[92] On this basis, they argue that allowing children sexual freedom is a human-rights matter: "...letting children 'do' sexual pleasure in their own way is vital for their sense of their own agency" and "a matter of gender and sexual justice."[93] Drawing heavily on the ideas of Foucault—especially as they are repackaged as "Queer Theory"—the authors urge readers to abandon "outdated" frameworks, pointing out that other sexual categories (such as homosexuality) were once pathologized but later normalized. In their view, the "truth" is that "heteronormative and cisnormative assumptions [traditional views of sexuality]" serve no higher good beyond constraining natural and harmless "expressions of pleasure."[94]

This is only a sampling of the works on this topic. While some haven't been without critical responses, they remain genuine, influential contributions to the academic discourse. Published in peer-reviewed journals and books put out by universities, these writings are cited and discussed in undergraduate and graduate-level courses examining sexual ethics. Michel Foucault's ideas form the central foundation for theoretical exploration at public universities across the West. By their own admission, the normalization of homosexuality set a culture-shaping precedent, equipping these "scholars" with arguments they believe should extend to legitimizing adult-child sexual relationships.

You Must Choose Pride or Humility

I know that critics will take issue with the connections I'm making. Even though the studies cited above have appeared in mainstream academic publications, they will dismiss them as "fringe." Likewise, though employed at leading universities, the academics who argue that acceptance of homosexuality should serve as a precedent for legitimizing adult-child sexual relationships will also be dismissed as marginal. They will hope we forget that the ideas of Foucault, the most cited intellectual in modern academia, are the foundation on which all gay and trans advocacy builds.

Harkening back to my earlier causal chain observations, they will claim that the growing disinterest in marriage is due to other factors, that the hyper-sexualization of children's spaces and media is due to other factors, that the erosion of parental rights is due to other factors, that the rise in youth LGBT identification—and the related mental distress—reflects other factors, and that the push for trans rights now endangering women's spaces is linked to other factors. I'm willing to concede: there are always other factors at play. But I'm no longer willing to pretend that the legalization and celebration of homosexuality wasn't one of them—and likely the main one.

To put it bluntly: I've been forced to take my own advice found at the conclusion of Chapter 9. I had to give up what *I wanted* to be true and "find the humility to see that our past political leaders were not religious tyrants driven to intolerance by blind faith, but instead men acting in accord with a cache of unique, time-honored wisdom."

I'm now convinced "that wisdom gave them the ability to see that civilization survives on a knife's edge and that changes made under the guise of tolerance and acceptance can destroy it." More than that, I've come to see that tolerance is a vice, not a virtue, when it's used to elevate what Christianity and Western custom, in their long history, never did.

The hardest truth to face is that our political and cultural leaders sometimes promote poison as progress. Every so often the changes they advocate are right, but when their crusades demand tearing up Christian-based standards that held firm for millennia, they are usually dead wrong. Time is the judge—and the verdict from the last half a century doesn't rule in their favor.

Christians who take the Bible as the ultimate authority will easily accept this conclusion about the roots of cultural decline. Most begin with the conviction that God's moral order is the foundation of truth and human well-being. So, anything outside that order—no matter how culturally celebrated—must ultimately harm individuals and society. However, as always with Traditional Conservatism, non-believers can also arrive at the same conclusion via facts and reason and, in this case, a little humility.

About humility: Across all cultures and all times—our current age being the only exception—laws and customs prohibited homosexuality; at the very least, it was deemed unfit for public display or celebration. As mentioned at length in Chapter 10, in addition to the Old and New Testaments, other major religious texts, the classic works of Greek philosophy, Roman jurisprudence, and Enlightenment thought, all felt compelled to caution against the practice, citing its ability to weaken the bonds of society if promoted. They spoke from firsthand knowledge; they saw the effects in their own day. How inflated must one's ego be—how infected by *Pride* must one be—to reject thousands of years of distilled wisdom for the cultural contrivances of a couple of generations?

Laws Restricting Homosexuality—Theological Groundwork

Before we get to politics—specifically, how a traditional conservative government would approach homosexuality—let's discuss some religion. (Given both relate to sexuality, it looks like we're about to cross off the entire list of "things never to mention at a dinner party.") Today, some "believers" claim that "Christianity doesn't see homosexuality as a problem"; others go with the more radical revisionist version: "Christianity actually sees homosexuality as a good thing." Both are false. I recognize that non-Christian readers may find this discussion a bit too much like "inside baseball." However, as with many sections of this book, consider it another free lesson in Christian theology necessary to understand why Traditional Conservatism takes the stands that it does.

The prohibition against homosexual acts is found in several passages of scripture, including Leviticus 18:22, Leviticus 20:13, Romans 1:26–27, 1 Corinthians 6:9–10, and 1 Timothy 1:10, while the expected model for sexual unions as a man and a woman joined in marriage is affirmed in Genesis 2:24, Matthew 19:4–6, Mark 10:6–9, Ephesians 5:22–33, 1 Corinthians 7:2–4, and Hebrews 13:4.

Starting in the mid-twentieth century, some interpreters—more advocates than scholars—introduced new ways of understanding Scripture's prohibitions against homosexuality. The first among them was Derrick Sherwin Bailey (1910–1984), an English Anglican priest who led the Moral Welfare Council of the Church of England from 1951 to 1955 and became recognized as the Church's leading authority on sexual ethics. Though trained as a historian, there is no evidence that Bailey was an expert in biblical languages.

Despite this, his most influential work, the 1955 book *Homosexuality and the Western Christian Tradition*, challenged traditional interpretations. He argued that biblical condemnations of same-sex intercourse were mistranslations and, in fact, referred only to specific exploitative practices rather than to homosexuality itself. Furthermore, he maintained that the Old Testament account of God's destruction of Sodom concerned the residents' lack of hospitality rather than homosexual behavior—even though the text does not mention inhospitality while explicitly describing same-sex acts.

Following the lead of Bailey, revisionists continue to make their case using selective readings, strained reinterpretations of key passages, and appeals to cultural context designed to overturn the plain meaning of scripture. They ignore the first chapter of Paul's letter to the Romans (we will see why in a moment) and focus particularly on reinterpreting the term *arsenokoitai*, found in Paul's first letter to the Corinthians 6:9 and in 1 Timothy 1:10.

In the First Letter to the Corinthians (6:9), we read, "Do not be deceived: neither the sexually immoral, nor idolaters, nor adulterers, nor men who practice homosexuality [arsenokoitai], nor thieves...

will inherit the kingdom of God," while the verse in Timothy lists arsenokoitai among sinful, prohibited behaviors.

These activists claim that arsenokoitai should not be translated as "homosexual" but as "sexual exploiter," "male prostitute," or "practitioner of pederasty" (sex between a man and a boy). They insist that the Apostle Paul, who coined the term by combining the Greek words for "male" (arsen) and "bed" (koite), wasn't referencing *consensual* same-sex relationships. Thus, in their view, translating it as "homosexual" today is wrong. However, this retelling contradicts 2000 years of consistent interpretation and even the vast majority of scholarship today.

Additionally, their argument fails because it rests on the assumption that Paul condemned only forced or exploitative homosexuality while blessing consensual acts. In reality, Paul never mentions coercion as a factor; in 1 Corinthians 6:9, he condemns the acts themselves, clearly targeting voluntary sexual relations between men.

Elsewhere, Paul is even clearer. In Romans 1:26–27, Paul unequivocally condemns all consensual same-sex relations: "women exchanged natural relations for unnatural, and the men likewise gave up natural relations with women and were consumed with passion for one another." The verbs "exchanged" and "gave up" indicate deliberate choice, not coercion. Most tellingly, Paul emphasizes that they were "consumed with passion." Someone forced into same-sex intercourse would be consumed with dread, not passion. This shows that Paul is describing people acting of their own free will.

If the surveys are correct,[95] more and more North Americans who consider themselves Christians are willing to accept terrible scholarship and abandon 2000 years of religious tradition so that they might better fit in at dinner parties. I realize that, as a former promoter of the "Christianity and homosexuality are pals" myth, I'm not in much of a position to judge. However, I will make one concession in my defense. When I was advocating this falsehood, I didn't try to convince others that scripture said something that it did not—I knew that the best scholarship showed Christianity did not, and never had, accepted homosexual practices as benign.

My line of argument was blunter and more intellectually honest: I said, "I choose to ignore the content that I don't like." Spoken like a true academic.

Laws Restricting Homosexuality—The Bare Minimum

As proposed in the previous chapter, any law crafted by traditional conservatives—whether addressing homosexuality, obscenity, blasphemy, the Christian Sabbath, abortion, or similar issues—must meet a fundamental standard. At a minimum, no statute of the state should endorse or celebrate behaviors that Christian morality deems unacceptable. Actions viewed by scripture and Christian tradition as destructive to the public good should not receive neutral or favorable treatment from the law.

A traditional conservative may uphold this view either because he believes Christian principles are divinely inspired or because historical and social-scientific evidence demonstrates that Christianity uniquely fosters individual and societal flourishing. Regardless, he recognizes that any deviance from the absolutes of the faith that informs the political philosophy inevitably brings social disorder. With that moral north star as our compass, I will steer, as best I can, through the cultural minefield that challenging homosexuality has become. In its simplest form, and echoing the fundamental standard, Traditional Conservatism holds that, at a minimum, the state must neither endorse nor celebrate homosexuality. Homosexual behavior should not receive neutral or favorable treatment under the law but should be discouraged by the state—not through outright derision, but through the explicit promotion of heterosexual norms and practices, accompanied by the deliberate and mandated exclusion of homosexual behavior from public endorsement or institutional support. At the same time, in recognition of individual liberty, Traditional Conservatism would hold that these restrictions apply only in the public sphere. Guided by the tenets of the philosophy, the state doesn't police the private lives of same-sex-attracted individuals, provided they act peacefully, lawfully, and respect established societal norms when in public. Furthermore, those who comply with the law and public proprieties are entitled to the same full protection of the state and impartial treatment under the law as any other citizen. However, they may not use their personal liberty to promote or advance homosexuality in society.

For progressive critics who will no doubt declare that such a policy is ripped directly from the Nazi handbook, I have to point out that, in practice, this model is nearly identical to the program instituted in 1993 by President Bill Clinton—a Democrat and icon of the political Left.

Wanting to address homosexuality in the military, Clinton implemented the "Don't Ask, Don't Tell" policy. That measure allowed gay individuals to serve in the armed forces provided they didn't openly declare or promote their sexuality. For its part, the military refrained from prying into their private lives.[96] It was a compromise sold as tolerance but that, in reality, functioned as a strict boundary to keep homosexuality from being normalized within the institution.

However, in 2011, after years of lobbying by activists and politicians more concerned with ideological symbolism than military readiness, the policy was repealed.[97] President Obama and Congress, backed by cultural elites and activist groups, forced the military to abandon a workable balance in favor of open celebration—turning what had been a disciplined force into another battlefield for progressive social engineering.

Under a traditional conservative government, the prohibition on same-sex-attracted people from advancing homosexuality, together with the state's refusal to give homosexual behavior public endorsement or institutional support, would manifest in several concrete ways.

Marriage would again be restricted to heterosexual couples, eliminating legal recognition and access to marital benefits for homosexuals. While homosexuals would still retain general civil liberties, the special legal recognition and institutional privileges added since the 1980s would be removed. Accordingly, an individual promoting homosexuality in their workplace, school, or through their housing wouldn't be protected from removal. Fostering and adoption rights for same-sex couples would be prohibited.

A Reality Check

To those wailing in outrage that homosexuals would be barred from employment, schools, or housing for explicitly promoting their lifestyle, I direct you to the countless examples of anti-Christian discrimination documented throughout this book. In particular, recall the final section of Chapter 10, which explained that public homosexuality and public Christianity cannot coexist. When homosexuality is publicly celebrated, Christianity is inevitably punished. The past decade alone has supplied more cases than one could count of Christians fired, expelled, or pushed out simply for articulating the doctrines of their faith in public.

To those brimming with fury over the idea that same-sex couples would be banned from fostering and adopting children, let me speak of a deeper anger. Countless Christians—myself included—have been reduced to tears as some of the most loving among us have been barred from caring for the most needy and broken children. Because they faithfully proclaim and live the full message of Christ, godless social workers inform them they are ineligible. Thousands of Christians are denied the right to care for society's most vulnerable children, yet we are expected to ignore the consistent body of research showing that children raised by Christian parents achieve the best outcomes,[98] while those raised by same-sex couples experience some of the worst.[99]

We are also expected to overlook the peer-reviewed studies demonstrating that Christian families have the lowest levels of in-home abuse,[100] whereas homosexuals have, at best, an equivocal record according to past research.[101] Flying in the face of these statistical realities, in virtually every jurisdiction of North America, it's illegal to apply any additional scrutiny to the fostering applications of homosexuals.[102] On the other hand, Christians who apply to become foster or adoptive parents *do* face additional vetting, often leading to their exclusion.

In multiple American states, and throughout all of Canada—in allegiance to LGBT doctrine—child welfare agencies now require *prospective* foster and adoptive parents to affirm a child's sexual orientation, gender identity, and expression—even in a hypothetical scenario.[103] These "affirming care" policies, justified as protections for LGBT youth, function as ideological purity tests. It's now the case that

Christian parents who uphold traditional teachings on sex and gender are excluded from fostering or adoption *before* a child even enters their care. In short, devout Christian faith has become a disqualifying trait in the eyes of the state.

What a curious inversion that so many accept without question. Indeed, no public arena demonstrates more clearly that Christian rights and homosexual rights cannot coexist than the fostering and adoption systems across the United States and Canada.

The specific cases are numerous, though only a few make the headlines. In 2023 in Oregon, a Christian mother hoping to adopt out of the foster parent system was asked how she would respond if a foster child identified as transgender. She said she couldn't agree to facilitate gender-transition interventions or use pronouns inconsistent with biological sex. The state denied her adoption application outright.[104] In 2024, Vermont news reports told of two Christian families stripped of their foster licenses for refusing to comply with similar ideological requirements, even though no child identifying as LGBT was in their care.[105] Even more recently, various Christian couples in Massachusetts have been refused a license to foster children because they wouldn't pledge to affirm a hypothetical LGBT child's identity.[106]

As a foster parent myself, I know firsthand the hostility that Canada's child welfare agencies can direct at Christians. In my home city, six families from a single evangelical church—who had been fostering children—were cut loose by the local Children's Aid Society simply for making explicitly Christian statements in a private social media chat. If this happens with regularity in my city, largely invisible to the public, it's happening everywhere, but under the radar. As in the U.S., in Canada it's only when Christian parents take legal action that these cases make the news.

Media covered a Christian couple in Alberta who, despite years of providing loving foster care, were denied the chance to adopt because the agency said their Christian convictions did not align with the requirement to affirm LGBT beliefs.[107] Similarly, in Hamilton, Ontario, a Christian couple had their foster children removed and their license revoked after they refused to sign an agreement committing to affirm a hypothetical child's gender identity and use preferred pronouns.[108] In an especially bizarre case, another Christian couple lost their foster children because their faith prevented them from teaching the Easter Bunny as real. Their social worker confirmed the children were well cared for, including participating in Easter egg hunts, but their refusal to turn Easter into a story about a rabbit rather than the resurrection was deemed sufficient to render them "unfit." A later court decision would allow them to continue as foster parents; however, their previous foster children, with whom they had developed loving, secure relationships, were never returned and were siphoned back into the system.[109]

As these examples show, it's a zero-sum game. If society celebrates the norms and values of homosexuality, it will not celebrate the norms and values of Christianity. The critics will scream: "You are trying to put homosexuality back in the closet!" The traditional conservative has to unashamedly, without wavering, answer, "Yes." Unless homosexuality is back in the closet, Christianity is forced to inhabit that space, and in its absence, women, children—indeed all of society—suffer.

However, this is not a trade-off where homosexuals have to suffer so that the rest of society does not. Within the Christian paradigm, the homosexual is not meant to suffer either.

To Die to Self is Gain

I'm deeply indebted to the work of Reverend Sam Allberry, a same-sex attracted man and pastor who does not practice homosexual acts, and whose insights[110] have greatly shaped my understanding of these issues.

The world insists that if someone experiences homosexual attraction, the only route to a fulfilled life is same-sex dating, sex, and romantic partnership. Anything short of that, we are told, is tragic self-denial: a sentence of repression, loneliness, and muted despair. Homosexuals who, by choice, refuse to act on their attraction—a practice typical among same-sex attracted Christians who believe scripture calls them to celibacy—are condemned by society. The cultural verdict against them is merciless; they are told that they are choosing misery over authenticity, sacrificing their only chance at love for an outdated rulebook.

That is the world's story, but as many Christians who walk this road will testify, it's entirely untrue.

The same-sex attracted Christian trusts this astonishing promise from Jesus: "The thief comes only to steal and kill and destroy; I have come that they may have life, and have it to the full" (John 10:10). He did not add, "provided you are heterosexual and married." He did not carve out exceptions for those who will never have sex or experience romantic partnership. Fullness of life, he insisted, is found in him—not in any earthly relationship we gain or lose. The psalmist had already discovered the same reality centuries earlier: "You make known to me the path of life; you will fill me with joy in your presence, with eternal pleasures at your right hand" (Psalm 16:11). According to

Christian doctrine, fullness is a Person, not a sexual status.

This is why, in the Christian context, the supposed tragedy of celibacy so often fails to materialize. When a same-sex attracted believer says no to sexual expression out of loyalty to Christ, they may brace themselves for a trying time, yet many discover that the door of intimacy they feared would close forever is the very one through which abundance enters. They find themselves surprised by joy.

They find, first, a deeper intimacy with Christ than they knew was possible. The heart that once ached for a human lover discovers that the One who made it is not a cold consolation prize but the one for whom it was ultimately designed. Certain longings may remain, but they are lifted into something larger. The energy once given to chasing or imagining romance is redirected toward knowing Jesus, serving his people, and pouring themselves into kingdom work. Many say their spiritual senses grow more and more awake.

They find, second, that the church—when it lives even imperfectly as the family of God—offers a depth of belonging no romantic relationship could match. Brothers and sisters who pray through the night, who show up when depression hits, who celebrate holidays and birthdays together, who adopt one another's parents, who become aunts and uncles to one another's children—these are not "substitutes" for family; they are family. Lifelong singleness does not equate to loneliness when the body of Christ takes seriously its call to be a household in which no one stands alone.

They find, third, a freedom and flexibility for ministry that many married believers quietly envy. Without the (entirely good) responsibilities of spouse and children, they can travel on short notice, sit up all night with a suicidal friend, open their homes to the broken, and take risks for the gospel that feel almost heroic even to themselves. Paul was not theorizing in 1 Corinthians 7 when he said singleness can be an advantage for undivided devotion to the Lord; countless believers live this every day and find he was exactly right.

None of this makes the road effortless. Desires remain. Periods of loneliness come. Weddings can still sting, Valentine's Day can still wound, and the flesh continues to want what it wants. But the crucial point is this: the ache that remains is not the ache of a life half-lived, but the ache of a heart being enlarged, of desires being reordered toward their true end. The real tragedy would be gaining the romantic relationship the world insists is essential while forfeiting the Relationship without which all other joys collapse into ashes.

Therefore, in the understanding of the Christian faith, giving up homosexual practice is not a loss for the same-sex attracted believer, but a trade—and a profoundly lopsided one—of lesser pleasures that cannot satisfy for the surpassing worth of knowing Christ Jesus as Lord. And many discover, often to their own astonishment, that his promise of abundant life was not exaggerated. He really is enough—more than enough. He is everything.

Making No One Happy

Throughout this chapter I've focused mostly on critics outside the traditional conservative movement, prefacing numerous sentences with hedging phrases like "Critics will argue" or "Skeptics will say." But there will also be voices within the political tent who will be dissatisfied with the strategy I have out-lined for addressing homosexuality. One group will say I have gone too far, and the other, not far enough.

I know that certain supporters of the philosophy—such as those who accept Traditional Conservatism's ideas on their historical and empirical merits, not because they consider themselves practitioners of the Christian faith—will want the message further diluted. It's particularly tough for such supporters. To publicly call for the removal of homosexuality from the public sphere will require an unassailable boldness—the very kind afforded by a bond with the risen Christ—and historical and empirical evidence may prove inadequate to generate that level of bravery.

To justify their call for retreat, they might point out that some of the most outspoken and influential voices on the political right today are, in fact, homosexuals. They could cite well-known stalwarts like Peter Thiel, Douglas Murray, and Dave Rubin. After producing their list of gays advancing the causes of the Right, they will ask: "Isn't the movement of Traditional Conservatism politically weaker if it doesn't make room for individuals like them?" The answer is that the movement does make room for them, especially given that its requirements ask for little change in what most of these men are already doing. From my viewing of their online material they do not seek to advance homosexual behavior in the public sphere and thus align with the core premise of Traditional Conservatism as it applies to homosexuality. Would they agree to rolling back the special status currently afforded to LGBT individuals as a protected class while retaining general rights to security of person and equality before the law? Perhaps not. For some, the removal of legal recognition of same-sex unions and prohibitions on fostering and adoption may be too much.

However, as these are non-negotiable to the project of Traditional Conservatism, one would hope that an appeal to the common good, supported by ample evidence proving that appeal to be credible, might bring them onside. One concession that I believe traditional conservatives should make is a grandfather clause pertaining to gay marriage and gay adoption. At the formation of a traditional conservative government, I believe it would be ill-advised to disassemble families already constituted.

Then there are those who will feel I have not gone far enough. They will be members of the traditional conservative fold who are deeply rooted theologically and whose identities are likely intimately fused with the classical Reformed tradition. Trusting presuppositionally in the truth of God's Word (if you know what that means, you're likely one of them), these supporters of the political movement are willing to endorse its goal of aligning the laws of the state with Christian norms and values even without historical or empirical evidence to justify that stance. They may believe that the approach I've outlined on this matter turns the soft theonomy promoted by Traditional Conservatism from "soft" to so pliable that it's more jiggling jelly than judicious judgment. Their concerns are nothing new. In fact, their calls for a stricter application of classical Reformed theological principles in governance—essentially a push for hard theonomy rather than soft—have clear historical precedents.

Abraham Kuyper, the Reformed theologian and former Prime Minister of the Netherlands, to whom we are indebted for his clarifications on the application of sphere sovereignty, faced similar petitions when launching his own version of a traditional conservative government. Critics on the Right believed his administration's approach to applying Christian principles in public life was too restrained and insufficiently faithful to earlier expressions of classical Reformed theology. Specifically, they urged him to adhere more closely to older confessional statements, such as the Belgic Confession of the 1560s.[111] A strict alignment with those formulations would have required the state to severely punish the public practice of non-Christian religions, suppress activities deemed heretical, and more broadly enforce measures designed to uphold the true faith and restrain perceived religious error.[112]

Kuyper's response is instructive, and its example resonates with Traditional Conservatism's own approach to embedding Christian norms and values within governance. Writing in 1890, Kuyper began his rebuttal by rejecting earlier Reformed theologians' calls for radical coercion—and even the execution—of heretics. He characterized these as remnants of Roman Catholic practice rather than principles grounded in the New Testament.[113] While acknowledging the early Reformed theologians as invaluable contributors who advanced the church's understanding of Christianity's role in the world, Kuyper emphasized that they were still shaped by the Catholic traditions and culture in which they had been raised.[114]

Stating what he and his supporters *do* stand for, he declared [with my own light adaptation into contemporary English]:

> We would rather be considered not Reformed and insist that men ought not to kill heretics, than that we are left with the Reformed name as the prize for assisting in the shedding of the blood of heretics...
>
> We do not at all hide the fact that we disagree with Calvin, our Confessions, and our Reformed theologians... We admit that someone who represents us in the church as deviating from the Confessions is telling the truth about us. Notwithstanding this serious objection which we do not consider lightly, we would nevertheless continue frankly to insist: In the name of the Lord, we will not harm heretics [literally "we do not erect a

scaffold for the heretic"].[115]

I hate to pass the buck, but if anyone objects to how Traditional Conservatism handles some of the culture's most controversial issues, they can really blame Kuyper. As he rejected harm to heretics then, Traditional Conservatism today seeks applicable accommodations.

Kuyper's willingness to shape his political approach to the realities of a pluralistic society—holding firm on divine morality while allowing flexibility in temporal punishments—reflects an implicit recognition that anything more radical would be doomed to fail among contemporaries of diverse worldviews. But it also reflects something more important: It acknowledges the transforming power of Jesus' death and resurrection, under which the penalties prescribed in the Old Testament can be prudently adapted and moderated for our own age. This is not cultural cowardice, nor is it an arrogant attempt to ignore God's moral requirements whenever they become inconvenient or clash with modern liberal norms. (I've played that game before and refuse to repeat it.) Rather, this willingness to temper justice with mercy rests on a deeper conviction: Christ can redeem even the most fallen person, and our laws should leave space for that possibility.

Endnotes for Chapter 4

1. Voddie Baucham, "The Biblically Informed Case against Homosexuality" (video), Semper Reformanda Conference, October 27, 2014, YouTube video, 1:02:45, https://www.youtube.com/watch?v=EAC6vuhOHAQ; Marshall Kirk and Hunter Madsen, *After the Ball: How America Will Conquer Its Fear and Hatred of Gays in the 90's* (New York: Doubleday, 1989).

2. For example, Erin Perse, "Rob Hoogland: Canada Prisoner of Conscience," *The Post Millennial*, January 3, 2022, https://thepostmillennial.com/rob-hoogland-canada-prisoner-of-conscience.

3. For example, Brett Pallotto, "State College-Area Man Charged for Burning Pride Flag during Pride," *Centre Daily Times*, June 9, 2025, https://www. centredaily.com/news/local/crime/article308213780.html.

4. Andrea Ross, "Thousands in Vancouver Rally against Police Violence as George Floyd Protests Shake U.S.," *CBC News*, June 1, 2020, https://www. cbc.ca/news/canada/british-columbia/vancouver-police-protest-1.5592620.

5. "The Wet'suwet'en Conflict Disrupting Canada's Rail System," *BBC News*, February 20, 2020, https://www.bbc.com/news/world-us-canada-51550821; Emma McIntosh, "Wet'suwet'en Solidarity Blockades Were a 'Blip' in the Canadian Economy, Budget Watchdog Says," *Canada's National Observer*, March 13, 2020, https://www.nationalobserver.com/2020/03/13/news/wetsuweten-solidarity-blockades-were-blip-canadian-economy-budget-watchdog-says.

6. Larry Humber, "Meeting of Canadian and Italian Prime Ministers at Art Gallery of Ontario Cancelled Due to Protest," *The Art Newspaper*, March 4, 2024, https://www.theartnewspaper.com/2024/03/04/justin-trudeau-giorgia-meloni-art-gallery-ontario-protest-israel-hamas.

7. Angelica Toy, "BREAKING: Derek Reimer Arrested after Refusing Court-Ordered Apology," *Rebel News*, December 3, 2025, https://www.rebelnews. com/derek_reimer_arrested_after_refusing_court_ordered_apology.

8. David M. Haskell, *Through a Lens Darkly: How the News Media Perceive and Portray Evangelicals* (Toronto: Clements Academic, 2009), 1.

9. Smithsonian Institution, "Marsha Johnson, Sylvia Rivera, and the History of Pride Month," *Smithsonian Magazine*, June 7, 2021, https://www.si.edu/ stories/marsha-johnson-sylvia-rivera-and-history-pride-month.

10. Funders for LGBTQ Issues. *Forty Years of LGBTQ Philan-thropy: 1970-2010*. New York: Funders for LGBTQ Issues, 2012. https://lgbtfunders.org/wp-content/uploads/2018/04/40years_lgbtqphilanthrophy.pdf

11. Voddie Baucham Jr., *It's Not Like Being Black: How Sexual Activists Hijacked the Civil Rights Movement* (Washington, DC: Regnery Faith, 2024).

12. Ibid.

13. Marshall Kirk and Hunter Madsen, *After the Ball: How America Will Conquer Its Fear and Hatred of Gays in the '90s* (New York: Doubleday, 1989).

14. Ibid, 167.

15. Ibid., xxvi.

16. For example, Kirk and Madsen, *After the Ball*.

17. Tom W. Smith et al., *General Social Surveys, 2008–2018* [data file and codebook] (Chicago: NORC at the University of Chicago, 2018), https://gss.norc.org/.

18. *All Families Are Equal Act (Parentage and Related Registra-tions Statute Law Amendment)*, 2016, S.O. 2016, c. 23 – Bill 28 (assented to 13 December 2016), https://www.ontario.ca/laws/statute/s16023.

19. Susan L. Brown, Wendy D. Manning, and Kathryn K. Payne, "Trends in Relationship Formation and Stability in the United States: Dating, Cohabitation, Marriage, and

Divorce," *Child Trends*, May 19, 2020, https://www.childtrends.org/publications/trends-in-relationship-formation-and-stability-in-the-united-states-dating-cohabitation-marriage-and-divorce; Benjamin Gurrentz, "For Young Adults, Cohabitation Is Up, Marriage Is Down: Living with an Unmarried Partner Now Common for Young Adults," *U.S. Census Bureau*, November 15, 2018, https://www.census.gov/library/stories/2018/11/cohabitation-is-up-marriage-is-down-for-young-adults.html.

20. U.S. Census Bureau, "America's Families and Living Arrangements: 2023" [press release], 2023, https://www.census.gov/newsroom/press-releases/2023/ families-and-living-arrangements.html.

21. Center for American Progress, "The Economic Status of Single Mothers," August 7, 2024, https://www.americanprogress.org/article/the-economic-status-of-single-mothers/.

22. W. Bradford Wilcox, "Why Marriage Matters: A Natural Law Perspective on Marriage and Family Life" (video), Wheatley Institution, Brigham Young University, Provo, UT, January 27, 2011, YouTube video, 1:02:45, https:// www.youtube.com/watch?v=W1CwlUkb-2o.

23. Robert L. Spitzer, "Can Some Gay Men and Lesbians Change Their Sexual Orientation? 200 Participants Reporting a Change from Homosexual to Heterosexual Orientation," *Archives of Sexual Behavior* 32, no. 5 (2003): 403–17.

24. Mark Regnerus, "How Different Are the Adult Children of Parents Who Have Same-Sex Relationships? Findings from the New Family Structures Study," *Social Science Research* 41, no. 4 (2012): 752–70.

25. D. Paul Sullins, "Invisible Victims: Delayed Onset Depression among Adults with Same-Sex Parents," *Depression Research and Treatment*, 2016, article 2410392, https://doi.org/10.1155/2016/2410392; Paul Sullins, "Emotional Problems among Children with Same-Sex Parents: Difference by Definition," *British Journal of Education, Society & Behavioural Science* 7, no. 2 (2015): 99–120, https://doi.org/10.9734/BJESBS/2015/15823.

26. Tristin Hopper, "Canadian Economist Never Knew He Would Become Centre of a U.S. Firestorm over His Research on Same-Sex Parenting," *National Post*, March 28, 2014, https://nationalpost.com/news/canadian-economist-never-knew-he-would-become-centre-of-a-u-s-firestorm-over-his-research-on-same-sex-parenting.

27. Ibid.

28. Suzanna Diaz and J. Michael Bailey, "Rapid Onset Gender Dysphoria: Parent Reports on 1655 Possible Cases," *Archives of Sexual Behavior* 52, no. 3 (2023): 1031–43, https://doi.org/10.1007/s10508-023-02576-9 (retracted; see retraction note: Suzanna Diaz and J. Michael Bailey, "Retraction Note: Rapid Onset Gender Dysphoria: Parent Reports on 1655 Possible Cases," *Archives of Sexual Behavior* 52, no. 8 (2023): 3441, https://doi.org/10.1007/ s10508-023-02699-z).

29. American Psychological Association, "Answers to Your Questions: For a Better Understanding of Sexual Orientation and Homosexuality," 2008, https://www.apa.org/topics/lgbtq/orientation.

30. W. D. Erickson, N. H. Walbek, and R. K. Seely, "Behavior Patterns of Child Molesters," *Archives of Sexual Behavior* 17, no. 1 (1988): 77–86.

31. Paul Cameron, Kirk Cameron, and Kay Proctor, "Homosexuality and Child Molestation: A Review of the Evidence," *Psychological Reports* 57, no. 3 (suppl.) (1985): 1227–36.

32. For example: Gene G. Abel et al., "Self-Reported Sex Crimes of Nonincarcerated Paraphiliacs," *Journal of Interpersonal Violence* 2, no. 1 (1987): 3–25; Paul Cameron et al., "Child Molestation and Homosexuality," *Psychological Reports* 58, no. 1 (1986): 327–37; Kurt Freund and Robert J. Watson, "The Proportions of Heterosexual and Homosexual Pedophiles among Sex Offenders against Children: An Exploratory Study," *Journal of Sex & Marital Therapy* 18, no. 1 (1992): 34–43; Paul Cameron et al., "Child Molestation and Homosexuality," *Psychological Reports* 58, no. 1 (1986): 327–37.

33. Hilary Cass, *Independent Review of Gender Identity Services for Children and Young People: Final Report* (London: NHS England, 2024), https://cass. independent-review.uk /final-report/; Alex R. Dopp et al., *Interventions for Gender Dysphoria and Related Health Problems in Transgender and Gender-Expansive Youth: A Systematic Review of Benefits and*

Risks to Inform Practice, Policy, and Research (Santa Monica, CA: RAND Corporation, 2024), https:// www.rand.org/pubs/research_reports/RRA3223-1.html.

34. Leor Sapir, "'We're All Just Winging It': What the Gender Doctors Say in Private," *The Free Press*, December 3, 2025, https://www.thefp.com/p/were-all-just-winging-it-what-the.

35. For example: Parents Defending Education, "GLSEN: Gay, Lesbian & Straight Education Network," n.d. , https://defendinged.org/resources/glsen-gay-lesbian-straight-education-network/; Cathy Ruse, "Sex Education in Public Schools: Sexualization of Children and LGBT Indoctrination," *Family Research Council*, 2020, https://downloads.frc.org/EF/EF20E22. pdf; Peter Sprigg, "Homosexuality in Your Child's School," *Family Research Council*, 2006, https://downloads.frc.org/EF/EF06K26.pdf.

36. Ibid.

37. For example, New Jersey Department of Education, "Transgender Student Guidance for School Districts," n.d., https://www.nj.gov/education/safety/sandp/climate/docs/Guidance.pdf; California State Legislature, "Assembly Bill No. 1955," 2024, https://leginfo.legislature.ca.gov/faces/billTextClient.xhtml?bill_id=202320240AB1955; Avon Maitland District School Board, "Administrative Procedure 398: Gender Identity," n.d., https://www.amdsb. ca/apps/pages/ap398; Toronto District School Board, "Guidelines for the Accommodation of Transgender and Gender

Non-Conforming Students and Staff," n.d., https://www.tdsb.on.ca/About-Us/Innovation/Gender-Based-Violence-Prevention/Accommodation-of-Transgender-Students-and-Staff.

38. For example, Sue-Ann Levy, "Levy: Schools Aren't in Session but That Won't Stop the Radical Activists," *True North*, July 21, 2022, https://tnc. news/2022/07/21/levy-radical-school/.

39. For example, Waterloo Region District School Board, "Kyne Uses Math to Bring Students Together for Pride Month," *WRDSB*, June 17, 2022, https:// www.wrdsb.ca/blog/2022/06/17/kyne-uses-math -to-bring-students-together-for-pride-month/.

40. Barbara Kay, "When Gender Rights Only Protect Those Who Do Not Fit Stereotypes," *National Post*, April 9, 2022, https://nationalpost.com/opinion/ barbara-kay-in-ontario-schools-gender-rights-only-protect-those-who-do-not-fit-stereotypes; Maura Walsh, "Parents Lose Appeal over School's Gender Identity Notification Policy," *Education Week*, February 19, 2025, https:// www.edweek.org/policy-politics/parents-lose-appeal-over-schools-gender-identity-notification-policy/2025/02.

41. Alesha Perkins, "Non-Binary Teacher Cites Personal Safety Concerns to Avoid Director's Child, Sparking Legal Action," *Substack*, December 7, 2025, https:// aleshaperkins.substack.com/p/non-binary-teacher-cites-safety-concerns.

42. Joseph Backholm and Travis Morrison, "Is America Really Getting Gayer?," *Family Research Council*, March 15, 2022, https://www.frc.org/get. cfm?i=PV22C03.

43. Jeffrey M. Jones, "What Percentage of Americans Are LGBTQ+?," *Gallup*, August 6, 2025, https://news.gallup.com/poll/332522/percentage-americans-lgbt.aspx.

44. GLAAD, *Where We Are on TV 2023–2024: Representation in Kids & Family Programming* (New York: GLAAD, 2024), https://glaad.org/ whereweareontv23/representation-in-kids-and-family-programming/.

45. Concerned Women for America, *Netflix Report* (Concerned Women for America, December 2025), https://concernedwomen.org/wp-content/ uploads/2025/12/CWA-Netflix-Report.pdf.

46. Harper Keenan and Lil Miss Hot Mess, "Drag Pedagogy: The Playful Practice of Queer Imagination in Early Childhood," *Curriculum Inquiry* 51, no. 2 (2021): 165–182, https://doi.org/10.1080/03626784.2021.1954876.

47. Ibid., 174.

48. Ibid., 173.

49. College Fix Staff, "USC Professors Promote 'Drag Pedagogy' for K-12 Teacher Prep Programs," *The College Fix*, December 14, 2025, https:// www.thecollegefix.com/usc-professors-promote-drag-pedagogy-for-k-12-teacher-prep-programs/. For com-

plete study, see: Theodore R. Burnes and John Pascarella, "Centering Celebratory Drag Pedagogies in Queer- and Genderqueer-Evasive K-12 Educator Preparation Programs," *International Journal of Qualitative Studies in Education* (October 2025), https://www. tandfonline.com/doi/full/10.10 80/09518398.2025.2572459.

50. Ibid.

51. Ibid.

52. The Trevor Project, *2022 National Survey on LGBTQ Youth Mental Health*, 2022, https://www.thetrevorproject.org/s urvey-2022/.

53. Centers for Disease Control and Prevention, *Youth Risk Behavior Survey: Data Summary & Trends Report, 2011–2021*, 2022, https://www. cdc.gov/healthyyouth/data/yrbs/pdf/ YRBS_Data-Summary-Trends_ Report2023_508.pdf.

54. Jesse Singal, "How the Fight over Transgender Kids Got a Leading Sex Researcher Fired," *New York Magazine*, February 7, 2016, https://www. thecut.com/2016/02/fight-over -trans-kids-got-a-researcher-fired.html.

55. Ann Coulter, "Blame Social Media, Guns, Vacuums—Anything but Transgenders," *Townhall.com*, September 17, 2025, https://townhall.com/columnists/anncoulter/2025/09/17/ columnistsanncoulter20250917blame-social-media-guns-va cuums-anything-but-transgenders-n2663529;   Brooke

Singman, "Charlie Kirk's Assassin Lived with Transgender Partner Who Now Cooperating with FBI, Sources Say," *Fox News*, September 13, 2025, https://www.foxnews.com/politics/charlie-kirks-assassin-lived-transgender-partner-who-now-cooperating-fbi-sources.

56. Alliance Defending Freedom, "Indiana Music Teacher Forced to Resign over Pronoun Usage Asks Court to Uphold Religious Accommodation," *ADF Legal*, October 1, 2021, https://adflegal.org/press-release/indiana-music-teacher-forced-resign-over-pronoun-usage-asks-court-uphold-religious; Matthew Lavietes, "Professor Who Wouldn't Use Trans Student's Pronouns Wins $400K Settlement," *NBC News*, April 22, 2022, https://www.nbcnews.com/nbc-out/out-news/professor-wouldnt-use-trans-students-pronouns-wins-400k-settlement-rcna24989; Liberty Counsel, "Teacher Wins Settlement Over Refusing Pronoun Policy," *Liberty Counsel*, October 4, 2024, https://lc.org/newsroom/details/100424-teacher-wins-settlement-over-refusing-pronoun-policy.

57. For example: Association for Reformed Political Action (ARPA) Canada, "Bill C-6 (Conversion Therapy) Passes through the House of Commons," *ARPA Canada*, June 22, 2021, https://arpacanada.ca/articles/bill-c-6-conversion-therapy-passes-through-the-house-of-commons/; Association for Reformed Political Action (ARPA) Canada, "Federal Liberals Retable Criminal Ban on 'Conversion Therapy' with Major Legal Implications for Pastoral Ministry,"

October 1, 2020, https://arpacanada.ca/articles/federal-liberals-retable-crimin al-ban-on-conversion-therapy-with-major-legal-implications -for-pastoral-ministry/.

58. Erin Perse, "Father Jailed after Referring to Biological Female Child as His Daughter," *The Post Millennial*, March 16, 2021, https://thepostmillennial. com/rob-hoogland-canada-prisoner-of-conscience.

59. Rudy Ticzon, "What's in a Name? $18,000 Awarded to Transgender Man Who Was Misgendered and Deadnamed at Work," *Koskie Minsky LLP*, March 8, 2024, https://kmlaw.ca/whats-in-a-name-18000-awarded-to-trans gender-man-who-was-misgendered-and-deadnamed-at-wor k/.

60. Field Law, "Substantial Damages Awarded for Refusal to Use Proper Pronouns," *Field Law*, 2024, https://www.fieldl aw.com/insights/publication/ Substantial-Damages-Awarded-for-Refusal-to-Use-Proper-Pronouns.

61. Tristin Hopper, "FIRST READING: The Canadians Being Punished by the State for Not Believing in Gender Ideology," *National Post*, February 20, 2026, https://nationalpost.com/opinion/canadians-being -punished-by-the-state-for-not-believing-in-gender-ideology.

62. Ibid.

63. Singal, "How the Fight over Transgender Kids."

64. Hilary Cass, *Final Report: Independent Review of Gender Identity Services for Children and Young People* (2024), https://cass.independent-review.uk/final-report/; Society for Evidence-Based Gender Medicine, "The Final Cass Review and the NHS England Response: Summary and Analysis," 2024, https://segm.org/Final-Cass-Report-2024-NHS-Response-Summary.

65. See California Family Council, "Dozens of Gender-Confused Male Inmates Are Living in Female Facilities in California," April 3, 2023, https://www.californiafamily.org/2023/04/dozens-of-gender-confused-male-inmates-are-living-in-female-facilities-in-california/; Alysia Root, "Blue States Called Out by Women's Group for Ignoring Risks Posed by Transgender Inmates," *Fox News*, January 9, 2025, https://www.foxnews.com/us/blue-states-called-out-womens-group-ignoring-risks-posed-transgender-inmates.

66. Mia Hughes and Peter Copeland, "Prison-Onset Gender Dysphoria: A New Low for Women's Dignity," *Macdonald-Laurier Institute*, December 10, 2024, https://macdonaldlaurier.ca/prison-onset-dysphoria-a-new-low-for-womens-dignity-mia-hughes-and-peter-copeland-for-inside-policy/.

67. Chris Pandolfo, "3rd-Strike 'Trans' Rape Suspect Prompts Rebellion against CA Law after Attack in Women's Prison," *Fox News*, June 3, 2024, https://www.foxnews.com/us/third-strike-trans-rape-suspect-prom

pts-rebellion-against-ca-law-after-attack-womens-prison.

68. Matt Huston, "Transgender Inmate Accused of Rape," *Illinois Times*, February 26, 2020, https://ww w.illinoistimes.com/news-opinion/ transgender-inmate-accused-of-rape-11867999.

69. Kate Ruff, "Ex-Prisoner Sues WA State DOC, Saying It Didn't Protect Her from Sex Assault by Cellmate," *News Tribune*, January 3, 2025, https://www. thenewstribune.co m/news/local/article297816883.html.

70. Karen Finlay, "Parole Decision Confirms Another Male Prisoner Was Violent towards Incarcerated Women," *Women Are Human*, April 19, 2022, https://www.womenarehuman.com/parole-decision-confir ms-another-male-prisoner-was-violent-towards-incarcerated -women/.

71. Anonymous, "Male-Bodied Rapists Are Being Imprisoned with Women. Why Do So Few People Care?," *Quillette*, October 12, 2019, https://quillette. com/2019/10/12/male-bodied-rapists-are-being-imprisoned-with-women-why-do-so-few-people-care/.

72. For example, Carl R. Trueman, "The Slippery Slope from Gender to Pedophilia," *The American Conservative*, July 12, 2023, https://www.theamericanconservative. com/the-slippery-slope-from-gender-to-pedophilia/; Cheryl K. Chumley, "Told You So: Conservatives Have Warned over and over Where LGBTQ Narrative Will Lead," *The*

Washington Times, May 28, 2023, https://www.washin gtontimes. com/news/2023/may/28/told-you-so-conserva-tives-have-warned-over-and-ove/.

73. Houssem Guesmi, "Reckoning with Foucault's Alleged Sexual Abuse of Boys in Tunisia," *Al Jazeera*, April 16, 2021, https://www.aljazeera.com/opinions/2021/4/16/rec koning-with-foucaults-sexual-abuse-of-boys-in-tunisia.

74. Michel Foucault, *The History of Sexuality, Volume 1: An Introduction*, trans. Robert Hurley (New York: Pantheon Books, 1978; originally published 1976); see also Michel Foucault, *Discipline and Punish: The Birth of the Prison*, trans. Alan Sheridan (New York: Vintage Books, 1995; originally published 1975).

75. Michel Foucault, Jean-Paul Sartre, and Simone de Beauvoir, "Appel à la commission chargée de réviser le Code pénal pour la révision de certains textes régissant les rapports entre adultes et mineurs [Appeal to the Commission in Charge of Revising the Penal Code for the Revision of Certain Texts Governing Relations between Adults and Minors]," *Le Monde*, January 26, 1977, 23.

76. Michel Foucault, "The Danger of Child Sexuality," interview by Guy Hocquenghem and Jean Danet, in *Politics, Philosophy, Culture: Interviews and Other Writings, 1977–1984*, ed. Lawrence D. Kritzman, trans. Alan Sheridan et al. (New York: Routledge, 1988), 271–85; originally published 1978.

77. J. McCoy, "Your Students May Not Have Read the Syl-

labus. But This Tool Did," *Katina Magazine*, March 24, 2025, https://katinamagazine.org/content/article/resource-reviews/2025/open-syllabus-analytics-review; Joseph Karaganis, dir., *Open Syllabus Project: Syllabus Explorer 2025* (Columbia University, n.d.), https://t.co/Nz2lIgf4po.

78. Theo Sandfort, *Pedophilia and the Gay Movement* (Binghamton, NY: Harrington Park Press, 1990).

79. Gert Hekma, "A History of Sexology: Social and Historical Aspects of Sexuality," *Journal of Homosexuality* 20, no. 1–2 (1991): 173–93.

80. Edward Brongersma, *Loving Boys: A Multidisciplinary Study of Sexual Relations between Adult Males and Minors*, vol. 2 (Elmhurst, NY: Global Academic Publishers, 1990).

81. Gayle S. Rubin, "Thinking Sex: Notes for a Radical Theory of the Politics of Sexuality," in *Pleasure and Danger: Exploring Female Sexuality*, ed. Carol S. Vance (New York: Routledge, 1984), 267–319.

82. Hubert Kennedy, "The 'Third Sex' Theory and Its Consequences," *Journal of Homosexuality* 29, no. 2–3 (1995): 111–29.

83. Bruce Rind, Philip Tromovitch, and Robert Bauserman, "A Meta-Analytic Examination of Assumed Properties of Child Sexual Abuse Using College Samples," *Psychological Bulletin* 124, no. 1 (1998): 22–53.

84. Gilbert Herdt, *Sambia Sexual Culture: Essays from the Field*

(Chicago: University of Chicago Press, 1999).

85. Allyn Walker, *A Long, Dark Shadow: Minor-Attracted People and Their Pursuit of Dignity* (Oakland: University of California Press, 2021).

86. Prachi V. Parwani, "Revisiting Consent under POCSO: From a 'Fixed-Age' Rule to a 'Competence-Based' Standard," *NUJS Law Review* 16, no. 2 (2023): 322–62.

87. Michael Rees and Jonathan Ichikawa, "Sexual Agency and Sexual Wrongs: A Dilemma for Consent Theory," *Philosophers' Imprint* 24, no. 1 (2024): 1–23.

88. Cosmin Dzsurdzsa, "SICK: Federal Grant Paid Ped*philes for Disturbing Sex Research," *Juno News*, June 12, 2025, https://www.junonews.com/p/ sick-federal-grant-paid-pedphiles.

89. Ibid.

90. Ibid.

91. Deevia Bhana and Stefan Lucke, "Childhood Sexualities: On Pleasure and Meaning from the Margins," *Sex & Sexualities* (2025), https://doi. org/10.1177/30333717251375994.

92. Ibid., 3.

93. Ibid., 5.

94. Ibid., 7.

95. For example, Pew Research Center, "Most U.S. Christian

Groups Grow More Accepting of Homosexuality," December 18, 2015, https://www. pewresearch.org/short-reads/2015/12/18/most-u-s-christia n-groups-grow-more-accepting-of-homosexuality.

96. Sarah Pruitt, "Once Banned, Then Silenced: How Clinton's 'Don't Ask, Don't Tell' Policy Affected LGBTQ Military," *HISTORY*, May 28, 2025, https://www.history.com/articl es/dont-ask-dont-tell-repeal-compromise.

97. Ibid.

98. For Christians with best outcomes see, W. Bradford Wilcox, "Why Marriage Matters: A Natural Law Perspective on Marriage and Family Life" (video), Wheatley Institution, Brigham Young University, Provo, UT, January 27, 2011, YouTube video, 1:02:45, https://www.youtube.com/watch ?v=W1CwlUkb-2o.

99. For homosexual parents with some of the worst outcomes, Mark Regnerus, "How Different Are the Adult Children of Parents Who Have Same-Sex Relationships? Findings from the New Family Structures Study," *Social Science Research* 41, no. 4 (2012): 752–70; D. Paul Sullins, "Invisible Victims: Delayed Onset Depression among Adults with Same-Sex Parents," *Depression Research and Treatment*, 2016, article 2410392, https://doi. org/10.1155/2016/2410392.

100. Christopher G. Ellison et al., "Race/Ethnicity, Religious Involvement, and Domestic Violence," *Journal of Marriage and Family* 69, no. 5 (December 2007): 1222–1242; Soy-

oung Yoon et al., "Parents' and Children's Religiosity and Child Behavioral Adjustment among Maltreated and Non-maltreated Children," *Journal of Child and Family Studies* 27, no. 9 (September 2018): 2896–2907; Harold G. Koenig, Dana E. King, and Verna Benner Carson, *Handbook of Religion and Health*, 2nd ed. (New York: Oxford University Press, 2012), 366–368.

101. Paul Cameron, "Child Molestations by Homosexual Foster Parents: Illinois, 1997–2002," *Psychological Reports* 96, no. 1 (2005): 227–30; Paul Cameron, "Molestations by Homosexual Foster Parents: Newspaper Accounts vs Official Records," *Psychological Reports* 93, no. 3 (2003): 793–802; Kurt Freund and Robin J. Watson, "The Proportions of Heterosexual and Homosexual Pedophiles Among Sex Offenders Against Children: An Exploratory Study," *Journal of Sex & Marital Therapy* 18, no. 1 (Spring 1992): 34–43.

102. See this official directive prohibits any form of discrimination or harassment in the licensing process—including the imposition of greater or different vetting standards on gay men—and mandates that all applicants receive "fair and equal access" to licensing: California Department of Social Services, "Written Directives to Resource Families and Foster Family Agencies Regarding Non-Discrimination and LGBTQ+ Youth and Families," All County Letter No. 23-71 (September 28, 2023), 2, https://www.cdss.ca.gov / Portals/9/Additional-Resources/Letters-and-Notices/ACL/2023/23-71.pdf.

103. For the US see Movement Advancement Project, "Foster Care Laws & Regulations," *LGBTQ+ Map*, n.d., https://www.lgbtmap.org/equality-maps/ foster_care_laws; Association for Reformed Political Action (ARPA) Canada, "Bill 89 Pushes Gender Ideology in Child Services," June 1, 2017, https:// arpacanada.ca/articles/bill-89/.

104. Shaanth Nanguneri, "Oregon LGBTQ Foster Care Safeguards Violate Free Speech, Federal Appeals Court Says," *Oregon Capital Chronicle*, July 28, 2025, https://oregoncapitalchronicle.com/2025/07/28/oregon-lgbtq-foster-care-safeguards-violate-free-speech-federal-appeals-court-says/.

105. Lola Duffort, "Conservative Legal Group Sues Vermont over LGBTQ-Affirming Foster Care Rules," *Vermont Public*, June 6, 2024, https://www.vermontpublic.org/local-news/2024-06-06/conservative-legal-group-sues-vermont-over-lgbtq-affirming-foster-care-rules.

106. Hannah Reale, "Do Foster Parents Have to Affirm LGBTQ+ Kids? The State Says 'Yes,'" *WGBH News*, September 19, 2025, https://www.wgbh.org/news/ local/2025-09-19/do-foster-parents-have-to-affirm-lgbtq-kids-the-state-says-yes; CBS Boston, "Massachusetts Foster Parents Lose License after Refusing to Sign Gender Affirming Policy: 'We Simply Can't Agree to Go against Our Christian Faith,'" October 10, 2025, https://www.cbsnews.com/boston/ news/massachusetts-foster-parents-dis-

crimination/.

107. John Cotter, "Edmonton Christian Couple Says Adoption Nixed over Views on Sexuality," *CBC News*, November 7, 2017, https://www.cbc.ca/news/ canada/edmonton/edmonton-christian-adoption-homosexuality-1.4391853.

108. Anugrah Kumar, "Ontario Passes Law Allowing Gov't to Seize Children from Parents Who Oppose Gender Transition," *Christian Post*, June 4, 2017, https://www.christianpost.com/news/ontario-passes-law-government-seize-children-parents-oppose-gender-transition.html.

109. Adrian Humphreys, "Christian Couple That Lost Foster Children for Refusing to Lie about Easter Bunny Wins in Court," *National Post*, March 7, 2018, https://nationalpost.com/news/canada/requirement-to-say-easter-bunny-is-real-violated-couples-charter-rights-court.

110. Sam Allberry, *Is God Anti-Gay?* (Wheaton, IL: Crossway, 2013); Sam Allberry, *7 Myths About Singleness* (Wheaton, IL: Crossway, 2016).

111. James R. Wood and C. Shaffer, "How Abraham Kuyper Lost the Nation and Sidelined the Church," *Ad Fontes Journal*, August 22, 2023, https:// adfontesjournal.com/church-history/how-abraham-kuyper-lost-the-nation-and-sidelined-the-church/.

112. Christian Reformed Church in North America, "Belgic

Confession: Article 36—The Civil Government," 2011, https://www.crcna.org/welcome/beliefs/ confessions/belgic-confession#toc-article-36-the-civil-government.

113. Abraham Kuyper, "A Pamphlet Concerning the Reformation of the Church," *The Standard Bearer* 62, no. 15 (1986; originally published 1890), https:// sb.rfpa.org/a-pamphlet -concerning-the-reformation-of-the-church-30/.

114. Ibid.

115. Ibid.

5

Political Activism for Traditional Conservatism

The Self-Castrated Clergy

In the first and second centuries AD, as Christianity spread rapidly through the Roman Empire, it faced stiff competition from three other religions. One was Mithraism, a secret cult for men—especially soldiers—that honored the warrior god Mithras and his cosmic battles. The other two were public, co-ed faiths that centered on female deities and their consorts: Isis, with her lover Osiris, and Cybele, with her lover Attis. In both myths, the male companions were castrated. Osiris was gelded by an enemy, while Attis castrated himself in a frenzy of devotion and submission to Cybele.

In real life, Cybele's priests, called the *Galli*, copied Attis' mythical act as part of their faith. During wild festivals—especially the *Dies Sanguinis,* or "Day of Blood," in the spring—new recruits to the Galli would work themselves into trances through music, dance, and sometimes drugs, and use sharp tools made from flint or pottery shards to emasculate themselves. The removal of their testicles was viewed as a way to serve Cybele more completely; the marks of their masculinity were regarded as barriers to fully honoring the divine feminine.[1]

Though worship of Cybele died out before the 400s AD, many of today's *Christian* clergy bear a striking resemblance to this ancient priesthood of the divine feminine. Most—even those who call themselves conservative Protestant pastors—still practice a kind of symbolic self-castration. Afraid of offending the modern "divine feminine," or at least the feminized sensibilities of our age, they preach a meek, carefully domesticated Christianity, one that would never dare rise up politically or prophetically against unchristian practices for fear of being called unkind. The Jesus they preach is a soft, sentimental figure who just wants everyone to get along in the name of "inclusivity"—a far cry from the real Jesus of history and scripture.

The true Christ was physically and temperamentally unyielding. His body was hardened by years of working with stone and wood and by walking miles each day. His words were as powerful as his hands, able to cut through the hypocrisy and moral cowardice of his own cultural elites and religious pretenders. He rebuked the leaders of his day as "fools" (Matthew 23:17), a "brood of vipers" (Matthew 12:34), and "whitewashed tombs" (Matthew 23:27). He never spoke to gain approval but called out sin with uncompromising authority.

So many pastors today are—physically and temperamentally—unlike the real Jesus. These pastors have cut away the vigorous, combative, masculine part of their faith, leaving a gelded gospel. Their only harsh words are for those in their own circle who fail to meet their standards of *niceness*; those outside the church who openly defy Christian principles are met with silence—or even indulgence.

In another area of compromise, these clergy—today's gelded Galli—treat the Christian's relationship to government as one-sided, if they address it at all. Citing Paul in Romans chapter 13: 1-2, they say Christians are obligated to give the governing authorities unqualified submission. But they never speak of the reciprocal obligation the authorities bear to deserve that compliance. Because Paul, in this particular letter, did not explicitly say, "Of course, this is a general rule I'm giving, but please use the entirety of inspired Scripture to navigate specific situations," these shepherds pretend there is no more to the matter and leave their congregations to the wolves.

Interestingly, many of these same pastors are not completely brainless—that is, they are capable of sound reasoning—when the idea of submission is applied to the family rather than the state. In Ephesians 5:22–24 and Colossians 3:18, Paul tells wives to submit to their husbands without adding any conditions or exceptions. Yet every Christian pastor—including conservative Protestants—understands that an abusive husband is not owed respect or obedience. Although Paul does not state this explicitly, they rightly conclude that because a husband is commanded to love his wife—even to the point of death—an abusive man has broken the covenant, and the obligation no longer applies.

Before the great feminization of Christianity—a process that took hold in the 1960s and coincides with the dawn of the Post-War Consensus discussed in Chapter 6—clergy of almost all denominations understood that rules similar to those guiding a wife's submission to her husband were to be applied to governing authorities. Submission was not absolute: there was a time to resist, and even a time to take up arms and rebel. Because they knew their Bibles and their history, these pastors of the past were able to clearly instruct the congregations under their care.

Their Bibles showed them that God's servants did not submit to tyranny: Moses defied Pharaoh, Esther risked her life before King Xerxes, Daniel stood firm before King Darius, and the Apostles refused to yield to the Jewish governing council, the Sanhedrin. History confirmed the same pattern: Martin Luther confronted Emperor Charles V, John Knox resisted Mary I of England and Mary Queen of Scots, English Puritans defied King Charles I, and the Americans stood against King George III.

The effect of such clear preaching—common before the 1960s—was transformative: the average man in the pew was prepared not only to resist spiritual enslavement but also to confront its political and physical varieties. It was such preaching that enabled some laymen within the church, armed with these moral "marching orders," to emerge as political leaders for Traditional Conservatism, while others in the congregation, shaped by the same vision, became its committed soldiers.

Today, thanks to the emasculated messages coming from the gelded Galli, we have too few men who can lead—or even follow. They have been trained to welcome but not cast out. They know how to be "nice" but have no idea how or when to be fierce. They cannot define their principles, and therefore they cannot defend them. If the conservative movement in the West is weak, it's because the clergy are doubly so.

In Chapter 1, I clarified that "to champion Christianity is to champion Traditional Conservatism—they rise or fall together. As Christianity grows, so does Traditional Conservatism." Conversely, the fall of conservatism in the West—and with it Western culture—is similarly linked to the decline of Christianity, which, in turn, is disproportionately the fault of the gelded Galli. This bears repeating: from the earliest flowering of Christianity in the West, the sermons of pastors served as the blueprint for the deeds of their people—especially their most capable and courageous men. If conservative movements across the English-speaking world today lament the limits of their leaders (as most do), they should trace the line of blame back to the cowardice of their clergy.

If we hope to restore what has been lost, we must first see it in its full strength. The past shows what faith, courage, and discipline can do—and gives us the standard we must pursue. Among historical examples, the English Puritans and the Revolutionary Americans—who shared essentially the same Reformed Christian doctrine—demonstrate how, according to Christian understanding, citizens must react to a political regime drifting toward despotism. Both precedents show that a threshold exists when submission to authority must end and active resistance, even armed uprising, may rightly begin.

The English Puritans: When Revolution Becomes Duty

Between 1642 and 1651, the Puritans of England and their supporters took up arms against the government of Charles I in what has come to be known as the English Civil War. Their victory established that the king could not govern without the consent of the people's elected representatives, laying the foundation for England's later constitutional monarchy. Although proudly political, the seventeenth-century Puritans were first and foremost a religious movement, rooted in the Reformed teachings of Calvinism. They wanted to see holdover Catholic practices—still at work in the Protestant Church of England—replaced with biblically based theology, simpler worship, and greater moral rigor.

Politically, as Reformed Christians, the Puritans had beliefs that were distinct from those of Catholics and even other Protestants. In particular, their radical doctrinal emphasis on the Sovereignty of God—which held that Christ, not any man, is the true King over everything and all people—allowed them to moderate their deference to human rulers.

Because the Puritans, as Calvinists, saw those of inherited high status—even royalty—as equally accountable to God's authority and as having no greater intrinsic worth or rights than the average man, they alone among Christians clearly and forcefully asserted that "all men are created equal." If a noble claimed descent from princes or dukes, any Reformed believer could remain unimpressed; after all, he himself was a son of the King of the universe. The historian of Calvinism, Professor Loraine Boettner, captures this attitude, writing:

> The Calvinist feared God; and fearing God he feared nobody else. Knowing himself to have been so chosen in the councils of eternity and marked for the glories of heaven he possessed something which dissipated the feeling of personal homage for men and which dulled the luster of all earthly grandeur.[2]

This distinct understanding of humanity profoundly shaped the Calvinist conception of liberty. Because Christ alone was King, they held that a person's freedom—and his rights to life, property, and happiness—derived not from earthly rulers but from God Himself. Liberty, thus understood, was not a privilege granted by the state but a divine endowment inseparable from human dignity. Consequently, when governing authorities sought without just cause to suppress those God-given freedoms, they ceased to act lawfully—they violated God's laws—and could rightly be resisted.

In addition to their unique political views on the worth and rights of every man, Puritan Calvinists promoted a system of representative, republican-style administration modeled after the governing structure of their own churches for the governing of a nation. By extension, the administrative order of their churches was patterned after the Roman

Republic.

"Republic" comes from the Latin phrase "res publica," which literally translates to "public thing." It refers to a governing structure in which political power is held by the people at large, through elected representatives. The ancient Roman Republic was one of humanity's first great experiments in self-government. However, it failed. While power was supposed to come from the people through elected officials rather than from kings or emperors, over the centuries ambition and corruption hollowed out Rome's republican ideals. Eventually, the Roman *Republic* collapsed into the Roman *Empire*, where emperors ruled with absolute power and the old institutions became empty symbols.

When developing his Reformed theology in the 1500s, John Calvin revived the idea of republican government—both in the structure of his churches and in broader ideas about national governance—with the aim of improving on the Roman model. In his Institutes of the Christian Religion, Book IV, Chapter 3, Sections 4–15, he outlined a Presbyterian model of church polity as a small-scale republic governed by elected representatives. Ministers (pastors) and elders were to be chosen with the consent and election of the congregation, but once selected, decisions were made by councils of these representatives. Authority resided in these elected bodies under the supreme rule of Scripture, with higher assemblies known as presbyteries and synods providing oversight and accountability. Calvin's model differs from congregational models where the full congregation exercises direct and ultimate authority.[3] Regarding nations, in Book IV, Chapter 20 of his *Institutes*, he argued that magistrates (civil rulers) derive authority from God but must be subordinate to law and the people's consent.[4]

Calvin believed his form of republicanism improved on the Roman model because it took for granted that people are fallen and sinful and cannot be trusted with unchecked authority. Accordingly, it asserted that authority belongs not to *individuals* but to *offices*. These offices were to be defined by law, accountability, fair elections, and term limits. In short, Calvin replaced personal rule with institutional rule. Calvin's insistence that divine law, not religious or temporal rulers, holds ultimate authority stood in sharp contrast to the thinking of the time. Calvin inverted the contemporary idea that "the king is law" into "the law is King," meaning that rulers themselves stand under a higher law that reflects the will of God.

A century after Calvin, Scottish Reformed theologian Samuel Rutherford made this concept famous in his 1644 treatise *Lex, Rex,* or, translated from the Latin, *Law is King*.[5] Rutherford argued that rulers derive their authority from a covenant with the people, and that breaking that covenant is grounds for resistance.[6] His book and its ideas reflect the dominant political thought of the Puritans of England during their revolution against King Charles I.

Despite taking up arms, the English Puritans battling the crown were not wild-eyed insurrectionists. They were disciplined, devout, and—above all—*law-abiding*. Most were loyal subjects who believed, at least initially, that a godly monarch could and should govern in accordance with divine and constitutional law. For decades, they pleaded, petitioned, and prayed for reform within the framework of England's ancient constitution.

But their goodwill was tested severely under King Charles I, who ascended the throne in 1625. Beginning in 1629, Charles dissolved Parliament and ruled for eleven years without it—a period known as the "Personal Rule." During that time, he taxed his subjects but gave them no political voice or accountability. He silenced his critics and filled the English churches with bishops whose ceremonies reflected a Catholic assault on the Protestant sensibilities of the majority.[7]

Even so, the Puritans did not turn to rebellion but endured disenfranchisement, fines, and censorship, patiently seeking reform through the writing of tracts, the preaching of sermons, and the sending of petitions rather than through the sword. They waited—believing that enduring obedience and lawful lobbying were the marks of Christian citizens.

The Puritans felt justified in taking up arms only after King Charles I escalated from political and religious oppression to open physical aggression and the unlawful use of force against his political opponents. Beginning in the late 1630s, many Puritans and their allies were harmed, imprisoned, or executed by agents of the Crown acting under its authority. In 1637, for example, three Puritan writers—William Prynne, Henry Burton, and John Bastwick—were fined, publicly mutilated (their ears cut off and cheeks branded), and imprisoned by order of the Star Chamber, a royal court acting under the king's command.[8]

The decisive turning point came in 1642, when Charles personally entered the House of Commons with armed guards in an attempt to arrest five members of Parliament who were Puritans or Puritan supporters. Shortly thereafter, he began raising troops and attempting to seize the guns and ammunition of the Puritan-led faction.[9]

In the view of Puritan leaders and their allies in Parliament, the king's actions—physical punishments and imprisonment of Puritan critics, the attempted arrest of parliamentary representatives, the amassing of troops, and the seizure of arms—made clear that Charles had abandoned lawful rule in favor of coercion. They argued that when a monarch resorted to physical force against the constitution and the people, the obligation of obedience no longer applied, and defensive resistance—carefully considered and long avoided—became a moral and political necessity.

The American Patriots: When Revolution Becomes Duty

Leopold von Ranke (1795–1886) was a pioneering German historian widely regarded as one of the founders of modern historiography. While much of his work focused on the Reformation in Europe, when he turned his scholarly gaze to the New World, he concluded that "John Calvin was the virtual founder of America."[10] By this Ranke meant that the vast majority of Americans at the time of the country's founding were devout Calvinists and that their beliefs were the foundation of the country's customs, policies, and laws.

Of the roughly three million inhabitants living in the 13 colonies during the American Revolution, about 900,000 were Reformed Presbyterians (of Scots-Irish heritage), 600,000 were Reformed Congregationalists (of English Puritan heritage), and 400,000 were members of German, Dutch, and French (Huguenots) Reformed churches.[11] About 450,000 Americans were Anglicans.[12] Though Anglicans were officially supporters of the monarchy, some American members of this denomination, including men like George Washington, were sympathetic to Calvinistic doctrine.[13] Importantly, the Reformed faith of these early American citizens—and especially the Reformed faith of most of their political leaders—imbued the American experiment with core doctrines of covenantal governance, providential liberty, and resistance to tyrannical authority. As with the Puritans, these principles inspired a desire for a constitutional order that reflected John Calvin's vision of a godly commonwealth ruled by divine law rather than capricious royal will. Some historians note that the American Revolutionaries of the mid-1700s were not as patient as the Puritans a century before them. Under the burden of heavy British taxes imposed without commensurate political representation, colonists were inclined to move beyond political petitions to sporadic, militant actions against local governing officials. In the ten years leading up to the start of the revolution in 1775, there were over 70 instances where colonists physically harmed British personnel, although there was no general "call to arms," and the intent was to cause pain and embarrassment, but not death.[14] By 1770, British forces had begun to escalate retaliation, and in March of that year, British sentries in Boston fired into a mob, killing five and wounding six. This marked the British government's first use of deadly force against unarmed civilians.[15]

The formal taking up of arms by Americans in organized warfare, marking the start of the Revolution, resulted from British aggression. In April 1775, British troops marched on the towns of Lexington and Concord, Massachusetts, to seize colonial arms and arrest suspected rebels. Combined with earlier acts of physical repression, the colonists viewed this coordinated effort by the Crown to confiscate weapons and imprison political leaders as justification for rebellion.[16] The American patriots of the Revolution typically framed their cause using language drawn from Calvinist political thought, particularly as articulated in Samuel Rutherford's *Lex, Rex*.[17] They also drew on the example and works of John Winthrop (1588–1649), an English Puritan leader and pastor who fled his homeland to become the first governor of the Massachusetts Bay Colony. His sermons, available in published form to the colonists, emphasized that rulers are accountable to divine law and provided an intellectual and theological precedent that Americans in the mid-1700s adapted to justify resistance to

British authority.[18]

Meanwhile, some of the less religious among them appealed to John Locke's theory of the social contract as a justification for resisting unjust authority.[19] Ironically, Locke's ideas were simply secular reworkings of the doctrines of his deeply Calvinist upbringing. His parents were devout Puritans, and his father, a lawyer, had fought for the Puritan side in the English Civil War. From birth, Locke was immersed and educated in a Reformed moral framework that emphasized covenant, obedience to divine law, and the moral accountability of rulers. In Locke's philosophical thought, Calvinist principles were cut from their religious moorings to become the less resilient notion of the *consent of the governed* (the problems arising from this disconnect were explored in Chapter 6).[20]

Those Americans who justified their armed rebellion with Calvinist political ideas did so easily because their Presbyterian and Congregationalist pastors regularly taught Reformed resistance theory from the pulpit. Historian Gary Steward's book, *Justifying Revolution: The American Clergy's Argument for Political Resistance, 1750–1776*, provides an exhaustive account of this widespread phenomenon.[21]

Unafraid to discuss the cultural crises unfolding around them, these ministers of the Gospel recognized it as their sacred duty to intertwine politics and religion. They understood that every aspect of society bears political significance and that Christ's sovereign authority extends over it all. Unlike pastors today who say, "I don't want to get political," these colonial clergy recognized the utter nonsense of such a statement: the Christian faith began with a political declaration—"Christ is Lord, and thus Caesar is not"—and grew because of it.

As early as 1750, Jonathan Mayhew, a Congregationalist minister in Boston, began instructing his parishioners on when they should rise against the English king.[22] In his sermon *"Discourse Concerning Unlimited Submission,"* delivered on the anniversary of Charles I's execution by the English Puritan government (January 30, 1649), he emphasized resistance as a moral imperative under tyrannical conditions, rather than a general call for rebellion against any governmental failings.[23] He clarified, "The king is as much bound by his oath not to infringe the legal rights of the people, as the people are bound to yield subjection to him. From whence it follows that as soon as the prince sets himself above the law, he loses the king in the tyrant."[24]

Several pastors vividly illustrated Reformed resistance theory in the early days of the Revolution. Reverend John Carmichael, a Presbyterian in Pennsylvania, preached a sermon titled *A Self-Defensive War Lawful* on June 4, 1775, declaring: "We desire to be as we were in the beginning of the present unhappy reign—we have tried every lawful peaceable means in our power—but all in vain! ...Therefore, you can, gentlemen soldiers, appeal to God for the justice of your cause."[25] Carmichael also urged soldiers to fight without hatred, blending revolutionary zeal with Calvinist ethics.[26]

Reverend Samuel Langdon, a Congregationalist pastor and president of Harvard, delivered his homily *Government Corrupted by Vice and Recovered by Righteousness* on May 31, 1775, in Massachusetts. He denounced British tyranny as a moral corruption requiring resistance, noting that petitions had failed and the king "reasoned only by the roar of his cannon."[27]

Similarly, Reverend William Stearns, a Congregationalist in New Hampshire, preached *A View of the Controversy Subsisting between Great Britain and the American Colonies* on May 11, 1775. He proclaimed, "If ever there was a call in providence to take the sword, there now is—Therefore to arms!—to arms!"[28] Citing Judges 5:23 and Jeremiah 48:10, Stearns framed resistance as a divine command.[29]

Many pastors not only preached but actively supported the fight as soldiers. In front of his Reformed church in Virginia, Reverend Peter Muhlenberg famously shed his robe to reveal a uniform and then proceeded to enlist other men in the war effort. Presbyterian minister James Caldwell in New Jersey supplied hymnals to his male congregants to use for wadding when loading their muskets.[30] (In doing this, he may have stepped outside Reformed doctrine: pastors were permitted to preach against tyranny and offer counsel, but physical preparation for battle was supposed to remain at arm's length from church activity.)

A striking example of Calvinist political thought expressed in written form is the *Mecklenburg Resolves*, adopted on May 31, 1775, in Mecklenburg County, North Carolina. Drafted by Presbyterian leaders from local congregations, the Resolves served as a proto-Declaration of Independence, outlining the unlawful acts of the British Crown, renouncing its authority, and establishing local committees of self-governance. Reflecting the Calvinist belief in citizens' rights under divine law, the document is said to have provided a practical framework for the American Declaration of Independence, which followed a year later. That document, written by Thomas Jefferson, echoed many of the same principles but, consistent with Jefferson's more secular leanings, omitted the explicit scriptural references found in the Mecklenburg Resolves.[31]

British observers scornfully recognized the Reformed clergy's central role in the colonists' uprising, popularly calling the conflict the "Presbyterian Rebellion" rather than the American Revolution.[32] Furthermore, in acknowledgment of their influence, Reformed clergy were mockingly called the "Black Robed Regiment" by the British, referencing both their black clerical gowns and their leadership in the patriot cause.[33]

Other Elements of Reformed Resistance Theory

Neither the Puritans of the 17th century nor the American Patriots of the 18th century saw their actions as offensive rebellions but as defensive restorations. Both believed they were defending their inherited rights as Englishmen—rights grounded in legal tradition but ultimately rooted in God's immutable sovereignty and thus beyond human repeal. When their rulers stripped them of these rights and then sought to disarm, imprison, or physically harm them for insisting on their restoration, these peaceful Calvinists (and their allies) felt justified in taking up arms against their oppressors.

When we examine the criteria deemed sufficient to justify armed uprising, we notice an ironic juxtaposition: when rulers removed or attempted to remove the means by which ultimate physical resistance was possible, these Christians resorted to the ultimate forms of physical resistance. Expressed as an even simpler axiom: when the government pursues actions that make physical rebellion impossible, physical rebellion becomes possible (that is, morally permissible). Fascinatingly, even in uprising, the English Puritans and American Patriots carefully policed their actions. Their doctrinal code allowed the restoration of godly order in society but not destruction through militant chaos (an interesting contrast to today's progressives). To ensure order in uprising, these reluctant rebels appealed to the Reformed principle of "lesser magistrates."[34] The principle held that when a supreme ruler became tyrannical, lower-ranking, lawfully constituted authorities—not private individuals acting on impulse—were authorized to interpose, defend the people, and, if necessary, lead a measured resistance to restore legitimate rule. By appealing to these lesser magistrates, Christians could honor their duty to submit to governing authorities (as commanded in Romans 13) while refusing allegiance to those who had placed themselves in opposition to God's higher law.[35]

In addition to their commitment to principled rebellion—seen most clearly in their insistence on acting under the guidance of lesser magistrates—the Reformed dissenters of England and America drew on a broader body of Resistance Theory that helped them navigate the many pressures that arose in conflict with the state. Besides rejecting laws that compelled them to sin, they held that believers could also refuse laws unjustly restricting personal freedom, thus blocking them from fulfilling their God-given calling.[36]

Furthermore, they believed it legitimate to use every lawful means—from legal appeals to public protest—to restrain governmental overreach, pointing to the Apostle Paul's own example of asserting his rights as a Roman citizen when he faced unlawful treatment (Acts 22:25–29; 25:10–12). They affirmed that while it was not sinful to endure imprisonment or enslavement, neither was it wrong to flee or escape unjust captivity, as seen in the Apostle Peter's angelic release from prison (Acts 12:6–11).

They also recognized that unjust mandates could be resisted covertly and discreetly—without the knowledge of authorities—following biblical precedents like Gideon secretly threshing wheat to evade Midianite oppression (Judges 6:11). And they maintained that explicit, public noncooperation was itself ethically valid when dealing with commands that violate God's moral order, following Jesus' own refusal to legitimize unjust authority when he stood before Pilate in solemn silence (John 19:10–11).[37]

This Calvinist foundation was rooted in fearless trust in God's providence. It was expressed through moral discipline, a duty to speak uncomfortable truths, and a recognition of the worth and potential of every individual, no matter how common. Together, these convictions help explain why Britain, and later America, rose to unmatched prosperity and influence. Because they feared God, they feared no man; because they believed themselves bound to Him in covenant, they took bold risks in work, exploration, and governance, confident that success or failure alike unfolded according to His plan.

In Britain, these convictions helped fuel the rise of constitutional government, the Industrial Revolution, and global leadership in commerce, science, and culture. When those same Reformed ideals—in even purer form—took deep root in the American colonies, they produced a nation whose civic virtue, enterprise, and respect for individual rights led it to surpass even Britain in power and prosperity. Their success was made visible in the material but rested on the moral, as research corroborates.

The first studies into the impact of Reformed theology on national prosperity were conducted at the turn of the 20th century. Max Weber, the pioneering German sociologist, in his seminal work *The Protestant Ethic and the Spirit of Capitalism* (1905), offered a systematic framework for understanding how Reformed doctrine helped shape economic, and, to a lesser extent, social success in certain European nations. He argued that Calvinist beliefs led adherents to pursue diligent labor and disciplined lives as signs of divine favor. Moreover, their emphasis on individual calling—expressed in the recognition of every person's worth—encouraged innovation, initiative, and active participation in public life. Yet he cautioned that as societies secularized, the spiritual foundations of this ethic could weaken, threatening the moral framework that sustained liberty and prosperity.[38] His warning now appears prescient.

Preparing the Field Before Planting the Seeds

This entire book is an effort to avoid the hollowing out of moral authority and civic virtue that Weber warned could follow the erosion of a nation's Christian foundations. As liberty and prosperity in the West decline, we see the prophetic value of his words, but we can take heart knowing that Traditional Conservatism provides a path out of the cultural chaos. While the Puritans and American patriots who took up arms against tyranny offer a model for the gravest of circumstances, the aim of this book is to ignite a renewal in the United States and Canada before society is driven to such extremes.

Up to now, this book has shown that the political project of Traditional Conservatism and the norms and values of Christianity that inspire its principles are needed for individual and national flourishing. Having established what must be restored and why, the focus now moves from aspiration to implementation, examining the noncombatant methods and approaches that can bring these ideals to life.

In the spirit of full transparency, I should warn that the advice in this "how-to" guide is unlikely to succeed fully on its own. In essence, my advice for non-military political activism starts in the middle; that is, it presupposes prior preparation. For maximum impact, certain preconditions must be met—or, at the very least, implemented simultaneously. Think of it this way: We are farmers about to plant seeds; the more carefully we cultivate the soil, the greater the harvest those seeds will yield.

Churches for Community Building

I began this chapter by pointing out the failings of contemporary clergy to provide theological guidance that addresses the culture, and I return to that general idea now. For the principles of Traditional Conservatism to become widely accepted, intentional communities united by the principles of the philosophy must be strengthened and new ones established. It's within shared life, not abstract argument, that conviction gains strength. When people live out these principles together—raising families, serving neighbors, and gathering side by side in common cause—the ideas cease to be theoretical, becoming visible, tangible, and persuasive. A philosophy embodied in community becomes nearly unassailable because it proves its truth through the flourishing of those who live by it.

Small, independent communities united by a clear common worldview have two key advantages. First, they can thrive in times of social disorder. When external shocks occur—such as persecution or hardship in one community—the damage does not spread through the whole network. Instead, others observe, learn, and adjust. Those that endure refine their practices, applying the lessons learned to strengthen the wider group. Because authority and experience are distributed, hardship becomes an opportunity for growth, and the shared worldview gives them a common purpose that encourages adaptation and improvement.

Second, these communities grow and spread easily—what we call "scalable"—because they function like modular building blocks and require few resources to establish. Like a Lego set, independent communities can snap together into a larger structure without needing a master architect to oversee everything. The shared worldview serves as the instruction manual that each group follows, allowing new groups to form and connect seamlessly without centralized control.

Scalability here is not about unchecked growth but organic replication—new nodes can join the network, amplifying its impact exponentially. Unlike hierarchical organizations that bloat with bureaucracy as they expand, these communities preserve efficiency through peer-to-peer interaction and minimal overhead.

As the examples from the Puritans and the Reformed pastors of the American Revolution show, churches are in many ways closely suited to this purpose. Churches are, by definition, intentional communities with deep connections. Within conservative Protestantism, especially the Reformed tradition, they are independent bodies holding a similar worldview. Just as the Puritans and Patriots demonstrated, when pastors teach a biblically faithful, conservative message that presents political advocacy as a duty, not a sin, cultural engagement arises from both expectation and deliberate training.

I am not advocating for churches to become political headquarters, but they should serve—intentionally and expectantly—as community hubs that gather and inspire a like-minded political community, which will organize and implement political action outside of religious services. The best churches already function as community hubs, but they must also cultivate a self-aware-ness of their political responsibility.

Not every sermon must be a rallying cry against some explicit aspect of the culture war, but messages generally should equip members with the norms and values of historic Christianity, along with a sense of political responsibility, which will make traditional conservative activism both possible and effective. The unbreakable law is this: only as the churches of America and Canada rise will Traditional Conservatism rise with them.

Let the Church be for Worship

I hope that my readers are both Christians and non-Christians. For a moment, I must address the Christians directly.

For a church, the importance of maintaining the right balance between the internal task of proclaiming the Word and the external task of encouraging political activism cannot be overstated. While the church might inspire political engagement, Sunday worship, weekly Bible studies, and prayer meetings cannot be exchanged for political rallies and strategy sessions. Outside of religious services, church members must participate in political movements, but if the church itself becomes primarily a political movement, it stops being the church. If theology is reduced to political theory, it loses its power to heal human hearts and bring a better life now and a perfected life for eternity. Churches—pastors and believing congregants—must repeatedly affirm that the political actions they inspire, though necessary, are not where they place their hope or trust. Their hope and trust rests in the sovereignty of God alone. When change comes, it comes because God wills it. Political effectiveness must never be confused with Christian faithfulness. Whether change comes in one's lifetime or not, God is good. For the Christian, political activism can be a genuine work of faith, yet it must never become a substitute for faith. It must not be allowed to slide into a new form of works-righteousness. If we begin to believe that activism itself will save a nation, we have merely fashioned a theology of works—and such a theology cannot stand. The church's first and constant task is to proclaim that the Christian's unique and most powerful weapon is always the death and resurrection of Jesus Christ, which alone brings forgiveness and transformative power through the Holy Spirit. In obedient response to that gospel, Christians will do whatever is required to see God's kingdom come on earth as it is in heaven—yet they never forget that their actions do not and cannot defeat evil. Only God defeats evil, and he has already done it through the cross and resurrection.

This distinction is crucial for how we approach a book like this. My willingness to engage non-believers on their own terms—inviting them to embrace the political project of Traditional Conservatism as a rational choice rather than a matter of faith—does not in any way diminish the paramount importance of religious commitment. On the contrary, allegiance to the Christian faith is the foundation upon which true flourishing rests. Traditional Conservatism, in its deepest sense, cannot achieve lasting success unless the majority of its adherents are believing Christians. Any endeavor that focuses solely on resistance, strategy, or activism, while neglecting the proclamation of the Gospel, is ultimately destined to fail. Political engagement apart from spiritual formation is not merely insufficient but a framework built on sand, incapable of supporting the enduring good to which Traditional Conservatism aspires. Yet the reverse is also true: proclamation that refuses to engage in costly action—to endure prosecution, fines, or imprisonment—quickly degenerates into "cheap grace." Writing during World War II, Dietrich Bonhoeffer used this term to describe the religious outlook of German Christians who prayed for their Jewish neighbors but stood by as they were rounded up and sent to Nazi death camps.[39] These realities should not be separated. Authentic Christian proclamation has always produced activism, and faithful activism has always invited persecution. This pattern is neither accidental nor avoidable; it is simply the cost of discipleship. The church must neither forget nor flee from it.

The Right Church—Even for Non-Christians

While most churches could meet the criteria of community hubs with the potential for both resilience and scalability, not every church is prepared to accept the full cost of discipleship. Of little use are those in which affirming pep talks and group therapy sessions make up the bulk of the sermons, and where the sum of the theology amounts to the Billy Joel lyric, "Don't go changing... I love you just the way you are."

These sanctuaries of sterility managed by the gelded Galli should be abandoned to die the death they deserve. The ideal church for the revival that North America requires will be known by its fruits. The sermons and public documents will show explicit evidence of *uncomfortable* cultural engagement. In any church worth attending, a review of the pastor's posted messages should make clear its Christian response to radical gender ideology, homosexuality, marriage, abortion, pornography, prostitution, public education, and other typically taboo subjects. This will not be every sermon, of course, but it will be easily evident. The church's doctrinal statements will be equally clear with regard to their stand on such specific matters. Finally, there should be evidence of activism organized by the church but performed outside its walls. Yes, this includes works of service and charity, but also bold public actions that challenge progressive orthodoxy—the kinds of efforts that provoke opposition and attempts at suppression. Asking Christians to commit to church membership in congregations with sound doctrine and active cultural engagement is of grave importance. When believers gather with others who are equally committed, they are strengthened against outside criticism and prepared to act with courage. In addition, a community formed around authoritative truth generates its own legitimacy and is more resilient under external pressure.

But what about supporters of Traditional Conservatism who arrive by the road of the head rather than the road of the heart? That is, what about those whose embrace of the political philosophy rests on its alignment with empirical evidence rather than divine truth? Should we expect them to join a biblically faithful church, even if they make no profession of Christian faith, in order to participate in an intentional community with a shared identity? Yes—non-Christians should absolutely consider joining a biblically faithful, conservative church, even if their initial commitment is intellectual rather than spiritual. For someone who appreciates the structure and rigor of Traditional Conservatism, this is a direct pathway to living within the moral framework that underpins the philosophy itself. Christianity is the source of those principles, and by joining a church, even as a non-believer, one becomes connected to the very foundations of the worldview one admires.

Non-Christians would be warmly welcomed, provided they are forthright about their own beliefs and do not seek to contradict the church's teachings. Far from being exclusionary, such congregations would extend genuine friendship and social support. To be sure, the members will openly encourage a relationship with Christ, but they see that for what it truly is: an expression of compassion. Their encouragement flows from a sincere desire for non-Christians to experience the best in this life and security in the next. The compassion is real. Studies consistently show that the closest and most enduring friendships are found within conservative Protestant congregations, meaning the social and relational benefits are significant[40]—there is essentially no downside.

Moreover, participation in a church community allows non-believers to observe, learn from, and experience the rhythms of moral and cultural formation in a way that cannot be replicated through political organizations or secular networks alone. Integration into such a community provides both intellectual and practical insight into how Traditional Conservatism thrives when rooted in principled, disciplined, and ethically coherent social structures.

For supporters of Traditional Conservatism who are strongly disinclined to belong to an actual church, they might attempt to create a church-like congregational community grounded in the principles of the political philosophy. However, such an effort would lack many of the essential features that give real church communities their resilience, leaving the resulting association less able to provide the same depth of loyalty, cohesion, or generational continuity.

Taking Control of Education

Related to generational continuity, an intentional community will collapse by the next generation if it does not invest in educational networks and other character-shaping institutions to ideologically train its children. This includes the creation of independent schools, homeschooling co-ops, tutoring programs, and clubs grounded in the worldview of the community. Accessible online curricula and webinars might be used to keep costs down and import the experience of others.

When such programs encounter resistance—whether through regulatory pressure or cultural antagonism—it should be seen as a positive. The push-back often strengthens parental and community commitment, helps solidify the network, and attracts like-minded families. It also shows that ideological opponents have noticed the program's success and feel threatened by it.

What is not an option is the use of the public school system—at least for children below high school age, who are still heavily involved in identity formation. Beyond providing academic results that fare no better, and typically worse, than those of homeschooled children,[41] attendance at public school is among the strongest variables leading someone to reject traditional Christian norms and values in adulthood.[42] While not the sole factor—parental modeling remains influential—public school attendance can lead to an apostasy risk 50% higher relative to faith-based alternatives.[43]

Media Presence and Cultural Outreach

A robust media presence is essential to influence the broader culture. Podcasts, YouTube channels, print publications, and social media platforms provide opportunities to present traditional conservative perspectives on faith, culture, and civic life. These channels should encourage participation from the community, including guest content, discussions, and events. Attempts at censorship or public criticism from ideological antagonists often have the opposite effect, amplifying the message and increasing engagement, turning opposition into a vehicle for growth.

As the traditional conservative community grows beyond small-scale media ventures, it should launch larger cultural institutions—such as television networks, publishing houses, music companies, and film studios—to reinforce its worldview. By supporting writers, filmmakers, and musicians who reflect its values, the community can create alternative cultural narratives that resonate with broader audiences. Again, criticism from mainstream culture often heightens the perceived authenticity and countercultural appeal of these initiatives, attracting individuals seeking depth and meaning.

Defining Political Activism

Early in this chapter I wrote that political activism cannot succeed without prior moral and institutional preparation—I described this as preparing the soil. Having shown that building intentional communities, reclaiming education, and developing a strong media presence are essential to that groundwork, we can now turn to the seeds of activism itself as we move from preparation to the practice of political engagement.

The word "activism" on its own means doing *something*. It's the opposite of doing nothing. Of course, you knew that. But what is it to do something political? It can mean running for office yourself, or helping with a campaign, and that is usually what we think of first. Certainly, that is part of it. But doing something political extends beyond running for office or assisting a political candidate.

To do something political is to engage in any public contest against a rival group or groups in an attempt to have your ideas, beliefs, and values triumph.

Political activism is doing something publicly that advances the interests of your group and undermines the interests of another group. There is a ridiculous line in *Talladega Nights: The Ballad of Ricky Bobby*: "If you ain't first, you're last." It's a joke in the movie, but politically the principle holds: if your ideas and values aren't winning, they're losing. They are being replaced with something else. Acknowledging that reality, political activism is about winning a war of words and even actions so that your ideas, beliefs, and values are reflected across society. But here is an important distinction: political activism does not involve physical violence or armaments; there are no fists, fires, knives, or guns. When a group uses weapons and violence in a power struggle against a rival group, that is *military* activism, or a military campaign, not political activism.

Recent examples of military activism masquerading as political activism include the Black Lives Matter riots that arose in the wake of George Floyd's death, almost every Antifa demonstration, and many recent pro-Palestinian/anti-Israel protests. As shown by the English Puritans and American Patriots, there is a time to take up arms—and clear conditions that must be met before doing so; however, that is the last resort, not the starting point of faithful resistance. A traditional conservative realizes that one desires to engage fully in political activism precisely because one wants to avoid military activism. We do not want to get to a point where the persecution against our children is so great, and our ability to use our words and our non-threatening actions is so restricted, that defensive military activism is the only remaining option. Given no choice, we must act defensively, but we do not want to get to that point.

Recalling the Words of Jesus

Of course, as has been mentioned elsewhere in this book, the Christians among the traditional conservatives voice an additional reason why they must commit to political activism: Jesus commands it.

In the *Lord's Prayer*, Jesus tells his followers that they must want the will of God to be enacted on earth (Matthew 6:10). That is impossible unless *their* political team significantly influences the laws of the land. Similarly, Christians are reminded in the Great Commission (Matthew 28:18–20) that "all authority in heaven and on earth" belongs to Jesus. He commands that every nation be discipled and taught "to observe all that [He] has commanded." Laws—the rules that govern a society's behavior—are nothing more than codified commands. To follow Christ consistently, Christians must insist that these laws reflect His standards. To accept laws that contradict His commands is to misunderstand what it means to follow Him.

Knowing that the followers of Christ must ensure that the standards of Jesus are reflected in the laws and cultural practices of their nation, those who claim to be Christians are left with a binary choice: Is the best way to achieve that to stay out of politics, or to go all in with the goal of significantly influencing the political process? Obviously, the latter.

Progressive Christians (and here "Christians" is used loosely) claim that devout believers seeking political influence are acting solely out of self-interest and a desire to lord it over others. But, like most of their ideas, this view is mistaken. True Christians do not pursue political power to dominate their opponents. They seek it out of love for their enemies and for their enemies' children. They are confident that when the teachings of Jesus win, everyone wins—even their opponents.

Winning, for traditional conservatives, begins by getting those dedicated to the principles of the philosophy elected to office and into other positions where policies are created. Politically, traditional conservatives need to be the people on the inside. Meals are made by the cooks in the kitchen; everybody else has to put up with what is served to them. To avoid a societal death from ideological malnutrition, we need to have the right cooks using the right recipe book.

Collective Activism

Later, I'll focus on the political activism of traditional conservatives as individuals, but to begin, I'm going to focus specifically on the political activism that can best be carried out collectively, especially by churches.

As a first step, within church communities, members need to be actively scouting for good people to advance as political candidates, policy wonks, and influencers. It's often said that the best candidate for politics is the person who does not aspire to it—that is, someone cut out for political leadership may be too humble to come forward without nudging. Churches can create an officer or a committee of *political nudgers* whose role is to look for individuals with political acumen long before election time.

They might look for a teen or young adult who stands out for his leadership; they should take his name and start a conversation. Once someone with political potential is conclusively identified from within a congregation or larger network of believers, the community should invest in training that person. Among other skills, he might be provided with the opportunity to become proficient in public speaking and in knowledge of current events, political theory, and the traditional conservative worldview. Securing a political mentor for him—ideally someone with strong traditional conservative bona fides and a record of legislative experience—would be invaluable.

Beyond recognizing and developing emerging political communicators within the church, equal attention must be given to how churches themselves communicate politically. Many churches avoid anything that might seem "political," fearing it could jeopardize their charitable status. In both the U.S. and Canada, governments have struck deals with churches in which staying tax free means staying silent on some aspects of politics.

In reality, however, the restrictions on what churches may do are quite limited. As we will see shortly, even some earlier constraints have recently been rolled back in the United States.

A larger discussion of the charitable status of churches is likely needed but will not happen here. I believe that at some point church leaders will need to decide if charitable status is more stick than carrot. Has it become the means by which the government quashes the prophetic voice of the church? Do church leaders now self-censor or tacitly commit to government initiatives that are anti-Christian under the cover of "I can't risk my charitable status"? This is a conversation that each church community should commit to in the immediate future. For now, we turn to the current rules of the game.

As mentioned, the political "thou shalt not" list is fairly short for churches and church leaders in both the U.S. and Canada. For example, the church (or pastor acting on behalf of the church) cannot provide direct financial support or indirect resource support to a political candidate or political party. Even providing things like free office space, church technology, or church staff is a no-no.

In Canada, a church, or a religious leader on behalf of his congregation, cannot endorse or denounce a particular political candidate or political party. Impartiality is the guiding principle when it comes to specific politicians and parties. That means no endorsing or denouncing political candidates or political parties in the Sunday sermon, church bulletins, emails from a church account, or electronic messages on a church's social media channels. However, the rules are now different in the U.S.

In July 2025, the U.S. Internal Revenue Service (IRS) announced a major change in how it enforces the Johnson Amendment, a 1954 law that limited political activity by tax-exempt organizations like churches. The new guidance allows churches to endorse political candidates during sermons or through customary church communications without automatically risking their tax-exempt status. Such endorsements must be in good faith, framed through a religious perspective, and focused on matters of faith.

While churches and church leaders in Canada still cannot criticize *political persons*, on both sides of the border—in both America and Canada—criticizing *political ideas* as they are presented in laws, policies, or decisions of government is fair game. This can be done from the pulpit or on any of the church's typical messaging platforms. In fact, if they choose, a church can go beyond traditional messaging platforms and reach out to the general public through billboards, neighborhood newsletters, or even media advertising. However, a caveat for Canadians is that the message of endorsement or criticism must only reference the law, policy, or political decision and not the politicians or political parties associated with it. Another caveat applies to both the U.S. and Canada. During an official campaign period, in the weeks before an election, some jurisdictions enact additional rules surrounding political messaging meant to influence the public. Churches and pastors should familiarize themselves with any extra regulations related to their geographical location.

A final note concerns churches using social media. When a church uses platforms like Facebook, X (Twitter), or YouTube to share or support a policy position, it must also monitor public comments.

In Canada, rules require churches to remove any comments that are partisan, false, misleading, or hateful—even without being prompted—to stay compliant. In the U.S., the IRS does not require the same proactive approach, but churches are still advised to monitor comments to avoid any appearance of illegal political campaigning and to follow general laws and platform policies.

Since churches and pastors are free to speak for or against government laws and policies—and in the U.S., even to critique politicians from a religious perspective—I recommend a rarely used but powerful method for doing so: protest rallies, more delicately described as advocacy events or civic assemblies. These opportunities for public witness have long been a consistent feature of my own political engagement.

Protest Rallies

A few years ago, I took part in a protest rally that gathered about a thousand parents to oppose the spread of radical gender ideology in local public schools. My own children were not in the public system and thus were not being pressured to declare pronouns, study LGBT pornography masked as young adult fiction, or endure lessons denying the reality of male and female. But many other children of unsuspecting parents were being exposed to these harmful ideas, and bringing that to light was a moral necessity. Our local event, held in front of City Hall, was part of a nationwide movement called the *Million Person March*—a series of rallies held across Canada on the same day.

I was the only university professor to help organize and then speak at our rally. Others were leaders of local parents' groups, and some were religious leaders. Among the clergy, none were Christian pastors; all were Muslim. The lack of Christian clergy taking a public stand for the *uncomfortable* truths of the faith is common across North America. Whether it's fear of social stigma or the unfounded fear of jeopardizing their charitable status, most Christian pastors are far more sheep than shepherds when it comes to controversial public witness. These pastors shirk their responsibility, choosing cowardice and comfort instead of publicly condemning profound cultural corruptions, such as the effort to steer vulnerable children toward unnecessary drugs and irreversible surgeries that mutilate healthy sex organs.

I often wonder whether these Christian clergy, who believe that a sermon with a vague reference to "problems in the culture" counts as bold witness, have ever considered that *they might qualify* as the servant beaten by the Master in Matthew 25:26–30, the lukewarm morsel that Jesus spits from His mouth in Revelation 3:16, and the goat sent to hell in Matthew 25:41–46.

Christ warned that anyone who harms a child would be better off with a millstone tied around his neck and thrown into the sea (Matthew 18:6). Made complicit by their silence, these cowardly clergy have feet entangled in the rope connected to that stone.

As a balance to my quoting scripture like a lethal machine gun, I'll offer one more biblical story in a conciliatory tone. The Apostle Peter—a man Christ hand-picked to lead the nascent Christian community—experienced moments when cultural pressure compromised his witness. Most famously, he denied knowing Jesus three times on the night of the Savior's arrest, fearing for his own safety and wanting to avoid the scorn of those around him (Matthew 26:69–75). Later, as a leader in the early church, Peter acted hypocritically by temporarily withdrawing from eating with Gentile believers when certain Jewish Christians were present (Galatians 2:11–14). He allowed social expectations to influence his behavior. In both instances, these lapses in courage and consistency show that even devoted followers can struggle to remain faithful under societal pressure.

Peter's story does not end in failure. After his moments of compromise, he repented and was restored. His example shows that past lapses are not final—courage and faithfulness can be renewed. Today's hesitant clergy would do well to reflect on this, letting it inspire bold, countercultural public witness. The clearest sign of such a change would be their active participation in—or even organization of—a civic gathering addressing a truly uncomfortable political issue: one that aligns with God's will but invites condemnation from progressives and criticism from the mainstream media.

Having more people with a traditional conservative worldview organizing protests is needed, but probably not for the reason you might expect. To be sure, it's unlikely that protests by Christian leaders specifically or traditional conservatives generally will immediately push governments to do something different. Nonetheless, protests do serve multiple purposes.

Their first purpose is to build courage in the like-minded. When supporters of Traditional Conservatism participate in a large public gathering with others who share their views, they become more willing to express their beliefs boldly afterward. Many people find it uncomfortable to state a politically unpopular opinion, but within the safety of a like-minded group, they are more likely to try. Sociologist Émile Durkheim remarked on the power of groups in his concept of "collective effervescence," the heightened emotional energy that arises from shared experiences.[44] Durkheim believed this energy could elevate individuals to new levels of bravery, because being swept up in the group's enthusiasm strengthens personal confidence and reinforces the sense that taking bold action is both possible and socially supported. Put more simply, collective courage begets individual courage, and once someone has expressed his or her belief publicly, doing so in smaller or less public settings becomes much easier.

The second purpose of a protest is to make your opponents nervous. In my experience, folks on the Left—progressives and secularists—become fearful with very little provocation. Research data corroborate just how mentally fragile they are, especially compared to devout Christians. In particular, they are ill-equipped to handle facts and arguments that contradict their positions. Such challenges send them into an existential meltdown, wherein they claim words are violence or that some group's existence is being erased. Unable to make a convincing argument, they resort to shouting over or physically hindering their opponents. We can use that.

As progressives overreact, make outrageous claims, and even resort to violence, the general public begins to see who they really are and what they really stand for. In short, they sabotage themselves. An area of sociology known as *social movement theory* provides insights into this phenomenon.

For a social movement to grow, it must attract ordinary, law-abiding people—not just professional activists. Most of society consists of everyday men and women seeking peace and prosperity for themselves and their families, far outnumbering the radicals. If a movement does not capture the "normies," it cannot succeed. People like soccer moms, accountants, and business professionals generally do not want to be associated with masked militants or violent demonstrations. Smashing windows, blocking traffic, or calling for the death of others turns them away.

But they will join—or at least support—movements that appear respectable. To drive home the point, picture this: on one side of the town square is a group of moms and dads engaged in collective singing, and on the other side are blue-haired protestors, masked, draped in black clothing, and engaged in collective screaming laced with profanity. Who do you want to stand beside? In summary, successful movements ease the fears of the public rather than adding to them, thus increasing their appeal. The behavior of leaders and members should reassure people that order and stability will follow as the movement grows. Chaos and violence—the hallmarks of leftist groups—undermine the chances of creating a lasting, influential movement.

For example, Harvard researchers studied different social movements and found that nonviolent campaigns are twice as likely to succeed as violent ones. Nonviolent movements led to political change 53% of the time, compared to just 26% for violent protests. Their success was largely due to attracting more participants from a wider range of people. Once enough people adopt the movement's ideas, they reach a tipping point and start to become mainstream.[45] A third reason why public protests are valuable tools for political movements is that they create an opportunity for citizens from outside your ideological community to become aware of a significant societal problem. Apart from a few headlines, the average person does not know what is happening nationally or even locally. If they get their news from MSNBC in the U.S. or CBC in Canada, they may actually believe the opposite of what is happening in their country.

That is to say, issues important to traditional conservatives seldom get accurate coverage. Thus, when done right, a civic rally organized by traditional conservatives can turn on a light for local people who knew nothing about an issue—or knew only one side of it—and might convince them to seek further answers.

Moving from the motivations for a public protest to its implementation, there are a few considerations to keep in mind. To be most effective, it should have a reliable turnout, and the messaging must be carefully managed. On the numbers side, do not publicly announce a rally until you already know that you have enough committed attendees to pull it off impressively. Holding a protest where few people show up can have the opposite effect on your opponents: it can encourage them.

Regarding controlling the message, when we held our local rally protesting radical gender ideology in the schools, we followed strict protocols. We made clear to supporters what would be said. We had sheets with talking points that identified the problem and worded it in a way that attacked no person but took issue with policy. We provided proof of the problem with graphic, memorable examples from local schools. We also articulated the specific solutions we wanted to see. Above all, we repeatedly reminded our supporters to behave in a way that would make onlookers think we were the reasonable ones in this battle. You can be loud and respectful at the same time. The media want to paint those with traditional worldviews as out-of-control bigots; careless messaging gives them the brush.

Political Debates

Protests can be organized at any time of year, but other forms of activism follow a fixed schedule. Elections present time-sensitive opportunities. In the run-up to an election, political candidates are often obligated to participate in debates. While most of these events are organized by media outlets (if national) or, if local, by chambers of commerce or civic organizations, there is nothing to prevent groups of traditional conservatives from inviting candidates and holding their own event. In fact, they should.

If protest rallies are the sledgehammer of political activism, debates organized and hosted by advocates of Traditional Conservatism are the scalpel. Church communities have a distinct advantage, since such events can be held in the sanctuary, hall, or gym of their place of worship. The only rule—according to the guiding legislation in the U.S. and Canada—is that the sponsoring group must, as a nod to impartiality, invite all the political candidates representing all the major parties. While not always officially defined, a "major party" is likely one that has candidates running across the country or across an entire state or province. It's up to organizers to decide which candidates from "non-major" parties will be invited to attend.

Some candidates with strongly progressive views may see little benefit in appearing before a crowd of traditional conservatives unlikely to vote for them. However, the rules allow the debate to proceed even if certain candidates decline. In fact, the event should still be held even if only one candidate participates. Doing so shames those who refuse to attend while giving the participating candidate—in all likelihood someone aligned with the traditional conservative worldview—uninterrupted time to speak to a sympathetic audience, which can greatly benefit their campaign.

For a community of traditional conservatives, hosting its own political debate is a unique opportunity to ask would-be civic leaders about the issues that almost never come up during events organized by secular organizations. The moderator at a debate organized by the chamber of commerce will never ask about a candidate's position on abortion, or whether they can answer "What is a woman?" If traditional conservatives do not organize the debate, those types of questions will never be asked.

And while organizing a debate allows a community to ask questions aligned with its core interests, it's important to remember that such an event should not be limited to one's own tribe. The goal should be to make it the most significant event of its kind in the town or city—one that draws all local citizens, giving them the opportunity to hear discussion of topics that the media and establishment politicians avoid.

When traditional conservatives serve as organizers, they hold the privilege of crafting not only the questions but also the background context that precedes each one. This background functions as a framing device—it sets the stage, provides key facts, and subtly guides how the audience interprets the issue before the candidate even responds. For example, before asking a question about abortion policy, organizers might first present statistics about late-term abortions. This approach educates the audience while anchoring the discussion in moral and factual clarity. In this way, the background context transforms a simple Q&A into a moment of public instruction, allowing attendees—many for the first time—to confront the deeper truths about issues such as abortion, child gender transition, or government-imposed discrimination against Christians.

I have a personal story that illustrates the need for debates run by traditional conservatives while also showing how sheltered from the facts most people really are. As my account demonstrates, the gatekeeping on certain hot-button issues is so significant that even some political candidates are in the dark.

In 2019, I was running as a federal political candidate and attended a local debate. While the event was not organized by traditional conservatives, at one point the questions did slant to the right. Someone from my campaign team was in the audience, and during the open mic session when questions from the floor were being taken, she asked all the candidates to discuss their personal position and their party's position on abortion. Before getting to her question, she provided some background on the issue, noting that since 1988, Canada has been the only Western country without any law on abortion. As such, it remains fully legal in all of Canada for any child in the womb to be killed at any time up until the point when he or she is delivered. What transpired after that question was jaw-dropping.

I answered, but two of the candidates from major left-wing parties would not, because they said the question—in particular, its background context—was false. They said it was untrue that Canada was without an abortion law. They accused the questioner and then me of spreading misinformation. They said, "Of course Canada has some restrictions on abortion," and I believe they were sincere in their ignorance. One of the doubters was a lawyer, and the other was a university professor.

Here's the lesson from this: if political candidates from elite professions have no idea what the facts are on hot-button issues, imagine how surprised ordinary citizens will be when they attend a debate organized by traditional conservatives and, perhaps for the first time, hear truths that challenge almost every progressive idea they have been led to believe.

Finally, when traditional conservatives host a political debate, a high-quality video recording should be made and shared across all social media platforms. The few hundred who attend in person could become several thousand viewers online. The chances of the event going "viral" increase if, in addition to posting the full debate, you and your team package and upload the more compelling moments as shorter clips.

Individual Activism

Our focus so far has been on collective activism; now we turn to work suited to the individual. The options are nearly endless, but as noted earlier, the gold standard for advancing the interests of traditional conservatives is electing them to office, so we will address that first. If you are not running yourself, consider assisting those who are.

Those running for political office need an executive board supporting their campaign. At minimum, they will need a campaign manager (typically someone with political knowledge and experience); a chief financial officer (sometimes known as the official agent—this person should know bookkeeping); a secretary or communications coordinator (who is competent to oversee internal and external messaging); and a field manager (to recruit, train, and manage the election campaign volunteers).

Outside the executive team, a campaign needs a squad of about 30 to 50 committed volunteers to deliver lawn signs and pamphlets. The more articulate among them go door-to-door promoting the candidate to neighbors. Some may also provide security or refreshments at campaign events.

Beyond the traditional roles on a campaign team, there is another position that is less conventional but increasingly required: the hidden or anonymous confederate. This person is on your team but doesn't make that public knowledge. These secret helpers go to debates and other multi-party campaign events and position themselves around the hall. During open question periods, they ask your candidate the questions he has been dying to answer, while asking competitors the questions they want to avoid.

The campaign team's confederates will also write positive letters to the editor or opinion pieces on behalf of their candidate, especially if he has been maligned. They will also regularly take to social media to boost their candidate, come to his defense when he is slandered, or point out the foibles of the other guys. Interestingly, psychological research, particularly *warranting theory*, shows that a rebuttal to a slander delivered by a more neutral third party—your confederate—is more effective than one coming from the candidate himself.[46] The needs and the potential benefits are great, so assisting in political campaigns should be a priority for individuals wanting to advance Traditional Conservatism. Outside a campaign team, the opportunities for individual political activism remain numerous.

Any citizen has the right to make a delegation before their local city council or school board. In fact, providing time for members of the community to speak directly to elected officials on issues of concern is an established part of these local government meetings.

If there is something going on in your municipality that is at odds with the principles of Traditional Conservatism, call the staff in charge of booking and get yourself put on the agenda. Knowing that you are slated to present gives you time to prepare, and you should. As per typical protocols, you'll only be given five to 10 minutes to say your piece. If you don't want your most important points cut off, write them down and practice delivering them within the time limit.

Of course, even carefully practicing to stay within the time limit doesn't guarantee you will actually be able to say everything you prepared. I once presented before the public school board in my region, laying out research showing that instruction rooted in critical race theory—the very approach these board officials were promoting—was harmful to students. Yet, as the video recordings clearly show, the chairman's stopwatch magically sped up, and what I was told was my full ten minutes was, in fact, about eight.

Examples of Individual Activism

In addition to the official opportunities for individuals to speak truth to power, some political activism performed as a solo venture relies on the principle of "be somewhere unexpected and do something unexpected." Because people are attracted to oddities and spectacle, a small stunt can have a large reach. Importantly, once attention is captured, have a rehearsed, carefully crafted message ready to deliver.

A clear example of the principle "be somewhere unexpected and do something unexpected" is the work of Chris Elston, known globally as "Billboard Chris." Elston stands outside legislatures, university campuses, and other busy public spaces wearing a sandwich board with short messages challenging radical gender ideology. Knowledgeable on the issue, he calmly engages anyone willing to talk—though some react with hostility. Elston records all his interactions, later sharing the most striking moments on major social media platforms, where they often go viral. His courage has helped shift public opinion and inspired politicians to introduce laws protecting children from hormone blockers and irreversible surgeries.

I've used the "be somewhere unexpected and do something unexpected" strategy myself with some targeted success. For example, I showed up at a local event where Justin Trudeau, then the Prime Minister of Canada, was slated to appear. While outside the venue, I traversed the waiting line of attendees, handing out small flyers in the form of business cards. In addition to the fruitful conversations I had, the cards directed people to a website explaining Trudeau's ethical breaches and dishonorable actions. A local TV news station thought my actions were novel and gave them some coverage.

Similarly, I once made a billboard out of a white tarp and stick-on letters and fastened it to the side of my van as I parked outside a political convention in full view of those going in. The sign directed attendees to a website that highlighted the weaknesses of their party on particular issues and asked them to consider whether loyalty to their party outweighed loyalty to the truth.

On another occasion, I planted myself outside a lecture hall on the campus where I teach. I had learned that a colleague had organized a special extracurricular presentation for students—and, to inflate attendance, he offered bonus marks in their regular courses for showing up. The invited speakers were far-left union leaders whose goal was to persuade students to oppose conservative political ideas and embrace socialist policies.

I stood just beside the lecture hall doors, handing out copies of peer-reviewed studies that refuted the claims the presenters were expected to make. Next to me, set on an easel, was a sign I had made that read, "If they only provide one side of the argument, it's indoctrination, not education. Do you wonder what else you're not being told?"

As students streamed past, most gladly accepted my handout materials, and several thanked me for being there. Some confided that much of their education felt like indoctrination and that they were surprised to learn that professors like me even existed. Because I recorded the event and posted it on social media, many people beyond the campus were encouraged and influenced as well.

This reinforces a simple rule for solo activism: always record what you do. Alert the media if you think they might cover it, but record it yourself regardless and release it onto the internet. You never know what results may arise.

Strategies for Gentle Controversy

Admittedly, solo activism that requires direct, face-to-face engagement with strangers in public—even when done politely and calmly—may feel like "a bridge too far" for some. Fortunately, for those who are more timid, there are temperate strategies that can help build confidence and strengthen courage over time. Even mild approaches can elicit gentle controversy and allow you to give gentle witness.

Do not underestimate the power of flying a flag, posting a small sign, wearing a T-shirt, or attaching a bumper sticker. Begin by finding a traditional conservative idea that resonates with you—it may appear as a statement, picture, or symbol—and display it for all to see. If a particular idea is presented as a coordinated effort and the participants are many, the results can be formative in a neighborhood, city, or beyond.

A large body of research in the area of *cultivation theory* has shown that what humans see repeatedly, they come to accept as normative;[47] they believe "this is the way the world is and always has been." Our opponents in the culture war know the power of such measures, which is why they have relentlessly lobbied to make sure you and, in particular, your kids, cannot enter any public space without passing some adulterated version of a rainbow. Related to the proliferation of pride flags, posters, and stickers in every public space, theologian and social commentator Doug Wilson provides this chilling insight: "One of the functions that flags perform is that they mark territory. They stake claims of sovereignty and ownership."[48]

As an individual, perhaps the most innocuous method of advocating your worldview in a public setting is the T-shirt. It provides two sides for a positive slogan affirming a traditional conservative conviction and travels wherever you do. But realize that what you consider an innocent T-shirt slogan might still significantly trigger others—especially if it makes specific references to Christianity.

For example, a few years ago, a high school student in the province of Nova Scotia was suspended for five days for wearing a T-shirt with the slogan "Life Is Wasted Without Jesus."[49] After being told to remove the shirt by the principal, the student wore it to class every day for several weeks, which led to the suspension. School board officials told the media that some non-Christian students and teachers found the T-shirt offensive because, apparently, nothing ruins a perfectly comfortable liberal worldview faster than being reminded that it might have room for improvement.[50]

Similarly, in 2023, a man walking through a Minnesota mall wearing a T-shirt that read "Jesus Saves" on the front and "Jesus Is the Only Way" on the back was ordered by security guards to remove it. Video showed security threatening to kick him out if he did not comply. One of the guards justified the action, saying, "Jesus is associated with religion, and it is offending people. People have been offended."[51]

A faith-neutral expression of the traditional conservative worldview was targeted that same year. A middle-school student in Massachusetts was removed from class for wearing a T-shirt that read "There Are Only Two Genders." School administrators said the message *could* violate rules against "hate speech," claiming it might make transgender or gender-nonconforming students feel unsafe.[52] Incredibly, myopic officials like these never seem concerned that students holding traditional conservative values are subject to feeling unwelcome and "unsafe" in environments saturated with Pride flags and LGBT propaganda.

In the Massachusetts incident, the student was sent home after refusing to change. He later returned wearing a second shirt reading "There Are CENSORED Genders" to protest the unequal treatment and was again barred from class. His family sued the school district, arguing that the actions violated his First Amendment rights. Between 2023 and 2024, both a federal district court and a federal appeals court upheld the school's decision.[53]

Individual Advocacy from a Distance

Not all individual advocacy risks confrontation. There are options for doing something political that allow for greater public distance and thus avoidance of angry face-to-face encounters. Creating a website dedicated to truth-telling is one such possibility. Let yourself brainstorm: Are people being kept in the dark about the reality of an issue or situation? Is one side of a story being told but not the other? If yes, you can set the record straight with a website presenting the facts.

Notice that I said your website should present "facts," not slander. If your online presence consists primarily of hurling nasty names at opponents, the public will likely view your arguments as weak—lacking evidence—and see you as cruel rather than concerned. But in Canada, and even in certain states in the United States, facts offered in good faith can still get you punished one way or another. Thus, anonymity may be most prudent.

It's possible to create a website without the public—or most investigators—easily discovering who built it, as long as you intentionally hide your digital trail. The basic method involves masking your internet connection with tools like a VPN, using an email address that isn't linked to your real identity, registering the domain through a privacy-focused service that keeps ownership details hidden, and hosting the site with providers that do not require personal information. Payments are typically made with privacy-preserving methods such as cryptocurrency, and the site itself must be built and maintained without including any personal metadata. In short, anonymity is achieved by layering tools and habits that break every link between the site and your real-world identity. However, no method is completely foolproof if authorities are determined and have the legal power to investigate—so post nothing that compromises your integrity.

If internet technology is not your strong suit, the same content that might go on a website could instead be published in the form of a newsletter or flyer. Distribution is more difficult; it will require hitting the streets and not just hitting "send" on the information superhighway. However, the old-school, direct-to-mailbox method may increase the odds that a particular audience—maybe a local neighborhood or parents of kids at a certain school—receives the message. If you are concerned about remaining anonymous, give careful thought to what you wear when canvassing in a neighborhood, as front door video surveillance is ubiquitous.

A couple of years ago, in my own neighborhood, there was quite an uproar when a newsletter was delivered house-to-house exposing some of the far-left gender and race nonsense that was taking place in our local schools. It also detailed which of our elected trustees and board administrators were promoting it. The wording of the document was neutral, but the factual examples were enough to allow the craziness to condemn itself.

The newsletter directed readers to a website for more information. It seems the anonymous team or individual who created the paper document had simultaneously launched a website with identical and additional material. Calls from the implicated board officials and their progressive supporters to shut down the website and find and punish the creators generated quite a few stories in the local press. That, in turn, caused many more residents to check out the website.

Playing the Long Game

For the traditional conservative movement to advance, its supporters must do more than vote for the lesser of two evils. They must work to create options that are principled, viable, and truly reflective of their values. Over the course of this chapter, I've outlined some of the political activities that can be applied immediately. But I'll now turn to a form of political activism that is a more intensive, longer-term solution.

If traditional conservatives across the West want to see their countries return to reflecting the norms and values of Christianity, they need to have more babies. By "have more babies," I mean having significantly more than the other side. Immigration policies that prioritize newcomers who already embrace Christian norms and values—and who are thus better able to assimilate into Western countries—are needed. However, greater fertility among a country's traditional conservatives is the key to complete and sustained political success. It's well known that Western countries are not producing children at a level sufficient to replace older generations who are dying. The replacement level, which is not being reached, would be a total fertility rate of 2.1 children per woman. The total fertility rate in the U.S. is currently 1.6, and in Canada it is 1.25.[54] Although countries of the West are leading in the downward race, this depopulation crisis is a worldwide phenomenon. Following current trends, in 50 years or so only 26 countries out of a world total of 195 will still have more births than deaths; almost all of them will be in Africa, and none will be Western nations.[55]

In terms of a remedy, if devout Christian families and other traditional conservative households in the U.S. and Canada began having at least four children each, each country's traditional conservative population would double about every 20 years.[56] It is a sacrifice, but Traditional Conservatism, echoing the Christian faith that inspires it, embraces the paradox: sacrifice for the greater good leads to the greatest fulfillment. Jesus' statement, "Lose your life and you will find it," is both outlandish and accurate.

For young couples today, committing to larger families involves more financial strain than in the past. Compared with the population at large, they will have less personal leisure, and even career ambitions—particularly for wives—may be constrained as they prioritize the needs of their children. Accordingly, older parents of these young couples are also called to sacrifice. They should look for opportunities to provide financial support, housing, or other practical assistance—much as was customary in earlier generations—to help ensure that the new family can thrive despite the challenges of raising multiple children. In my own home, we live this reality: we created an apartment in our basement where one of my sons, his wife, and my first grandbabies currently live. I can attest that our life satisfaction is greater because of it.

When it comes to the sacrifice of having more kids leading to greater fulfillment in life, there is ample sociological proof. For example, an impressive study out of Australia's Edith Cowan University found that parents with the most life satisfaction—that is, those most content with their life—are those who have four or more children.[57] Similarly, a massive Norwegian study of 114,500 children found that everyone in a larger family—parents and children—has better mental health compared to those in small families or those living alone.[58] Of course, we can also recall the scores of studies from Chapter 3 confirming that traditional conservative parents—in particular, devout Protestants—enjoy "higher quality relationships with their children characterized by fewer arguments, more warmth, and a stronger b ond."[59] Simply put, raising a large family in a traditional manner, grounded in Christian norms and values, leads both parents and children to greater joy in life and deeper affection for one another.

On the other hand, things are not as pleasant for those operating outside the ideals of Traditional Conservatism. Studies show that children, especially in larger broods, can reduce the life satisfaction of *secular, progressive* parents. For them, kids are seen less as a blessing and more as a burden on their personal freedoms and finances.[60]

As one might intuit from the secularists' and progressives' negative attitudes towards child-rearing, they are shrinking most of all across the West, and celebrating abortion and any manner of non-traditional union are contributing factors to their decline. Their crisis is an opportunity for traditional conservatives. However, having more children than them is only the first step in this larger, long-term strategy.

If traditional conservatives are to succeed politically, we must stop spreading ourselves thin across our nations. When your population is spread thin, your influence becomes thin. Instead, we must congregate and colonize a single geographical area and then move outward from that strongly established foothold. Small successes are needed for big successes. When traditional conservatives are the major force on a municipal council or school board, it does more than provide good governance and correct policy direction at the local level; it also trains leaders and campaign teams for success at the upper levels of government. Practically speaking, traditional conservative parents need to encourage their kids to stay close geographically. There may be times when the youth have to leave to start a new intentional community somewhere farther away, but for greatest political influence—and, I would argue, for the greatest happiness of human beings—the general rule should be that extended families grow together, multi-generationally, in one geographical area.

There is one moderating caveat that could influence this idea of geographic concentration. If the area that has served as the "home and native land" of your people for decades or centuries has become impossibly inhospitable to the advancement of traditional conservatism (and taking up arms seems the only other option), you may want to leave. But in such a case, follow the example of the Puritans who left England to build what would become America, and take as much of your extended family and wider community with you as you can.

Who Wins

If traditional conservatives can commit to the political strategies I've described in this chapter, including these final tactics—having bigger families, encouraging their children to stay geographically close, all while transmitting the norms and values of their movement—our gradual success in winning back society becomes probable. For a proximate example, we could look to the Amish.

The Amish are one of the fastest-growing religious groups in North America, and their growth happens without any external conversions. Through births alone, they double their population about every 22 years. Their devout daughters and sons—taught to value strong generational ties—remain in the same community as adults, and they start their own families of devout believers.[61] Families and the immediate church community oversee education and religious training.

Doubling their population every two decades requires the founding of a new Amish colony in the United States every three and a half weeks. When land availability and prices are favorable, new communities are established adjacent to existing ones. For these Christians, growth has been accelerating rather than diminishing in recent years; nearly two-thirds of all existing Amish settlements have been founded since 1990.[62]

As an example of an intentional community with conservative values mastering the recipe for exponential growth, the Amish are worthy of imitation. However, in an important regard, their example is dangerously flawed and thus not to be followed.

Outside their own enclaves, the cultural influence of the Amish is virtually zero. In theological terms, they do almost nothing to fulfill Jesus' Great Commission (Matthew 28:16-20). Believers are supposed to work to ensure that the norms and values of Christianity—Jesus' commands—shape the laws of nations; however, the Amish make no progress in that regard.

Why are they so ineffective? Because they deliberately avoid political activism.[63]

Interestingly, in North America and across the West, another group matches the exponential growth of the Amish: Muslims.

In the U.S. they are doubling about every 20 years, with a recent report by the Pew Research Center in Washington concluding that by 2050 "the U.S. Muslim population will replace Jews as the second largest religious group in America... as it reaches nearly twice the share of today." In Canada and parts of Europe, the increase is even greate r.[64]

Unlike the Amish, Muslims in Western nations are ferociously committed to political activism. Beyond their heavy involvement as organizers and participants in protest rallies, they are increasingly visible as elected officials—especially in major cities across the UK, U.S., and Canada. Muslim success in municipal elections—in places such as London, New York, and Calgary[65]—has been attributed in part to their concentrated communities and their consistent practice of voting as a bloc for their co-religionists.[66]

The remarkable expansion of the Muslim population in the West, paired with its aggressive political involvement, reminds us that a rival movement with its own version of non-Western "traditional conservatism" also has its sights set on cultural ascendancy.

Unlike Western Traditional Conservatism—restrained and shaped by the norms and values of Christianity—this Muslim alternative has little theological basis for insisting on equality before the law or love for enemies. In comparison, the prohibitions and compelled mandates likely to accompany a Muslim variant of traditional conservatism—should it achieve power—might make the modest and limited restrictions on public behavior associated with Western-style Traditional Conservatism appear inconsequential.

Critics may argue that an Islamic-derived form of traditional conservatism in the West would be a mild variant, unlike the authoritarian ideology that has destabilized Muslim migrants' countries of origin. This claim seems to be refuted by the research. The best sociological data show that a strong majority of Muslims in Western nations display little evidence of belief moderation and that most hold attitudes at odds with their adopted countries' core norms and values. For example, 74% of Muslim immigrants in Western Europe agree that "there is only one interpretation of the Koran." This does not suggest a flexible or modern outlook, especially when 60% also insist that "Muslims should return to the roots of Islam." Equally concerning, 64% agree that "the rules of the Koran are more important to me than the laws of the country I immigrated to," and 54% believe that "Western countries are out to destroy Islam."[67] Taken together, these findings provide strong evidence against the claim of widespread ideological moderation. For those who suggest that a tempering of attitudes among Muslims in the West is inevitable and that more time is simply needed, the data again point in the opposite direction. When researchers compare the responses of first-, second-, and even third-generation Muslim immigrants, they find that these concerning outlooks do not significantly moderate over time.[68] In fact, some studies suggest deeper cultural integration can heighten radical attitudes.

For example, the study titled "Threat, Anti-Western Hostility and Violence among European Muslims," published in the *International Journal of Intercultural Relations*, found that Muslims who had adopted the external trappings of assimilation—specifically the host country's language, customs, dress, and general social norms—reported the highest intentions of faith-inspired personal violence. Among the groups studied, Muslims residing in Britain expressed the greatest willingness to act aggressively in defense of their co-religionists against those they perceived as opposing cultural forces.[69]

To be blunt: longstanding integration, often assumed to ease alienation and soften oppositional identities, did not operate as a moderating force. On the contrary, greater cultural adaptation was associated with a greater willingness to endorse or personally engage in violence. These findings directly undermine the optimistic expectation that time and proximity will naturally temper extremist sympathies among Muslims in the West.[70]

While Muslim immigrants have benefited from Western openness, those represented in these research samples do not share their host nations' devotion to diversity and inclusion. Instead, they retain strong religious solidarity, in-group preference, and out-group hostility. Whatever one makes of this, these traits confer a strategic advantage on Muslims in the West. Though they stand in opposition to the norms and values of the countries that welcomed them, this competing form of traditional conservatism—the Islamic variant—may be better positioned for long-term cultural ascendancy than many of the fragmented and self-questioning ideologies currently dominant in the West. As shown in earlier chapters, the inherent weaknesses of progressivism and classical liberalism (including libertarianism) leave them vulnerable to collapse under the weight of their own contradictions. Their emphasis on individualism and permissiveness correlates with lower fertility, weaker communal bonds, and cultural erosion. Given enough time, it is likely inevitable that some form of traditional conservatism—rooted in the norms and values of one religious faith or another—will rise to become the dominant ideology of the West. All conservative movements tend to share certain built-in strengths, such as high fertility and deep loyalties to family, faith, and community.

And while they may share similar traits, not all forms of traditional conservatism produce the same outcomes. As this book has shown, only the version of Traditional Conservatism grounded in British common law and Christianity consistently and uniquely leads to progress. And, as I said at the very beginning, I'm for progress.

Are you?

Endnotes for Chapter 5

1. See William Smith, "Galli," in *A Dictionary of Greek and Roman Antiquities*, ed. William Smith (London: John Murray, 1875), 569–70, https://penelope. uchicago.edu/Thayer/E/ Roman/Texts/secondary/SMIGRA*/Galli.html.

2. Loraine Boettner, *The Reformed Doctrine of Predestination* (Grand Rapids, MI: Eerdmans, 1932), 383.

3. See John Calvin, *Institutes of the Christian Religion*, ed. John T. McNeill, trans. Ford Lewis Battles, vol. 2 (Philadelphia: Westminster John Knox Press, 1960), 1053–70.

4. Ibid., 1485–1521. The chapter does not use "nations" as a technical term but refers to them implicitly as political entities under civil magistrates, governed by laws and accountable to God's moral order.

5. John Coffey, *Politics, Religion and the British Revolutions: The Mind of Samuel Rutherford* (Cambridge: Cambridge University Press, 1997), 146–80.

6. Ibid.

7. Mark Kishlansky, *A Monarchy Transformed: Britain 1603–1714* (London: Penguin Books, 1996), 108–16; Kevin Sharpe, *The Personal Rule of Charles I* (New Haven, CT: Yale University Press, 1992), 50–130.

8. Kevin Sharpe, *The Personal Rule of Charles I* (New Haven, CT: Yale University Press, 1992), 719–26.

9. Ibid., 930–41.

10. Egbert Watson Smith, *The Creed of Presbyterians* (New York: Baker & Taylor, 1901), 119 (quoting Leopold von Ranke).

11. Bruce Gore, "Presbyterians and the American Revolution," YouTube video, 1:02:32, September 20, 2021, https://www.youtube.com/ watch?v=L9rxSyEWp2I.

12. Jon Butler, quoted in Erin Blakemore, "The Surprising Religious Diversity of America's 13 Colonies," *History.com*, July 25, 2022, https://www.history. com/articles/religion-13-colonies-america.

13. Gore, "Presbyterians and the American Revolution."

14. American Battlefield Trust, "Tarring and Feathering," *Battlefields.org*, https:// www.battlefields.org/learn/articles/tarring-and-feathering.

15. Richard Archer, *As If an Enemy's Country: The British Occupation of Boston and the Origins of Revolution* (New York: Oxford University Press, 2010), 186–204.

16. See David Hackett Fischer, *Paul Revere's Ride* (New York:

Oxford University Press, 1994), 99–150, 261–268; Robert A. Gross, *The Minutemen and Their World* (New York: Hill and Wang, 1976), 25–60.

17. Mark A. Noll, *America's God: From Jonathan Edwards to Abraham Lincoln* (New York: Oxford University Press, 2002), 73–75, 82–90.

18. Ibid., 53–55, 83–85.

19. Bernard Bailyn, *The Ideological Origins of the American Revolution*, enlarged ed. (Cambridge, MA: Harvard University Press, 1992), 27–31, 38–41, 55–60, 175–180.

20. See John Marshall, *John Locke: Resistance, Religion and Responsibility* (Cambridge: Cambridge University Press, 1994), 3–6, 18–22, 33–39, 155–157, 205–210.

21. Gary L. Steward, *Justifying Revolution: The American Clergy's Argument for Political Resistance, 1750–1776* (New York: Oxford University Press, 2021).

22. Ibid., 10–15.

23. Ibid., 11–12; see John Patrick Mullins, *Father of Liberty: Jonathan Mayhew and the Principles of the American Revolution* (Lawrence: University Press of Kansas, 2017), 45–60.

24. Jonathan Mayhew, *A Discourse Concerning Unlimited Submission and Non-Resistance to the Higher Powers*, repr. (Indianapolis: Liberty Fund, 2015), 33, https://oll.libertyfund.org/titles/mayhew-discourse-co

ncerning-unlimited-submission; see Steward, *Justifying Revolution*, 11.

25. John Carmichael, *A Self-Defensive War Lawful: Preached at Lancaster, on the 4th of June 1775* (Philadelphia: John Henry Miller for John Dean, 1775), 15, https://quod.lib.umich.edu/e/evans/N10950.0001.001.

26. Ibid.

27. Samuel Langdon, *Government Corrupted by Vice, and Recovered by Righteousness: A Sermon Preached before the Honorable Congress of the Colony of the Massachusetts-Bay in New England, Assembled at Watertown, on Wednesday the 31st Day of May, 1775* (Watertown, MA: Benjamin Edes, 1775), 26, https:// quod.lib.umich.edu/e/evans/N11171.0001.001/1:4?rgn=div1;view=fulltext.

28. William Stearns, *A View of the Controversy Subsisting between Great-Britain and the American Colonies: A Sermon, Preached at a Fast, in Marlborough in Massachusetts-Bay, on Thursday May 11, 1775* (Salem, MA: Samuel Hall, 1775), 21, https://quod.lib.umich.edu/e/evans/idno=N11443.0001.001.

29. Ibid.

30. Library of Congress, "Religion and the American Revolution," in *Religion and the Founding of the American Republic*, 1998, https://www.loc.gov/ exhibits/religion/rel04.html.

31. Jane Shaw Stroup, "The Mecklenburg Resolves," *North Car-*

olina History Project, John Locke Foundation, https://n orthcarolinahistory.org/ encyclopedia/the-mecklenburg-re-solves/.

32. Library of Congress, "Religion and the American Revolution."

33. Dan Fisher, *Bringing Back the Black Robed Regiment: Volume 1* (Oklahoma City: D. Fisher, 2015).

34. Steward, *Justifying Revolution*, 20–22, 26–27.

35. Ibid.

36. Ibid., 71-90.

37. Ibid. Also see: David VanDrunen, *Natural Law and the Two Kingdoms: A Study in the Development of Reformed Social Thought* (Grand Rapids, MI: Wm. B. Eerdmans Publishing Co., 2010), 212–219.

38. Max Weber, *The Protestant Ethic and the Spirit of Capitalism*, trans. Talcott Parsons (1930; repr., New York: Charles Scribner's Sons, 1958), esp. 54–57, 60–62, 102–104, 109–115, 172–183 (on Calvinist doctrines, providence, labor as proof of favor, individual calling, and secularization's erosion of the ethic's foundations).

39. Dietrich Bonhoeffer, *The Cost of Discipleship*, trans. R. H. Fuller, with some revision by Irmgard Booth (London: SCM Press, 1959; repr., New York: Touchstone, 1995), 43–56.

40. For example, Chaeyoon Lim and Robert D. Putnam, "Reli-

gion, Social Networks, and Life Satisfaction," *American Sociological Review* 75, no. 6 (2010): 914–933, https://doi.org/10.1177/0003122410386686.

41. For example, see: Lawrence M. Rudner, "Scholastic Achievement and Demographic Characteristics of Home School Students in 1998," *Education Policy Analysis Archives* 7, no. 8 (1999): https://doi.org/10.14507/epaa. v7n8.1999; Linda M. Barwegen et al., "Academic Achievements of Homeschool and Public School Students and Student Perception of Parent Involvement," *School Community Journal* 16, no. 1 (2006): 39–58; Brian D. Ray, "A Systematic Review of the Empirical Research on Selected Aspects of Homeschooling as a School Choice," *Journal of School Choice* 11, no. 4 (2017): 604–621, https://doi.org/10.1080/15582159.2017.1395638.

42. Lynn Swaner, Albert Cheng, Jonathan Eckert, "School Sector Influence on Graduate Outcomes and Flourishing" (Hamilton, ON: Cardus, 2024), Cardus Center for Faith in Education, https://www.cardus.ca/research/school-sector-influence-on-graduate-outcomes-and-flourishing/; Albert Cheng, Paul E. Hill, and Michael J. Petersen, "What Do Religious Schools Teach? A Survey of Religious Educators," *Journal of School Choice* 13, no. 1 (2019): 104–123, https:// doi.org/10.1080/15582159.2018.1537939; Ying Chen, Christine E. Cardinale, and Tyler J. VanderWeele, "School Types in Adolescence and Subsequent Health and Well-Being in Young Adulthood: An Outcome-Wide Analysis," *PLoS ONE* 16, no. 11 (2021): e0258723, https:

//doi.org/10.1371/journal.pone.0258723.

43. Ibid. See also Cardus Education Survey, "What Do Religious Schools Teach? A Survey of Religious Educators" (Hamilton, ON: Cardus, 2012), referenced in Dan Krause, *The Research Case for PK-12 Christian Schools* (Graceworks Ministries, 2023), https://graceworksministries.org/wp-content/ uploads/2023/09/The-Case-for-Christian-Education.pdf.

44. James J. Teevan, ed., *Introduction to Sociology: A Canadian Focus* (Toronto: Prentice-Hall Canada, 1986), 266–276.

45. Maria J. Stephan and Erica Chenoweth, *Why Civil Resistance Works: The Strategic Logic of Nonviolent Conflict* (New York: Columbia University Press, 2011), 9–14, 220–21.

46. For example: David C. DeAndrea and Matthew A. Vendemia, "The Influence of Self-Generated and Third-Party Claims Online: Perceived Self-Interest as an Explanatory Mechanism," *Journal of Computer-Mediated Communication* 24, no. 5 (2019): 223–39, https://doi.org/10.1093/jcmc/ zmz011; Maija F. Bjørklund and Øyvind Ihlen, "How Spokesperson Rank and Selected Media Channels Impact Perceptions in Crisis Communication," *Corporate Communications: An International Journal* 20, no. 4 (2015): 471–85, https://doi.org/10.1108/CCIJ-02-2014-0012.

47. Erik R. K. Hermann, Michael Morgan, and James Shanahan, "Television, Continuity, and Change: A Meta-Analysis of Five Decades of Cultivation Research," *Journal of Communication* 71, no. 4 (2021): 515–44, https://doi. org/10.109

3/joc/jqab018.

48. Douglas Wilson, "Rival Flag, Rival Nation," *Blog & Mablog* (dougwils.com), March 27, 2023, https://dougwils.com/books-and-culture/s7-engaging-the-culture/rival-flag-rival-nation.html.

49. "Student's 'Jesus' Shirt Sparks Feud with School," *CBC News*, May 3, 2012, https://www.cbc.ca/news/canada/nova-scotia/student-s-jesus-shirt-sparks-feud-with-school-1.1280427.

50. Ibid.

51. Allie Griffin, "Man Ordered to Remove 'Jesus Is the Only Way' Shirt at Mall of America," *New York Post*, January 16, 2023, https://nypost.com/2023/01/16/man-ordered-to-remove-jesus-is-the-only-way-shirt-at-mall-of-america/.

52. John Kruzel, "US Supreme Court Rejects Case About Student's 'There Are Only Two Genders' T-Shirt," *Reuters*, May 27, 2025, https://www.reuters. com/world/us/us-supreme-court-rejects-case-about-students-there-are-only-two-genders-t-shirt-2025-05-27/.

53. Ibid.

54. National Center for Health Statistics, "Births: Provisional Data for 2024," *Vital Statistics Rapid Release*, no. 38 (2025), https://www.cdc.gov/nchs/ data/vsrr/vsrr038.pdf; Statistics Canada, "The Daily — Fertility and Baby Names, 2024," September 24, 2025, https://www150.statcan.gc.ca/n1/dai

ly-quotidien/250924/dq250924d-eng.htm.

55. GBD 2021 Fertility and Forecasting Collaborators, "Global Fertility in 204 Countries and Territories, 1950–2021, with Forecasts to 2100: A Comprehensive Demographic Analysis for the Global Burden of Disease Study 2021," *The Lancet* 403, no. 10440 (2024): 2057–2099, https:// doi.org/10.1 016/S0140-6736(24)00550-6; Stephen Davies, "Population Decline Will Destroy the West as We Know It," *Telegraph*, March 26, 2024, https://www.telegraph.co.uk/news/2024/ 03/26/population-decline-should-terrify-the-west/.

56. For example: Sam Myers, "Across the Country, Amish Populations Are on the Rise," *Daily Yonder*, April 10, 2024, https://dailyyonder.com/amish-population-growth -rural-america/2024/04/10/.

57. Victoria Woollaston, "The Key to a Happy Family? Having Four Children: Parents of Larger Broods Happier with Their Lives," *Daily Mail*, September 16, 2015, https://www.dailymail.co.uk/sciencetech/article-3233796/ The-key-happy-family-Having-FOUR-children-Parents-larg er-broods-happier-satisfied-lives.html.

58. Bjørn Grinde and Kristian Tambs, "Effect of Household Size on Mental Problems in Children: Results from the Norwegian Mother and Child Cohort Study," *BMC Psychology* 4 (2016): 31, https://doi.org/10.1186/ s40359-016-0136-1.

59. Jonathan Rothwell, "Parenting Is the Key to Adolescent Mental Health," *Institute for Family Studies*,

November 30, 2023, https://ifstudies.org/blog/ parenting-is-the-key-to-adolescent-mental-health.

60. See Haya Stier and Amit Kaplan, "Are Children a Joy or a Burden? Individual- and Macro-level Characteristics and the Perception of Children," *European Journal of Population* 36, no. 2 (2019): 387–413, https://doi. org/10.1007/s10680-0 19-09535-y.

61. Sam Myers, "Across the Country, Amish Populations Are on the Rise."

62. Ohio State University, "A New Amish Community Is Founded Every Three-and-a-Half Weeks in US, Experts Estimate," *ScienceDaily*, July 27, 2012, https://www.sciencedai ly.com/releases/2012/07/120727131544.htm.

63. Erik Wesner, "Do Amish Vote? Republican or Democrat?," *Amish America*, June 3, 2024, https://amishamerica.com/d o-amish-vote/#political-office.

64. Pew Research Center, "The Future of World Religions: Population Growth Projections, 2010–2050," April 2, 2015, https://www.pewresearch.org/ religion/2015/04/02/religious-projections-2010-2050/.

65. In London, UK, Sadiq Khan became the city's first Muslim mayor when elected in 2016 and was re-elected in 2021 and 2024 for a historic third term, while in New York City, US, Zohran Mamdani was elected in November 2025 as the first Muslim and South Asian mayor at age 34, and in Calgary,

Canada, Naheed Nenshi served as the first Muslim mayor of a major North American city from his initial election in 2010 through re-elections in 2013 and 2017 until 2021.

66. For example: Becky Morton, "Pro-Gaza Candidates Squeeze Labour Vote in Some Constituencies," *British Broadcasting Corporation*, July 5, 2024, https://www.bbc.com/news/art icles/c9e9ydj215yo. (Details the five independent pro-Gaza wins in Muslim-heavy constituencies, attributing success to bloc voting dissatisfaction with Labour's Gaza stance.); WDET (Detroit Public Radio), "Dearborn Elects Mayor Abdullah Hammoud for Second Term," November 5, 2025, https://wdet.org/2025/11/05/dearborn-elects-m ayor-abdullah-hammoud-for-second-term/. (Covers Hammoud's landslide victory with over 60% of the vote, highlighting community endorsements and high turnout in the 40-55% Muslim/Arab area.)

67. Ruud Koopmans, "Religious Fundamentalism and Hostility against Out-Groups: Comparing Muslim Immigrants and Natives in Western Europe," *Journal of Ethnic and Migration Studies* 41, no. 1 (2015): 33–52, https://doi. org/10.1080/1 369183X.2014.935307.

68. Ibid.

69. Hajra Tahir, Jonas Rønningsdalen Kunst, and David Lackland Sam, "Threat, Anti-Western Hostility and Violence among European Muslims: The Mediating Role of Acculturation," *International Journal of Intercultural Relations* 73 (2019): 74–88, https://doi.org/10.1016/j.ijintrel.2019.08.

001.

70. Ibid.

Postscript—A Final Word and a Beginning

If you've reached this postscript, you've done more than finish a book. You've wrestled with an argument about how North American society can be restored—how it might recover unity, trust, justice, and prosperity. If you've been convinced that a resurgence of Traditional Conservatism is what's needed, a final step awaits. This postscript exists for one reason: to turn conviction into connection, and connection into action.

What you have encountered in these pages was never meant to be practiced in isolation, but to be embodied together. Beyond these words are others who have read what you have read and felt what you have felt—perhaps recognizing, "This names what I have been reaching for." This postscript is an invitation to find one another, to meet, to organize, to encourage one another, and to act together—locally and beyond. It also opens an ongoing channel between us, so that this book is not the end of the conversation but the beginning of a shared one. As a first step, our movement needs a name—something it's called and something we can call each other. The immediate thought might be to call the movement Traditional Conservatism and its followers traditional conservatives. While those labels are accurate, they leave the movement vulnerable to mischaracterization because both *traditional* and *conservative*—even when linked together—are already widely used in public discourse to describe positions, instincts, and coalitions that diverge in important ways from the specific philosophical commitments defined in this book.

We need a label that clearly signals that the form of traditional conservatism advanced by this movement is defined and disciplined by the framework set out in this book. The front cover states the crisis facing both America and Canada—*Christ or Collapse*. Inside, Part One is titled *Our Christian Foundation: Principles, History, & Rationale* and introduces the proposed solution. The back cover expresses the remedy most plainly: *Restoring the Foundation for a Flourishing Nation*. Together, these titles leave no ambiguity about the movement's purpose: restoring the Christian foundations on which unity, peace, and prosperity depend. For that reason, I propose we call our cause the **Foundationalist movement**, or simply **Foundationalism**, and its adherents **Foundationalists**. All Foundationalists are traditional conservatives, but not all traditional conservatives are Foundationalists.

A bit more clarification is needed. There's a branch of philosophy called epistemology, which studies how we come to know things. Within that field is a view known as foundationalism. It maintains that certain beliefs must be self-evident or verifiable, and that all other beliefs derive their justification from these basic truths—much as a house rests upon its foundation. I point this out because our Foundationalism is not that foundationalism. While there are similarities, the political Foundationalism advanced in this book is not intended as a direct extension, reinterpretation, or application of epistemological foundationalism. In some cases, the prefix "political" could be added for precision, but given the relatively low public profile of epistemological foundationalism—and the absence of any social movement associated with it—such a prefix is generally unnecessary when the term is used in context. Having established that we are (political) Foundationalists, I invite you, warmly and wholeheartedly, to take the next step to join us at <u>FoundationalistHub.org</u>

At FoundationalistHub.org you can join our mailing list to receive new writings, reflections, and announcements, including updates on conferences and conventions. You'll be added to a directory and matched with members in local and regional groups already meeting. Once you've found your people, you'll encourage one another, share experiences, and organize collaborative initiatives to advance the Foundationalist vision of traditional conservatism. It's important to note that not every group in this network will be newly formed; some communities may already exist and simply find renewed purpose or clarity through the Foundationalist vision. These groups don't need to reorganize or adopt a new name. It's enough that they mindfully put the Foundationalist principles into practice within their existing structures, deepening their impact and aligning their efforts with the broader enterprise.

And now, to work.